Python for AI: A Beginner's Guide to Coding Intelligence

Gilbert Gutiérrez

Artificial Intelligence (AI) is transforming the world at an unprecedented pace, revolutionizing industries ranging from healthcare and finance to entertainment and self-driving cars. At the heart of this revolution lies Python—an easy-to-learn, powerful programming language that has become the foundation of modern AI development. Whether you're a complete beginner with no coding experience or an aspiring AI enthusiast looking to take your first steps in machine learning, **Python for AI: A Beginner's Guide to Coding Intelligence** is the perfect starting point for your journey into the world of artificial intelligence.

This book is the first installment in the AI from Scratch series, a comprehensive step-by-step guide designed to help readers master AI concepts and techniques from the ground up. Through this hands-on and beginner-friendly approach, you will gain not only a solid understanding of Python programming but also a strong foundation in AI principles, tools, and real-world applications.

Who Is This Book For?

- Absolute beginners with no prior programming knowledge who want to learn Python and AI from scratch.
- Students and professionals looking to explore AI as a career path.
- Self-learners and tech enthusiasts who want to understand how AI models are built and deployed.
- Anyone interested in coding intelligence and building smart applications using Python.

What You Will Learn

This book is structured into four main parts, each progressively taking you deeper into the world of Python and AI. By the end of this journey, you will have a strong grasp of Python programming, AI fundamentals, and practical experience in building real-world AI applications.

Part 1: Python Foundations for AI

To build AI-powered applications, you first need to learn how to code in Python. This section introduces you to the basics of Python programming and essential tools used in AI development.

Chapter 1: Welcome to AI and Python

- Understanding Artificial Intelligence and its real-world applications.
- Why Python is the best programming language for AI.
- Setting up your development environment with Jupyter Notebook, VS Code, and Anaconda.
- Writing and running your first Python script.

Chapter 2: Python Basics: Writing Your First Code

- Variables, data types, and operators.
- Control structures: loops, conditionals, and functions.
- Error handling and debugging techniques.

Chapter 3: Data Structures for AI

- Working with lists, tuples, dictionaries, and sets.
- Understanding how data structures impact AI algorithms.

Chapter 4: Working with Libraries

- Exploring NumPy for numerical computing.
- Pandas for data manipulation.
- Matplotlib and Seaborn for data visualization.

Part 2: Essential AI Tools in Python

Once you're comfortable with Python, it's time to dive into the core concepts of artificial intelligence and machine learning. In this section, you will learn how AI models work, how to handle data, and how to train simple machine learning models.

Chapter 5: Understanding Data: The Fuel for AI

- The importance of data in AI and machine learning.
- Collecting, cleaning, and preprocessing data for AI models.
- Feature engineering techniques for improving AI accuracy.

Chapter 6: Introduction to Machine Learning

- What is machine learning? Supervised vs. unsupervised learning.
- How machines learn from data.
- Common ML algorithms and their applications.

Chapter 7: Getting Started with Scikit-Learn

- Using Scikit-Learn to implement simple machine learning models.
- Linear regression for prediction.
- Classification models and performance evaluation.

Chapter 8: Neural Networks Basics with TensorFlow & PyTorch

- Understanding artificial neural networks.
- Building a simple neural network with TensorFlow.
- Exploring PyTorch for deep learning.

Part 3: Hands-on AI Projects

This section is all about applying what you've learned to build practical AI applications. You'll work on three exciting projects that demonstrate real-world AI capabilities.

Chapter 9: Building a Simple Chatbot

- Introduction to Natural Language Processing (NLP).
- Creating a rule-based chatbot.
- Using machine learning to improve chatbot responses.

Chapter 10: Image Recognition with AI

- Understanding computer vision and image classification.
- Using pre-trained AI models for object recognition.
- Building a custom image classifier from scratch.

Chapter 11: AI for Predictions

- Understanding time-series forecasting.
- Training an AI model to predict stock prices or weather trends.
- Evaluating and improving prediction accuracy.

Chapter 12: Deploying Your AI Model

- Introduction to model deployment and APIs.
- Creating a web-based AI application with Flask.

- Deploying AI models to the cloud.

Part 4: Next Steps in AI Mastery

Now that you have a solid foundation in Python and AI, what's next? This final section introduces key ethical considerations in AI, advanced AI concepts, and the next steps in your learning journey.

Chapter 13: AI Ethics and Responsible Coding

- Understanding bias in AI models.
- Privacy, security, and responsible AI development.
- Guidelines for ethical AI programming.

Chapter 14: Advanced AI Topics Preview

- Deep learning and neural networks.
- Reinforcement learning and AI in gaming.
- AI in robotics and automation.

Chapter 15: Your AI Journey Ahead

- Roadmap to mastering AI.
- Recommended books, courses, and online communities.
- Building a portfolio and preparing for AI job roles.

Why This Book?

✓ **Beginner-Friendly Approach** – No prior programming knowledge is needed! This book introduces coding and AI concepts in an easy-to-understand way.

✓ **Hands-on Learning** – You'll work on real AI projects, making the learning process engaging and practical.

✓ **Step-by-Step Explanations** – Each concept is broken down into clear steps, ensuring a smooth learning curve.

✓ **Real-World Applications** – Learn how AI is used in chatbots, image recognition, and predictive analytics.

✓ **Future-Proof Your Skills** – AI is the future, and this book equips you with the knowledge to be part of the AI revolution.

Python for AI: A Beginner's Guide to Coding Intelligence is your gateway into the fascinating world of artificial intelligence. With clear explanations, hands-on projects, and real-world applications, this book provides everything you need to start coding AI with confidence.

Whether you dream of building intelligent applications, pursuing a career in AI, or simply want to explore the endless possibilities of artificial intelligence, this book is the perfect first step.

Your AI journey starts here.

Are you ready to code intelligence?

1. Welcome to AI and Python

Artificial Intelligence (AI) is no longer a concept of the future—it's here, transforming industries and shaping our daily lives. From voice assistants like Siri and Alexa to self-driving cars and recommendation systems, AI is revolutionizing the way we interact with technology. But what exactly is AI, and how does it work? In this chapter, you'll get an introduction to the fundamentals of AI, explore real-world applications, and understand why Python is the go-to programming language for AI development. You'll also set up your coding environment and write your first Python program, marking the beginning of your journey into AI-powered programming.

1.1 What is Artificial Intelligence?

Artificial Intelligence (AI) is a branch of computer science that focuses on creating systems capable of performing tasks that typically require human intelligence. These tasks include things like understanding natural language, recognizing images, making decisions, playing games, and even driving cars. Essentially, AI is the attempt to imbue machines with the cognitive abilities that humans possess, enabling them to mimic human thought and behavior. AI has been a rapidly advancing field, with new breakthroughs, tools, and applications emerging continuously.

At its core, AI is about creating algorithms and models that allow computers to learn from data and improve their performance over time without being explicitly programmed. It's not just about automating simple, repetitive tasks; rather, AI strives to enable machines to handle complex, dynamic tasks that require decision-making, reasoning, and problem-solving—skills that were once thought to be exclusive to humans.

Key Components of AI

There are several key components and technologies that make up AI. Below are some of the most important ones:

1. Machine Learning (ML)

Machine learning is a subset of AI and one of its most powerful tools. It involves training algorithms to recognize patterns in data, enabling them to make predictions or decisions based on that data. Unlike traditional software, which requires programmers to write specific rules, machine learning algorithms improve their performance automatically through experience. For instance, an algorithm can be trained on thousands of images to learn to recognize a cat by being fed images labeled as "cat" or "not cat."

Within machine learning, there are several types:

- **Supervised Learning**: The model is trained using labeled data (input-output pairs), which helps it make predictions or classifications on new, unseen data.
- **Unsupervised Learning**: The model is trained with data that has no labels, and the system tries to identify patterns, correlations, or clusters within the data.
- **Reinforcement Learning**: This involves training a system through trial and error. The model receives feedback based on actions it takes, learning which actions lead to desirable outcomes.

2. Deep Learning

Deep learning is a specialized subset of machine learning that uses neural networks with many layers (hence the term "deep"). These deep neural networks are designed to simulate the way humans process information in the brain. Deep learning has shown impressive results in complex tasks like speech recognition, image classification, and even generating new content (such as images or text).

Deep learning algorithms require vast amounts of data and computational power, but they are extremely effective in recognizing intricate patterns in large datasets, which has led to breakthroughs in fields like computer vision and natural language processing (NLP).

3. Natural Language Processing (NLP)

NLP is the branch of AI that deals with the interaction between computers and human languages. It allows machines to read, understand, and generate human language in a way that is meaningful. NLP is at the heart of virtual assistants like Siri and Alexa, as well as chatbots, language translators, and sentiment analysis tools.

NLP involves tasks such as text classification, language generation, machine translation, and named entity recognition. One of the key challenges in NLP is understanding the nuances, syntax, and meaning of human language, which can be highly contextual and ambiguous.

4. Computer Vision

Computer vision is another critical area of AI that focuses on enabling machines to interpret and understand visual information from the world, much like humans do. Using cameras and sensors, computer vision algorithms analyze images or videos, extract relevant information, and make decisions based on that data.

Applications of computer vision include facial recognition, autonomous driving (where cars recognize pedestrians, road signs, and other vehicles), and medical imaging (where AI systems can assist in diagnosing conditions by analyzing X-rays, MRIs, and other scans).

5. Expert Systems and Knowledge Representation

Expert systems are AI programs that use databases of expert knowledge to solve specific problems within a particular domain. They operate by using inference rules to make decisions, much like a human expert would in a given field. These systems often rely on large amounts of domain-specific data and structured reasoning processes.

AI models can also use knowledge representation techniques to capture knowledge about the world and reason about it. Logical representations, ontologies, and semantic networks are examples of methods used to structure and store knowledge in AI systems.

Types of AI

AI can be classified into three main types based on its capabilities:

1. Narrow AI (Weak AI)

Narrow AI, also referred to as Weak AI, refers to systems designed to perform specific tasks. These AI models are highly specialized and can outperform humans in the tasks they are designed for, but they cannot perform tasks outside their programmed capabilities. Examples of narrow AI include facial recognition systems, recommendation engines, and self-driving car technologies. While narrow AI is very powerful in specific contexts, it lacks generalization and cannot think or reason outside its trained domain.

2. General AI (Strong AI)

General AI, or Strong AI, is a more advanced form of artificial intelligence that aims to possess the cognitive abilities of a human across a wide range of activities. Unlike narrow AI, general AI would be able to perform any intellectual task that a human can do. It can think, reason, learn, and apply knowledge across different domains, exhibiting a level of flexibility and adaptability that is still a far-off goal in AI research.

Currently, general AI remains a theoretical concept, and we are still far from creating truly autonomous systems that can learn and function like a human mind.

3. Artificial Superintelligence (ASI)

Artificial Superintelligence refers to a form of AI that surpasses human intelligence in virtually every aspect, including creativity, problem-solving, and emotional intelligence. ASI would have the potential to independently enhance itself, learning and improving at a rate far faster than any human could. While ASI remains a topic of speculation and debate, its potential to reshape society is both fascinating and concerning.

Applications of AI

AI has a wide range of applications that are already shaping various industries, including:

- **Healthcare**: AI is used in medical diagnostics, drug discovery, personalized medicine, and even robotic surgery. AI-driven systems analyze medical data, identify patterns, and assist doctors in making more accurate diagnoses.
- **Finance**: AI is applied in fraud detection, algorithmic trading, credit scoring, and customer service automation. AI models can detect suspicious transactions, predict market trends, and automate decision-making processes.
- **Automotive**: Self-driving cars use AI technologies like computer vision, machine learning, and reinforcement learning to navigate roads, avoid obstacles, and make driving decisions.
- **Entertainment**: AI is used in recommendation engines (e.g., Netflix, Spotify), video games, and content creation. AI systems analyze user behavior to recommend personalized content and can even generate new music, art, or stories.

Challenges and Ethical Considerations

While AI presents immense potential, there are several challenges and ethical issues that must be addressed. One major concern is bias in AI, where algorithms may inadvertently reinforce existing societal biases, leading to unfair outcomes. For example, facial recognition systems have been found to have higher error rates for certain demographic groups, leading to concerns about discrimination.

There are also concerns around privacy and the impact of AI on jobs, as automation may replace jobs in fields like manufacturing, retail, and transportation. Finally, as AI continues to evolve, the potential for creating more autonomous systems raises questions about accountability and control, particularly in areas like military applications and decision-making systems.

Artificial Intelligence is a rapidly advancing field that has the potential to transform every aspect of society, from healthcare and transportation to education and entertainment. By developing systems that can learn from data, make decisions, and solve complex problems, AI is pushing the boundaries of what machines can do. While there are significant challenges and ethical considerations to address, the future of AI holds immense promise, and its impact on our world will only continue to grow. As we continue to advance in AI research and development, we are shaping a future where intelligent systems work alongside humans to solve some of the world's most pressing problems.

1.2 Why Python for AI?

When it comes to Artificial Intelligence (AI), choosing the right programming language is essential to the success of your projects. Among the many programming languages available, Python stands out as the top choice for AI development. In fact, it has become the de facto language for AI, machine learning, deep learning, and data science. But what makes Python so ideal for AI, and why has it become so widely adopted? In this section, we'll explore the reasons why Python is the preferred language for AI development, and how its unique features help streamline the process of creating intelligent systems.

1.1 Simplicity and Readability

One of Python's greatest strengths is its simplicity and readability. Python was designed to be easy to understand and use, which makes it an excellent choice for beginners and experienced developers alike. Its clean, readable syntax mimics human language, making it easier to write, debug, and maintain code. AI developers can focus on solving complex problems without getting bogged down by complicated syntax or convoluted code structures.

In comparison to languages like C++ or Java, Python allows developers to express complex algorithms in fewer lines of code. This simplicity is particularly important in AI, where algorithms can become quite intricate. Whether you're writing a basic machine learning algorithm or developing a deep learning neural network, Python's syntax allows you to focus on the logic of your program rather than getting distracted by syntax-heavy programming.

1.2 Extensive Libraries and Frameworks for AI

One of the main reasons Python is favored for AI development is its vast ecosystem of libraries and frameworks specifically designed for AI, machine learning, and data science. Libraries are pre-written code that help developers perform common tasks efficiently, saving time and effort. Python has an extensive collection of libraries that cater to different aspects of AI, such as data manipulation, machine learning, and deep learning.

Some of the most popular Python libraries for AI development include:

NumPy and Pandas: These libraries provide fast, efficient tools for data manipulation and analysis, enabling you to work with large datasets and perform mathematical operations with ease. Pandas is especially popular for handling structured data, while NumPy excels at working with numerical data and multi-dimensional arrays.

Matplotlib and Seaborn: These libraries are used for data visualization, helping you visualize trends, distributions, and patterns in data, which is a crucial step in AI projects.

Scikit-learn: Scikit-learn is one of the most widely used libraries for machine learning. It offers simple and efficient tools for data mining and data analysis, making it easy to implement common machine learning algorithms like regression, classification, and clustering.

TensorFlow and PyTorch: These are deep learning frameworks that are particularly popular for building and training neural networks. TensorFlow, developed by Google, and PyTorch, developed by Facebook, are both highly powerful and widely used in AI research and production applications. They provide tools for building complex deep learning models and have high-level APIs that simplify the implementation of neural networks.

Keras: Keras is a high-level neural networks API, written in Python, that runs on top of TensorFlow. It is known for being user-friendly and simplifying the process of designing and training deep learning models.

The rich collection of libraries and frameworks in Python allows developers to access state-of-the-art algorithms and tools, greatly accelerating the development process and enhancing productivity.

1.3 Community Support and Resources

Python's widespread popularity in AI has led to the development of a vibrant community of developers, researchers, and enthusiasts. The Python community actively contributes to the language by developing libraries, writing tutorials, and sharing solutions to common problems. This community support means that as you encounter challenges while working on AI projects, you'll have access to a wealth of resources, including documentation, forums, blogs, and video tutorials.

The open-source nature of Python also means that developers around the world contribute to its growth. Whether you're new to AI or an experienced developer, there are endless resources available to help you learn, troubleshoot, and collaborate with others. The large community also fosters a culture of collaboration and knowledge-sharing, which can be incredibly beneficial when solving complex AI problems.

1.4 Platform Independence

Python is a cross-platform language, meaning that Python code can run on multiple operating systems, including Windows, macOS, and Linux. This platform independence is especially valuable in AI development, as it allows you to run your code on different systems without having to worry about compatibility issues. This ensures that your AI applications can be deployed on a variety of devices and environments, making it more versatile for both development and production use.

Moreover, Python integrates seamlessly with other programming languages, databases, and systems. It can be used alongside languages like C++ for performance-intensive parts of AI models or integrated with big data tools like Hadoop and Spark for large-scale data processing.

1.5 Rapid Prototyping and Experimentation

AI development often involves trial and error, as developers iterate over different models, test algorithms, and fine-tune parameters to achieve the best results. Python's simplicity and flexibility make it an ideal language for rapid prototyping and experimentation. Developers can quickly test different approaches, modify existing models, and experiment with various algorithms without worrying about long compilation times or intricate syntax issues.

Python's interactive environment, such as the IPython shell and Jupyter Notebooks, also makes it easy to experiment with code in an iterative manner. You can execute small chunks of code, see immediate results, and visualize data—all in real-time—helping to speed up the development process and streamline experimentation.

1.6 Integration with Big Data Tools

AI often involves working with large datasets, and Python's ability to integrate with big data tools makes it particularly suited for AI applications. Libraries like PySpark allow Python to interact with Apache Spark, a popular framework for distributed computing. This makes it easier to process and analyze large datasets across multiple servers, a crucial step in many AI applications that require large-scale data processing.

Python's integration with other big data tools and databases (such as SQL, NoSQL, and Hadoop) makes it an ideal language for handling, storing, and analyzing massive amounts of data that are common in AI projects.

1.7 Flexibility and Versatility

Python is a general-purpose programming language, meaning it can be used for a wide range of applications, not just AI. This versatility allows developers to use Python in all stages of AI projects—from data collection and cleaning to model development and deployment. Whether you're working on a machine learning model, web development, automation, or a complex data analysis project, Python has the flexibility to meet your needs.

Furthermore, Python can be used in various domains such as robotics, natural language processing (NLP), computer vision, and automation, which makes it a versatile tool for AI developers working on a wide range of applications.

Python's combination of simplicity, powerful libraries, strong community support, and versatility makes it the perfect language for AI development. Whether you're building a machine learning model, developing deep learning systems, or creating a natural language processing tool, Python provides the tools and environment needed to succeed. Its ability to integrate with other technologies, work seamlessly with large datasets, and allow for rapid prototyping ensures that AI developers can stay focused on innovation rather than technical hurdles. This makes Python the go-to language for AI, helping developers accelerate their projects and bring innovative AI solutions to life.

1.3 Setting Up Your Development Environment (Anaconda, Jupyter, VS Code)

When you're starting to work with Artificial Intelligence (AI) and machine learning, having the right development environment is essential to streamline the process. A good setup allows you to easily manage libraries, run code, and track your work. In this section, we'll explore how to set up your development environment using three powerful tools commonly used in AI development: Anaconda, Jupyter Notebooks, and Visual Studio Code (VS Code). These tools are designed to make your workflow smoother and more efficient when building and deploying AI models.

1.3.1 What is Anaconda?

Anaconda is an open-source distribution of Python and R, specifically designed for data science, machine learning, and scientific computing. It simplifies package management and deployment, allowing you to easily install, manage, and update libraries and dependencies. Anaconda comes with several powerful tools out of the box, including Jupyter Notebooks and Spyder, which are widely used for AI and machine learning development.

Why Anaconda for AI?

- **Package Management**: Anaconda comes with the conda package manager, which helps you install and manage libraries and dependencies. This is especially useful for managing complex packages required for AI development, as it handles compatibility issues across different operating systems.
- **Environment Management**: One of the main reasons developers use Anaconda is its ability to create isolated environments. These environments allow you to separate different projects with their own dependencies and versions, making sure they don't interfere with each other.
- **Pre-installed Libraries**: Anaconda comes with a large set of data science and machine learning libraries pre-installed, including NumPy, Pandas, Matplotlib, Scikit-learn, and TensorFlow, so you don't have to install them manually.

Installing Anaconda

- Download the Anaconda installer from the official website for your operating system (Windows, macOS, or Linux).

- Follow the installation instructions, making sure to add Anaconda to your system's PATH variable during the installation process.
- After installation, you can launch Anaconda Navigator, a graphical interface for managing environments and libraries.

Creating a New Environment in Anaconda

Open Anaconda Navigator or use the Anaconda Prompt (for command-line users). To create a new environment, run the following command:

```
conda create --name myenv python=3.8
```

Replace "myenv" with your desired environment name and "3.8" with the version of Python you need.

Once the environment is created, activate it with:

```
conda activate myenv
```

Install the libraries you need by using the conda or pip command, such as:

```
conda install numpy pandas matplotlib
```

1.3.2 What is Jupyter Notebooks?

Jupyter Notebooks is an interactive web-based environment that allows you to create and share documents that contain live code, equations, visualizations, and narrative text. It is widely used by data scientists, AI practitioners, and machine learning engineers for experimentation, data visualization, and documentation.

Why Jupyter for AI?

- **Interactive Coding**: Jupyter Notebooks allow you to write code and execute it in small chunks, making it easier to test and experiment with different algorithms.
- **Real-time Visualization**: Jupyter is excellent for visualizing data. Libraries like Matplotlib, Seaborn, and Plotly can be used directly in a notebook to plot graphs, images, and more.

- **Documentation**: You can combine code with markdown and LaTeX, making it easy to document your process, explain your approach, and share results with others.

Running Jupyter Notebooks

Launch Jupyter: If you've installed Anaconda, you can easily launch Jupyter Notebooks from Anaconda Navigator or by running the following command in your terminal:

```
jupyter notebook
```

This will open the Jupyter Notebook interface in your web browser.

Create and Edit Notebooks: To create a new notebook, click the "New" button and select "Python 3". From there, you can start writing Python code in individual cells and execute them with Shift + Enter.

Visualizing Data: Use Jupyter to run code and instantly see the results. For example, you can plot graphs directly within the notebook to visualize machine learning results.

1.3.3 What is Visual Studio Code (VS Code)?

Visual Studio Code (VS Code) is a powerful, lightweight code editor developed by Microsoft. It's a versatile editor with a wide range of extensions that can support many programming languages, including Python. VS Code is favored for its customization options, intuitive interface, and robust debugging tools, making it a popular choice for AI and machine learning development.

Why VS Code for AI?

- **Code Editing Features**: VS Code offers intelligent code completion, error checking, and syntax highlighting, which makes it easier to write clean and error-free code.
- **Debugging**: VS Code has an excellent built-in debugger, which allows you to step through your code, inspect variables, and track the execution flow—ideal for AI development where debugging can be complex.
- **Extension Marketplace**: With a massive selection of extensions available, you can easily integrate tools like Jupyter, Docker, Git, and machine learning libraries into VS Code, enhancing its capabilities for AI development.

- **Integrated Terminal**: The integrated terminal within VS Code allows you to run scripts, execute commands, and manage environments without leaving the editor.

Setting Up VS Code for AI

Install VS Code: Download the latest version of Visual Studio Code from the official website.

Install Python Extension: Launch VS Code, open the Extensions panel (on the left sidebar), and search for the "Python" extension by Microsoft. Install it to get features like IntelliSense, syntax highlighting, and debugging for Python.

Set Up Python Environment: Once you have the Python extension installed, configure VS Code to use the Python interpreter from your Anaconda environment. You can do this by opening the command palette (Ctrl+Shift+P), typing "Python: Select Interpreter", and choosing the relevant environment.

Install Jupyter Extension: If you want to run Jupyter notebooks inside VS Code, install the Jupyter extension, which allows you to open, edit, and run Jupyter notebooks directly within the editor.

Run and Debug Code: You can open a Python file and run it using the integrated terminal, or use the built-in debugger to step through your code. To set breakpoints, click to the left of the line numbers, and start the debugger by pressing F5.

1.3.4 Integrating All Tools

Now that we've discussed the individual tools, it's important to understand how they can work together to optimize your AI development workflow:

- Anaconda manages your Python environments and packages, ensuring that all your dependencies are installed correctly without conflicts.
- Jupyter Notebooks provides an interactive environment for rapid experimentation, where you can visualize your data and tweak algorithms.
- VS Code acts as your primary code editor, providing powerful features like code completion, debugging, and version control integration.
- You can create and manage environments with Anaconda, work on AI models and run experiments in Jupyter Notebooks, and write and debug your code in VS Code—all while keeping everything in sync and organized.

Setting up a well-organized and efficient development environment is crucial when working with AI. By using Anaconda, Jupyter Notebooks, and VS Code, you can streamline your workflow and leverage powerful tools that will make your AI projects easier to manage, experiment with, and deploy. Anaconda helps with managing libraries and dependencies, Jupyter provides an interactive space for experimentation, and VS Code offers a robust code editing and debugging experience. Together, these tools will lay a strong foundation for your journey in AI development.

1.4 Installing Essential AI Libraries

One of the key steps in getting started with Artificial Intelligence (AI) is setting up the necessary libraries that will allow you to work with data, implement machine learning algorithms, and build intelligent systems. In this section, we will cover the essential AI libraries you will need, how to install them, and their roles in the AI development process.

Python is known for its vast ecosystem of libraries, which makes it easy to get started with AI and machine learning projects. Some libraries provide tools for mathematical operations, data manipulation, and visualization, while others offer advanced algorithms for machine learning, deep learning, and data processing. Let's walk through the installation of the core libraries that will serve as the foundation for your AI development.

1.4.1 NumPy: Numerical Computing

NumPy is the fundamental package for scientific computing in Python. It provides support for arrays and matrices, along with a wide variety of mathematical functions that can operate on these arrays. Many AI and machine learning algorithms require heavy mathematical computation, and NumPy is built to handle these tasks efficiently.

Why NumPy?

- **Efficient Array Operations**: NumPy arrays (ndarrays) are faster and more efficient than Python lists, especially when dealing with large datasets.
- **Mathematical Functions**: NumPy offers a variety of mathematical functions, including linear algebra operations, statistics, and random number generation, all of which are essential in AI.

Installing NumPy

To install NumPy, you can use either conda (if you're using Anaconda) or pip (Python's package installer). Run one of the following commands:

Using conda (recommended for Anaconda users):

```
conda install numpy
```

Using pip:

```
pip install numpy
```

1.4.2 Pandas: Data Manipulation and Analysis

Pandas is an open-source library for data manipulation and analysis. It provides easy-to-use data structures like DataFrames, which are perfect for handling and analyzing large datasets. Pandas is essential for cleaning, transforming, and processing data in AI projects.

Why Pandas?

- **Data Structures**: Pandas provides the DataFrame, a 2D data structure that's easy to manipulate, filter, and aggregate.
- **Handling Missing Data**: Pandas has built-in tools to handle missing data, which is common in real-world datasets.
- **Data Filtering**: Pandas allows for powerful data filtering, grouping, and aggregation, making it ideal for data preprocessing in machine learning and AI.

Installing Pandas

To install Pandas, use one of the following commands:

Using conda:

```
conda install pandas
```

Using pip:

```
pip install pandas
```

1.4.3 Matplotlib: Data Visualization

Matplotlib is a plotting library that provides a variety of ways to visualize data. Visualization is crucial in AI projects to understand patterns in data, evaluate model performance, and communicate results.

Why Matplotlib?

- **Data Visualization**: Matplotlib allows you to create line plots, bar charts, histograms, and scatter plots, among other visualizations.
- **Customization**: It provides extensive customization options to make your plots more informative and aesthetically pleasing.
- **Integration**: It integrates well with other libraries like NumPy and Pandas for easy plotting directly from your data.

Installing Matplotlib

To install Matplotlib, use either conda or pip:

Using conda:

```
conda install matplotlib
```

Using pip:

```
pip install matplotlib
```

1.4.4 Scikit-learn: Machine Learning Algorithms

Scikit-learn is one of the most widely used libraries for machine learning in Python. It provides a simple interface for training and evaluating a wide range of machine learning algorithms, including classification, regression, clustering, and dimensionality reduction.

Why Scikit-learn?

- **Wide Range of Algorithms**: Scikit-learn includes well-optimized implementations of various machine learning algorithms such as decision trees, support vector machines, random forests, K-nearest neighbors, and more.
- **Preprocessing and Evaluation Tools**: It includes tools for data preprocessing, feature scaling, cross-validation, and performance evaluation.
- **Easy to Use**: Scikit-learn's API is designed to be easy to learn and use, making it a great library for beginners and experts alike.

Installing Scikit-learn

To install Scikit-learn, use the following commands:

Using conda:

```
conda install scikit-learn
```

Using pip:

```
pip install scikit-learn
```

1.4.5 TensorFlow: Deep Learning Framework

TensorFlow is one of the most popular deep learning libraries developed by Google. It provides a comprehensive ecosystem for building and training machine learning and deep learning models. TensorFlow is known for its flexibility, scalability, and ease of use when building neural networks and working with large datasets.

Why TensorFlow?

- **Deep Learning**: TensorFlow is designed for creating and training deep learning models, such as artificial neural networks and convolutional neural networks (CNNs).
- **Scalability**: TensorFlow is highly scalable and can run on multiple CPUs and GPUs, making it ideal for large-scale AI projects.
- **TensorFlow 2.x**: The latest version of TensorFlow (2.x) provides an easy-to-use, high-level API (Keras) that simplifies the process of building and training deep learning models.

Installing TensorFlow

To install TensorFlow, use one of the following commands:

Using conda:

```
conda install tensorflow
```

Using pip:

```
pip install tensorflow
```

1.4.6 Keras: High-Level Deep Learning API

Keras is a high-level neural network API that runs on top of TensorFlow (or other backend engines). Keras simplifies the process of building deep learning models by providing easy-to-use abstractions for neural networks.

Why Keras?

- **Simplified Model Building**: Keras allows you to build complex neural networks with just a few lines of code.
- **Integration with TensorFlow**: Since Keras is now part of TensorFlow, it integrates seamlessly with TensorFlow's advanced features and GPU acceleration.
- **Modularity**: Keras provides pre-built layers and models, allowing you to quickly experiment with different architectures.

Installing Keras

Keras is included in TensorFlow 2.x, so there is no need to install it separately. If you have installed TensorFlow, Keras is already available.

1.4.7 PyTorch: Another Deep Learning Framework

PyTorch is another popular deep learning library, developed by Facebook, which is widely used in both research and industry. PyTorch is known for its dynamic computation graph and flexibility, making it a favorite among researchers.

Why PyTorch?

- **Dynamic Computation Graphs**: Unlike TensorFlow (prior to version 2.x), PyTorch uses dynamic computation graphs, which allow for more flexibility during model training.
- **Strong Community and Research Adoption**: PyTorch is widely adopted in the AI research community, making it ideal for experimenting with cutting-edge models.
- **GPU Acceleration**: Like TensorFlow, PyTorch supports GPU acceleration, allowing for faster model training.

Installing PyTorch

To install PyTorch, use the following commands based on your system configuration:

Using conda:

```
conda install pytorch torchvision torchaudio cudatoolkit=10.2 -c pytorch
```

Using pip:

```
pip install torch torchvision torchaudio
```

1.4.8 Installing All Libraries at Once

If you're using Anaconda, you can create a new environment and install all of the essential libraries for AI with a single command:

```
conda create -n ai-env python=3.8 numpy pandas matplotlib scikit-learn tensorflow
pytorch
```

This will create a new environment named ai-env and install Python 3.8 along with
NumPy, Pandas, Matplotlib, Scikit-learn, TensorFlow, and PyTorch in one go.

Installing essential libraries is an important step in getting started with AI development. In
this section, we've covered the most common libraries used in AI and machine learning:
NumPy, Pandas, Matplotlib, Scikit-learn, TensorFlow, Keras, and PyTorch. These
libraries will provide the foundational tools you need for tasks such as data manipulation,
visualization, machine learning, and deep learning.

By following the installation instructions and setting up these libraries, you'll be equipped
to start building AI models and working on real-world AI projects. Whether you are doing
simple data analysis or training complex neural networks, these libraries will be
indispensable to your development workflow.

1.5 Writing and Running Your First Python Script

Now that you have set up your development environment and installed the essential
libraries, it's time to write and run your first Python script. In this section, we'll guide you
through creating a simple Python script, running it, and understanding the basic structure
of a Python program. This is a crucial step in starting your journey with AI because it will
help you familiarize yourself with how Python code is written and executed.

1.5.1 Understanding the Python Environment

Python is an interpreted language, which means you write code in text files, and the
Python interpreter executes it directly. There are a few ways to interact with the Python
environment, and we'll look at the most common ones:

IDEs (Integrated Development Environments): These are applications where you can
write and run your Python scripts. Some popular IDEs for Python include VS Code,
PyCharm, and Spyder (available with Anaconda).

Text Editors: You can write Python code using simple text editors like Notepad++ or
Sublime Text, and then run the script via the command line.

Interactive Python Shell: The Python shell allows you to run Python code interactively, which is useful for testing snippets of code quickly.

Jupyter Notebooks: If you're using Anaconda or a similar setup, Jupyter Notebooks provide an interactive web-based environment that allows you to write Python code in cells and execute them one by one. This is especially useful for AI development.

1.5.2 Writing Your First Python Script

Let's start by creating a simple Python script. This script will print "Hello, AI World!" to the console. Follow these steps to write your first Python script:

Open Your Code Editor: Open your preferred Python IDE or text editor. For example, if you're using VS Code, open the editor and create a new file.

Write the Python Code: In the new file, type the following Python code:

```python
# This is a simple Python script that prints a message to the console
print("Hello, AI World!")
```

In this script:

- The print() function is used to output the message to the console.
- The # symbol indicates a comment. Anything after the # is not executed and is just there to explain the code.

Save the Script: Save the file with a .py extension (e.g., hello_ai.py). This is the standard file extension for Python scripts.

1.5.3 Running Your Python Script

Now that we have written our first Python script, let's run it.

Running the Script in VS Code

Open VS Code: If you're using VS Code, open the script file you just created (e.g., hello_ai.py).

Run the Script:

You can run the script by opening the integrated terminal in VS Code (by selecting Terminal > New Terminal).

In the terminal, type the following command and press Enter:

```
python hello_ai.py
```

If you're using Python 3 specifically, you might need to use:

```
python3 hello_ai.py
```

View the Output: After running the script, you should see the following output in the terminal:

```
Hello, AI World!
```

Running the Script in the Command Line

If you prefer using the command line, follow these steps:

Open the Command Line/Terminal:

On Windows, open the Command Prompt or PowerShell.

On macOS or Linux, open the Terminal.

Navigate to the Script Location: Use the cd (change directory) command to navigate to the folder where you saved the Python script. For example:

```
cd path/to/your/script
```

Run the Script: Type the following command and press Enter:

```
python hello_ai.py
```

You should see the same output:

```
Hello, AI World!
```

Running the Script in Jupyter Notebook

Launch Jupyter Notebook: If you're using Anaconda, you can launch Jupyter Notebook by typing the following command in the terminal:

```
jupyter notebook
```

Create a New Notebook: In the Jupyter interface, click on New (top-right) and select Python 3 to create a new notebook.

Write Code in Cells: In the first cell of the notebook, type:

```
print("Hello, AI World!")
```

Run the Cell: Press Shift + Enter to execute the cell. You should see the output displayed directly beneath the cell:

```
Hello, AI World!
```

1.5.4 Understanding Python Syntax

Let's break down the syntax of the script we just wrote:

- **print() function**: The print() function is one of Python's built-in functions. It is used to output information to the console.
- **Strings**: The text "Hello, AI World!" is enclosed in quotation marks. This is a string in Python. A string is any sequence of characters enclosed in either single (') or double (") quotes.
- **Comments**: Any text following the # symbol is a comment. Comments are ignored by the Python interpreter but are helpful for explaining code to human readers.
- **Whitespace**: Python relies on indentation (spaces or tabs) to define code blocks. In this simple example, there's no indentation needed beyond the function itself, but indentation is crucial for defining loops, functions, and classes.

1.5.5 Running a More Complex Python Script

Now, let's take it a step further and write a simple script that demonstrates variables, basic math, and printing results.

Create a New Python Script: Open a new file in your code editor and type the following code:

```python
# Python script demonstrating variables and basic math

# Define two numbers
num1 = 10
num2 = 5

# Perform basic math operations
sum_result = num1 + num2
diff_result = num1 - num2
prod_result = num1 * num2
div_result = num1 / num2

# Print the results
print("Sum:", sum_result)
print("Difference:", diff_result)
print("Product:", prod_result)
print("Division:", div_result)
```

Save and Run the Script: Save the file as math_operations.py and run it using the same steps as before.

The output will look like this:

```
Sum: 15
Difference: 5
Product: 50
Division: 2.0
```

In this script:

- We defined two variables num1 and num2 and assigned them values.

- We performed basic mathematical operations (addition, subtraction, multiplication, division).
- We used print() to display the results.

1.5.6 Common Python Errors and Troubleshooting

As you write and run Python scripts, you may encounter errors. Here are a few common ones and how to troubleshoot them:

SyntaxError: This occurs when Python encounters incorrect syntax in your script, like a missing parenthesis or extra spaces. Double-check the line where the error occurs to ensure that your syntax is correct.

Example:

```
print("Hello, AI World!"  # Missing closing parenthesis
```

NameError: This happens when you try to use a variable or function that hasn't been defined yet.

Example:

```
print(num1)  # NameError if num1 is not defined earlier
```

TypeError: This occurs when you try to perform an operation on incompatible data types.

Example:

```
num1 = "10"
num2 = 5
print(num1 + num2)  # TypeError because you're trying to add a string and an integer
```

In this section, we have walked through how to write and run your first Python script, which prints a message to the console and performs basic math. This foundational knowledge is essential for working with Python and understanding how to execute your code.

Whether you're writing a simple script or building complex AI models, knowing how to work with Python scripts is a crucial skill. By practicing writing and running Python code, you'll build the confidence to dive deeper into the world of AI and machine learning.

2. Python Basics: Writing Your First Code

Before diving into AI, you need a strong foundation in Python—the most popular programming language for artificial intelligence. In this chapter, you'll learn the core concepts of Python, including variables, data types, operators, and basic syntax. You'll explore control structures like loops and conditionals, which allow your code to make decisions and repeat tasks efficiently. Additionally, you'll get hands-on experience writing your first Python programs, understanding error handling, and debugging your code. By the end of this chapter, you'll have the fundamental coding skills needed to start building AI-powered applications.

2.1 Understanding Variables and Data Types

One of the core concepts in Python programming, especially for AI and machine learning, is understanding variables and data types. This section will introduce you to these fundamental building blocks of Python and explain how they are used to store, manipulate, and process data efficiently.

2.1.1 What Are Variables?

In programming, a variable is a symbolic name associated with a value. Variables allow you to store data and reference it throughout your code. Instead of hardcoding values directly into your program, you can assign values to variables and manipulate them as needed.

For example, in Python, you can define a variable to store a number:

```
age = 25
```

In this case, age is the variable name, and 25 is the value it holds. You can think of a variable as a container that stores data, which can then be accessed and modified as needed.

Rules for Naming Variables:

- A variable name must start with a letter (a-z, A-Z) or an underscore (_).

- The remaining characters in the variable name can be letters, digits (0-9), or underscores.
- Variable names are case-sensitive, meaning age, Age, and AGE are all different variables.
- Avoid using Python reserved keywords (like class, def, if, etc.) as variable names.

2.1.2 Data Types in Python

Each variable in Python is associated with a data type, which determines the kind of data the variable can store. Python supports several built-in data types, each used for different purposes. Below, we will explore the most commonly used data types in Python.

1. Integers (int)

An integer is a whole number, positive or negative, without a decimal point.

```
age = 25
height = -5
```

Integers are commonly used for counting, indexing, and performing arithmetic operations.

2. Floating-Point Numbers (float)

A float is a number that contains a decimal point or is expressed in scientific notation. It represents real numbers.

```
temperature = 23.5
pi = 3.14159
```

Floating-point numbers are important for representing continuous quantities, like measurements or probabilities, and are commonly used in AI models and calculations.

3. Strings (str)

A string is a sequence of characters, enclosed in either single (') or double (") quotes. Strings are used to represent text or alphanumeric data.

```
name = "Alice"
```

```
greeting = 'Hello, world!'
```

In AI, strings are often used to store textual data, like user input, labels for data points, or text from external sources such as files or databases.

4. Booleans (bool)

A boolean is a data type that can have one of two possible values: True or False. Booleans are typically used for decision-making and control flow in programs.

```
is_raining = True
has_permission = False
```

In AI, booleans are often used for flags, conditions, or to represent binary choices (yes/no, true/false).

5. Lists (list)

A list is a collection of items, which can be of different data types. Lists are ordered, meaning the items have a specific order, and they are mutable, meaning you can modify them.

```
fruits = ["apple", "banana", "cherry"]
numbers = [1, 2, 3, 4, 5]
```

Lists are very versatile and are frequently used in Python for storing data, especially when dealing with collections of related items, like data points in AI or machine learning algorithms.

6. Tuples (tuple)

A tuple is similar to a list but is immutable, meaning you cannot change its elements once it is created. Tuples are typically used for storing a fixed collection of items.

```
coordinates = (4, 5)
dimensions = (20, 30, 40)
```

Tuples are useful when you need a collection of items that should not be changed, such as coordinates in a 2D or 3D space or settings for an AI model that shouldn't be altered.

7. Dictionaries (dict)

A dictionary is an unordered collection of key-value pairs. Each key is unique, and it maps to a value. Dictionaries are mutable and are used for associating values with specific identifiers.

```
student = {"name": "John", "age": 20, "major": "Computer Science"}
person = {"first_name": "Jane", "last_name": "Doe", "age": 25}
```

Dictionaries are incredibly useful in AI, especially for representing structured data like JSON objects or to map features to values in machine learning models.

8. Sets (set)

A set is an unordered collection of unique items. Unlike lists and tuples, sets do not allow duplicates, and their elements are not indexed.

```
unique_numbers = {1, 2, 3, 4, 5}
unique_colors = {"red", "blue", "green"}
```

Sets are typically used when you need to store a collection of unique items, like eliminating duplicate values in a dataset or identifying unique categories in AI problems.

2.1.3 Type Conversion

Sometimes, you may need to convert one data type to another. This process is called type casting. Python provides several built-in functions for type conversion.

Examples of Type Conversion:

Integer to float: You can convert an integer to a float by passing it to the float() function.

```
x = 10
y = float(x)  # y becomes 10.0
```

Float to integer: You can convert a float to an integer using the int() function (which truncates the decimal part).

```
x = 10.75
y = int(x)  # y becomes 10
```

String to integer: If the string contains a valid number, you can convert it to an integer using int().

```
x = "25"
y = int(x)  # y becomes 25
```

Integer to string: You can convert an integer to a string using the str() function.

```
x = 30
y = str(x)  # y becomes "30"
```

2.1.4 Importance of Data Types in AI

Understanding the appropriate data type to use for different pieces of data is crucial in AI. Here's why:

Efficient Data Processing: Choosing the correct data type can lead to more efficient storage and faster computations. For instance, integers are faster for numerical calculations than floats, and lists are better for storing large amounts of data compared to strings.

Compatibility with Libraries: AI libraries and frameworks like NumPy, Pandas, and TensorFlow often expect specific data types. For example, a machine learning model may expect numerical inputs (integers or floats) and may not work properly with strings unless they are properly encoded or transformed.

Data Preprocessing: Many AI projects involve data preprocessing, where you may need to convert raw data into suitable formats. For example, text data might need to be tokenized or transformed into numerical features, and categorical data may need to be converted into one-hot encoding (using integers or booleans).

2.1.5 Common Operations with Variables and Data Types

As you work with variables, you'll often perform various operations on them. Below are some basic operations you can do with different data types:

Numeric Operations:

```
x = 10
y = 3
print(x + y)  # Addition
print(x - y)  # Subtraction
print(x * y)  # Multiplication
print(x / y)  # Division
print(x // y)  # Integer Division
print(x % y)  # Modulus
print(x ** y)  # Exponentiation
```

String Operations:

```
name = "Alice"
greeting = "Hello"
full_greeting = greeting + " " + name  # Concatenation
print(full_greeting)  # Output: "Hello Alice"
```

List Operations:

```
fruits = ["apple", "banana", "cherry"]
fruits.append("orange")  # Add an item to the list
fruits.remove("banana")  # Remove an item from the list
print(fruits)  # Output: ["apple", "cherry", "orange"]
```

Dictionary Operations:

```
person = {"name": "Alice", "age": 25}
person["age"] = 26  # Update a value
print(person)  # Output: {"name": "Alice", "age": 26}
```

Understanding variables and data types is fundamental to writing Python code, especially when working with AI and machine learning models. In this section, we've learned how to define variables, explore the different data types available in Python, and understand their significance in AI development. By practicing with these concepts, you'll be able to manage and manipulate data efficiently, which is essential for building AI systems and analyzing datasets.

2.2 Conditional Statements and Loops

Conditional statements and loops are two fundamental concepts in programming that allow you to control the flow of execution in your code. These structures are essential for making decisions, repeating tasks, and handling different cases based on varying conditions. Understanding how to use conditional statements and loops effectively is crucial for developing AI models and algorithms in Python. This section will explain these concepts and demonstrate how they can be applied to solve problems and create dynamic code in Python.

2.2.1 Conditional Statements: Making Decisions

A conditional statement allows you to run different pieces of code depending on whether a certain condition is true or false. The most common conditional statements in Python are if, elif, and else.

1. The if Statement

The if statement evaluates a condition, and if the condition is true, it executes the corresponding block of code. If the condition is false, the block is skipped.

Syntax:

```
if condition:
    # Code to execute if condition is true
```

Example:

```
age = 18
if age >= 18:
    print("You are an adult.")
```

In this example, the condition age >= 18 evaluates to True, so the message "You are an adult." is printed.

2. The else Statement

The else statement provides an alternative block of code to run if the if condition is false.

Syntax:

```
if condition:
    # Code to execute if condition is true
else:
    # Code to execute if condition is false
```

Example:

```
age = 16
if age >= 18:
    print("You are an adult.")
else:
    print("You are a minor.")
```

In this example, the condition age >= 18 evaluates to False, so the code under else runs and prints "You are a minor.".

3. The elif (Else If) Statement

The elif statement allows you to check multiple conditions. You can have as many elif statements as needed. If the if condition is false, the elif conditions are checked one by one in order. If none of the conditions is true, the else block is executed.

Syntax:

```
if condition1:
    # Code to execute if condition1 is true
elif condition2:
    # Code to execute if condition2 is true
else:
    # Code to execute if no conditions are true
```

Example:

```
age = 22
if age < 18:
    print("You are a minor.")
elif age >= 18 and age <= 21:
    print("You are a young adult.")
else:
    print("You are an adult.")
```

In this case, the age is 22, so the condition for else will be true, and the program will print "You are an adult.".

4. Comparison Operators

To make conditions in if, elif, and else statements, you use comparison operators to compare values. The most common comparison operators are:

```
== : Equal to
!= : Not equal to
> : Greater than
< : Less than
>= : Greater than or equal to
<= : Less than or equal to
```

Example:

```
x = 5
y = 10
```

```
if x < y:
    print("x is less than y")
```

5. Logical Operators

In addition to comparison operators, Python provides logical operators to combine multiple conditions in one statement:

```
and: Returns True if both conditions are true
or: Returns True if at least one condition is true
not: Reverses the condition (returns True if the condition is false)
```

Example:

```
x = 5
y = 10
z = 15
if x < y and z > y:
    print("Both conditions are true")
```

2.2.2 Loops: Repeating Tasks

A loop is a way to execute a block of code repeatedly. Loops are useful when you need to perform the same operation multiple times, such as iterating through a dataset or running an algorithm until a condition is met. There are two main types of loops in Python: for loops and while loops.

1. The for Loop

A for loop iterates over a sequence (like a list, tuple, or range) and executes a block of code for each element in the sequence. The for loop is especially useful when you know the number of iterations in advance or want to iterate over a collection of data.

Syntax:

```
for variable in sequence:
```

```
    # Code to execute for each item in the sequence
```

Example:

```
fruits = ["apple", "banana", "cherry"]
for fruit in fruits:
    print(fruit)
```

This loop will print each fruit in the list fruits one by one:

```
apple
banana
cherry
```

Using range() with for Loops: The range() function generates a sequence of numbers, and you can use it with a for loop to iterate over a range of values.

Example:

```
for i in range(1, 6):  # Loop from 1 to 5
    print(i)
```

The output will be:

```
1
2
3
4
5
```

2. The while Loop

A while loop continues to execute a block of code as long as a specified condition is True. It is useful when you do not know the number of iterations in advance, and you want the loop to continue until a certain condition is met.

Syntax:

```
while condition:
    # Code to execute as long as the condition is true
```

Example:

```
count = 0
while count < 5:
    print(count)
    count += 1
```

This loop will print:

```
0
1
2
3
4
```

In this case, the condition count < 5 is checked before each iteration, and the loop will stop once count reaches 5.

3. Infinite Loops

A while loop can create an infinite loop if the condition always evaluates to True. Be cautious when using while loops to avoid this, as it can cause your program to run indefinitely.

Example:

```
while True:
    print("This will run forever!")
```

To stop an infinite loop, you need to use a break condition inside the loop or interrupt the program (usually with Ctrl+C).

4. break, continue, and else in Loops

- **break**: Exits the loop entirely, regardless of the loop's condition.
- **continue**: Skips the current iteration and moves to the next iteration of the loop.
- **else**: A loop can have an else block that is executed when the loop finishes all iterations without hitting a break.

Examples:

```
# Using `break`
for i in range(10):
    if i == 5:
        break  # Exit the loop when i equals 5
    print(i)

# Using `continue`
for i in range(5):
    if i == 2:
        continue  # Skip the iteration when i equals 2
    print(i)

# Using `else`
for i in range(5):
    print(i)
else:
    print("Loop finished!")
```

2.2.3 Practical Applications of Conditional Statements and Loops in AI

In AI development, conditional statements and loops are frequently used for tasks like:

- **Decision Trees**: In machine learning, decision trees use conditions (based on data features) to make decisions.
- **Data Preprocessing**: Loops are used to iterate over datasets and apply transformations or filter data points.
- **Model Training**: Loops are used in training machine learning models, where an algorithm iterates over multiple epochs to update weights and improve predictions.
- **Optimization Algorithms**: Many AI optimization algorithms, like gradient descent, use loops to iteratively adjust model parameters based on the data.

2.2.4 Conclusion

Conditional statements and loops are essential tools for controlling the flow of your program. With if, elif, and else, you can make decisions based on varying conditions. For and while loops allow you to repeat tasks, which is crucial for handling large datasets and iterating through the steps of AI models. Mastering these constructs will enable you to write dynamic and efficient code, a critical skill for AI development. By practicing these concepts, you'll gain the flexibility to build more complex logic and implement algorithms effectively in your AI projects.

2.3 Functions and Modular Programming

In Python, functions and modular programming are key concepts that allow you to write clean, reusable, and organized code. Functions allow you to group related operations under a single name, making your code more readable and easier to maintain. Modular programming, on the other hand, is the practice of breaking down a program into smaller, manageable pieces (modules), each handling a specific task. Both concepts are essential for developing scalable and maintainable AI programs. This section will explore functions, how to define and use them, and how modular programming can improve your code structure.

2.3.1 What Is a Function?

A function is a block of code that only runs when it is called. Functions help you avoid repetition in your code, as you can write a block of logic once and reuse it wherever needed. Functions can accept inputs (called parameters or arguments), and they can also return a result (output).

Basic Syntax of a Function

The syntax for defining a function in Python is:

```
def function_name(parameters):
    # Code block
    return result   # Optional, depending on whether the function needs to return something
```

- def is the keyword used to define a function.
- function_name is the name you give to the function.

- parameters are values you pass to the function (also called arguments).
- The code block is the set of instructions that the function executes.
- return is used to send a value back to the caller (if needed).

Example: Defining and Calling a Function

```
def greet(name):
    return "Hello, " + name + "!"

# Calling the function
message = greet("Alice")
print(message)
```

Output:

```
Hello, Alice!
```

In this example:

- The function greet() takes a parameter name and returns a greeting message.
- We call the function with the argument "Alice", and it returns the greeting string, which is then printed.

Functions Without Return Values

Functions do not always need to return a value. Sometimes, they perform an action, such as printing something or modifying data, and do not need to send any value back to the caller.

```
def print_welcome():
    print("Welcome to the world of AI!")

# Calling the function
print_welcome()
```

Output:

```
Welcome to the world of AI!
```

In this case, the function print_welcome() prints a message but does not return anything.

2.3.2 Function Parameters and Arguments

Functions can accept parameters (also known as arguments) that allow you to pass values to the function. There are several ways to pass parameters to functions in Python:

1. Positional Arguments

Positional arguments are values you pass to a function in the order in which the parameters are defined.

```
def add(x, y):
    return x + y

result = add(5, 3)  # 5 is assigned to x, and 3 is assigned to y
print(result)
```

Output:

```
8
```

2. Keyword Arguments

With keyword arguments, you specify the names of the parameters when calling the function, which allows you to pass arguments in any order.

```
def multiply(a, b):
    return a * b

result = multiply(b=4, a=3)  # Passing arguments in any order
print(result)
```

Output:

3. Default Arguments

You can define default values for parameters, so if a caller does not provide a value, the function uses the default.

```
def greet(name="Guest"):
    return "Hello, " + name + "!"

print(greet())  # Uses the default value "Guest"
print(greet("Alice"))  # Uses the provided value "Alice"
```

Output:

```
Hello, Guest!
Hello, Alice!
```

4. Variable-Length Arguments

Sometimes, you may not know how many arguments a function will receive. Python allows you to handle this with variable-length arguments using *args and **kwargs.

- *args is used to pass a variable number of non-keyword arguments (like a list of values).
- **kwargs is used to pass a variable number of keyword arguments (like a dictionary of key-value pairs).

Example: Using *args

```
def add_numbers(*args):
    return sum(args)

result = add_numbers(1, 2, 3, 4, 5)
print(result)
```

Output:

In this example, the function add_numbers() takes any number of arguments, and it returns the sum of those numbers.

Example: Using **kwargs

```
def print_info(**kwargs):
    for key, value in kwargs.items():
        print(key + ": " + str(value))

print_info(name="Alice", age=25, occupation="Engineer")
```

Output:

```
name: Alice
age: 25
occupation: Engineer
```

Here, print_info() can accept any number of keyword arguments and print them in a readable format.

2.3.3 Return Values and Multiple Returns

Functions can return a value (or multiple values). You can use the return keyword to send a result back to the caller. A function can also return multiple values as a tuple.

Example: Single Return Value

```
def subtract(x, y):
    return x - y

result = subtract(10, 4)
print(result)
```

Output:

Example: Multiple Return Values

```
def calculate(x, y):
    sum_result = x + y
    product_result = x * y
    return sum_result, product_result  # Returning both sum and product

result = calculate(4, 5)
print(result)  # Output: (9, 20)
```

In this case, calculate() returns both the sum and the product as a tuple. You can then access these values in your program as needed.

2.3.4 Modular Programming: Breaking Down Your Code

Modular programming is a software design technique that divides a program into smaller, independent modules. Each module typically performs a specific task or handles a part of the program's logic. Modular programming promotes code reusability, makes your code easier to debug, and improves maintainability.

Benefits of Modular Programming:

- **Reusability**: You can reuse the same function or module in different parts of your code or even in different projects.
- **Maintainability**: Smaller modules are easier to maintain. If something goes wrong, it's easier to find and fix the problem.
- **Separation of Concerns**: By separating functionality into different modules, you ensure that each module does one thing, making it easier to understand and debug.
- **Collaboration**: In team environments, different team members can work on different modules independently, making development faster and more efficient.

Creating Modules in Python

You can create your own modules in Python by simply placing functions, classes, and variables in separate .py files. Each file can then be imported into other files.

Example: Creating a Module

Create a file called math_operations.py with the following functions:

```
# math_operations.py

def add(x, y):
    return x + y

def subtract(x, y):
    return x - y
Use the module in another Python file:
python
Copy
Edit
# main.py
import math_operations

result1 = math_operations.add(5, 3)
result2 = math_operations.subtract(10, 4)

print(result1)  # Output: 8
print(result2)  # Output: 6
```

In this example, the math_operations module contains two functions, add() and subtract(). These functions are imported and used in main.py.

2.3.5 Functions in AI Development

Functions and modular programming are particularly useful in AI development for several reasons:

- **Data Preprocessing**: Functions can be used to process datasets, such as cleaning data, encoding labels, or normalizing values, by encapsulating each preprocessing step in a function.
- **Model Evaluation**: Functions are useful for splitting datasets, training models, evaluating performance, and tuning hyperparameters.

- **Reusability**: In AI projects, you often reuse the same functions for various tasks, such as feature extraction, model training, and result visualization. Creating functions for these tasks makes your code modular and reusable.

2.3.6 Conclusion

Functions and modular programming are essential concepts for writing clean, reusable, and maintainable Python code. Functions help to organize and simplify your program by grouping related tasks, while modular programming allows you to break your program into smaller, manageable parts. These principles are crucial in AI development, where you often need to work with large datasets, complex models, and various data preprocessing and evaluation tasks. By mastering functions and modular programming, you can make your AI code more efficient, organized, and scalable.

2.4 Handling Errors and Debugging Your Code

In any programming language, including Python, errors are an inevitable part of the development process. Whether you're working on a small script or a complex AI system, understanding how to handle errors and debug your code is critical to ensuring that your program runs smoothly. Python provides a range of tools for identifying, managing, and fixing errors, making the debugging process easier and more efficient. This section covers error handling in Python, the different types of errors you might encounter, and strategies for debugging your code.

2.4.1 Understanding Errors in Python

Errors, also called exceptions, are issues that occur during the execution of a program. These errors can prevent the program from running successfully. Python categorizes errors into different types, and understanding these categories is essential for handling them effectively.

Types of Errors in Python:

Syntax Errors: These occur when the code does not follow the correct syntax of Python. Syntax errors prevent the program from running altogether.

Example:

```
print("Hello, world!"  # Missing closing parenthesis
```

Runtime Errors: These occur when the program is running, but something goes wrong, such as dividing by zero, trying to access an undefined variable, or using an incorrect data type.

Example:

```
x = 10 / 0  # Division by zero
```

Logical Errors: These are the most difficult to detect because the program runs without crashing, but the output is incorrect. Logical errors are typically caused by flaws in the program's logic.

Example:

```
def add_numbers(a, b):
    return a * b  # Incorrect operation, should be addition
```

NameError: This occurs when a variable is referenced before it has been defined or when a variable name is misspelled.

Example:

```
print(variable_not_defined) # NameError because 'variable_not_defined' is not defined
```

TypeError: This occurs when an operation or function is applied to an object of inappropriate type.

Example:

```
x = "hello" + 5  # You can't concatenate a string and an integer
```

IndexError: This occurs when you try to access an element in a list or tuple that is out of range.

Example:

```
my_list = [1, 2, 3]
print(my_list[5])  # IndexError because index 5 is out of range
```

ValueError: This occurs when a function receives an argument of the correct type but an inappropriate value.

Example:

```
x = int("hello")  # ValueError because "hello" cannot be converted to an integer
```

2.4.2 Handling Errors with Try and Except

Python provides a powerful way to handle errors using try and except blocks. The idea is to "try" to run a block of code that might raise an error, and if an error occurs, it is "caught" by the except block, allowing the program to continue running smoothly.

Basic Syntax:

```
try:
    # Code that may raise an error
except ErrorType:
    # Code to handle the error
```

Example: Handling a Division by Zero Error

```
try:
    x = 10 / 0
except ZeroDivisionError:
    print("You can't divide by zero!")
```

Output:

```
You can't divide by zero!
```

In this example, the division by zero raises a ZeroDivisionError, and the program prints a message instead of crashing.

Catching Multiple Types of Errors:

You can catch multiple types of errors in a single try block by adding multiple except clauses.

```
try:
    x = int("hello")  # This will raise a ValueError
except ZeroDivisionError:
    print("You can't divide by zero!")
except ValueError:
    print("Invalid value for conversion!")
except TypeError:
    print("Invalid type!")
```

Output:

```
Invalid value for conversion!
```

In this example, the ValueError is caught because the string "hello" cannot be converted to an integer.

Using the else Clause:

You can also use the else clause after the except block. The code inside the else block runs only if no error occurs in the try block.

```
try:
    x = 10 / 2
except ZeroDivisionError:
    print("You can't divide by zero!")
else:
    print("Division successful!")
```

Output:

```
Division successful!
```

Using the finally Clause:

The finally block is used to execute code that must run regardless of whether an exception was raised or not. It is often used to close files, release resources, or perform clean-up tasks.

```
try:
    file = open("data.txt", "r")
    content = file.read()
except FileNotFoundError:
    print("File not found!")
finally:
    file.close()  # Ensure the file is always closed, even if an error occurs
```

2.4.3 Debugging Techniques

Debugging is the process of identifying and fixing errors in your code. In Python, there are several techniques you can use to make the debugging process more effective.

1. Print Statements for Debugging

One of the simplest ways to debug your code is by using print() statements to output values of variables and track the flow of execution. This method is useful for understanding what's happening at different stages of your program.

```
def add(a, b):
    print(f"a: {a}, b: {b}")  # Debugging line
    return a + b

result = add(10, 5)
print(f"Result: {result}")
```

While this method can be effective for small programs, it can become cumbersome in larger codebases.

2. Using Python's Built-in Debugger: pdb

Python includes a built-in debugger called pdb (Python Debugger) that allows you to step through your code, inspect variables, and evaluate expressions during runtime. You can use it to pause the execution of your program at a specific point and interact with it.

Example:

```
import pdb

def add(a, b):
    pdb.set_trace()  # Pause the execution here
    return a + b

result = add(10, 5)
print(f"Result: {result}")
```

When the program hits pdb.set_trace(), it enters an interactive debugging session where you can type commands to inspect variables and control the flow.

```
n: Go to the next line of code.
s: Step into the function being called.
p: Print the value of an expression or variable (e.g., p a).
q: Quit the debugger.
```

3. Using an Integrated Development Environment (IDE)

Many Python IDEs, such as PyCharm, Visual Studio Code, and Jupyter Notebooks, come with built-in debugging tools that provide a graphical interface for stepping through your code, inspecting variables, and setting breakpoints. These IDEs allow you to easily control the flow of execution, monitor variables, and fix errors.

4. Unit Testing

Unit testing involves writing tests for individual units (functions or methods) of your code to ensure they work as expected. Python's built-in unittest module can help you write and run these tests.

```
import unittest
```

```
def add(a, b):
    return a + b

class TestAddition(unittest.TestCase):
    def test_add(self):
        self.assertEqual(add(2, 3), 5)  # Test that 2 + 3 equals 5

if __name__ == "__main__":
    unittest.main()
```

Using unit tests helps you catch errors early and ensures that your functions work as intended.

2.4.4 Best Practices for Debugging and Error Handling

- **Use Clear and Specific Error Messages**: When handling exceptions, provide clear and specific error messages to help identify the problem quickly.
- **Limit the Scope of Try Blocks**: Only wrap the code that might raise an exception inside a try block. This helps avoid catching unintended errors.
- **Test Your Code Regularly**: Use unit tests and debugging techniques throughout your development process to catch errors early.
- **Keep Code Simple**: Break complex logic into smaller, simpler functions. This makes it easier to identify errors and debug.

2.4.5 Conclusion

Handling errors and debugging are essential skills for any programmer, including those working with Python for AI development. By understanding different types of errors, using try and except to handle exceptions, and applying effective debugging strategies, you can identify and fix problems in your code quickly. Incorporating error handling and debugging techniques into your workflow will help you write more robust and reliable AI applications.

3. Data Structures for AI

Data is the backbone of artificial intelligence, and how you store, organize, and access that data is crucial for building efficient AI models. In this chapter, you'll explore Python's essential data structures, such as lists, tuples, dictionaries, and sets, which will help you manage and manipulate the data you'll work with in AI projects. You'll learn when to use each structure, how to perform operations on them, and why choosing the right data structure can make a significant impact on your model's performance. By the end of this chapter, you'll have the knowledge to handle complex datasets and start preparing data for machine learning and AI applications.

3.1 Lists and Tuples: Managing Collections of Data

In Python, managing collections of data efficiently is an essential skill, particularly when working with AI and machine learning. Two of the most commonly used data structures for handling collections of data are lists and tuples. These structures are both sequences that can hold multiple items, but they differ in terms of mutability, performance, and the scenarios in which they are used. In this section, we'll dive into the fundamentals of lists and tuples, understand their differences, and explore how to use them effectively for AI development.

3.1.1 Lists: Dynamic and Mutable

A list is an ordered collection of items that can store elements of any data type, such as integers, strings, or even other lists. Lists are mutable, meaning their contents can be modified after they are created. This makes them an excellent choice when you need to manipulate the data as you work with it, which is common in AI tasks like data preprocessing and manipulation.

Basic Syntax of Lists

In Python, lists are created by enclosing a comma-separated sequence of items within square brackets ([]).

```
# Creating a list
my_list = [1, 2, 3, 4, 5]
```

A list can store elements of different data types:

```
# List with mixed data types
mixed_list = [1, "hello", 3.14, True]
```

Accessing Elements in a List

You can access individual elements in a list using their index. In Python, indexing starts from 0, meaning the first element is at index 0, the second element at index 1, and so on.

```
my_list = [10, 20, 30, 40, 50]
print(my_list[0])  # Output: 10
print(my_list[3])  # Output: 40
```

Modifying Lists

Since lists are mutable, you can change their contents after creation. You can update an existing element, add new elements, or remove elements.

Changing an element:

```
my_list[1] = 25  # Change the second element (index 1)
print(my_list)  # Output: [10, 25, 30, 40, 50]
```

Appending elements:

You can add elements to the end of a list using the append() method.

```
my_list.append(60)
print(my_list)  # Output: [10, 25, 30, 40, 50, 60]
```

Inserting elements:

You can insert an element at a specific position using the insert() method.

```
my_list.insert(2, 15)  # Insert 15 at index 2
print(my_list)  # Output: [10, 25, 15, 30, 40, 50, 60]
```

Removing elements:

You can remove elements from a list using methods like remove(), pop(), or del.

```
my_list.remove(25)  # Remove the first occurrence of 25
print(my_list) # Output: [10, 15, 30, 40, 50, 60]

# Pop removes and returns an element at a given index
popped_item = my_list.pop(3)  # Removes the element at index 3 (40)
print(popped_item)  # Output: 40
print(my_list)  # Output: [10, 15, 30, 50, 60]
```

Slicing lists:

Slicing allows you to extract a part of the list. It uses the format list[start:end] where start is the index where slicing begins, and end is the index where slicing ends (but the element at end is not included).

```
my_list = [1, 2, 3, 4, 5]
sliced_list = my_list[1:4]
print(sliced_list)  # Output: [2, 3, 4]
```

Nested Lists

A list can also contain other lists as its elements. This is useful for creating multi-dimensional arrays or matrices, which are commonly used in AI tasks such as neural networks or datasets.

```
nested_list = [[1, 2], [3, 4], [5, 6]]
print(nested_list[1])  # Output: [3, 4]
print(nested_list[1][0])  # Output: 3
```

3.1.2 Tuples: Immutable Sequences

A tuple is very similar to a list, but the key difference is that tuples are immutable, meaning once created, their contents cannot be modified. Tuples are defined by enclosing items in parentheses (()), and like lists, they can hold elements of different data types. Because of their immutability, tuples are typically used to store data that should not be modified, such as fixed configuration values, coordinates, or return values from functions.

Basic Syntax of Tuples

```
# Creating a tuple
my_tuple = (1, 2, 3, 4, 5)
```

You can also create a tuple with a single element by including a comma after the value:

```
single_element_tuple = (5,)  # Comma is necessary to define a tuple with one element
```

Accessing Elements in a Tuple

Similar to lists, elements in a tuple can be accessed using their index.

```
my_tuple = (10, 20, 30, 40, 50)
print(my_tuple[0])  # Output: 10
print(my_tuple[3])  # Output: 40
```

Why Use Tuples?

While tuples are similar to lists, there are a few reasons why you might choose tuples over lists:

- **Immutability**: If you need a collection of data that should not change (such as fixed configuration parameters or function return values), a tuple is a better choice.
- **Performance**: Since tuples are immutable, they have a slightly better performance than lists in terms of memory usage and speed.
- **Safety**: Immutability makes tuples safer for use as keys in dictionaries (which require hashable objects) or elements in sets.

Working with Tuples

Because tuples are immutable, you cannot modify them in place. You cannot use methods like append(), insert(), or remove(). However, you can perform operations like concatenation and repetition.

```
my_tuple = (1, 2, 3)

# Concatenating tuples
new_tuple = my_tuple + (4, 5)
print(new_tuple)  # Output: (1, 2, 3, 4, 5)

# Repeating tuples
repeated_tuple = my_tuple * 2
print(repeated_tuple)  # Output: (1, 2, 3, 1, 2, 3)
```

You can also slice tuples in the same way you would slice lists.

```
my_tuple = (10, 20, 30, 40, 50)
sliced_tuple = my_tuple[1:4]
print(sliced_tuple)  # Output: (20, 30, 40)
```

3.1.3 Lists vs Tuples: When to Use Each?

While both lists and tuples are used to store collections of data, there are specific situations where one may be preferred over the other. The key factors to consider are mutability, performance, and use case.

Use Lists When:

- You need to modify the collection of data after creation (e.g., adding, removing, or updating elements).
- You are working with a dataset that needs to change over time, such as when training machine learning models where data can be dynamically updated.

Use Tuples When:

- The data should remain constant and unchangeable.
- You want to store fixed values (e.g., coordinates, configurations, or dates).
- You need to use the data as a key in a dictionary or as an element in a set.
- You are concerned about performance, as tuples are slightly more memory efficient than lists.

3.1.4 Using Lists and Tuples in AI Development

In AI development, both lists and tuples have their uses:

Lists are particularly useful for handling datasets, training sets, and managing data transformations. You may frequently use lists when processing data, storing features, or tracking iterations in training loops.

Tuples are helpful when working with fixed data such as configuration parameters, model evaluation metrics, or data points (e.g., a 2D point represented by (x, y) coordinates). They are also used when returning multiple values from a function, such as when performing a machine learning model's performance evaluation.

Example in AI:

```
# Tuple of model evaluation metrics (accuracy, precision, recall)
metrics = (0.85, 0.90, 0.87)

# List of features for machine learning model
features = [2.5, 3.1, 4.2, 5.0]
```

3.1.5 Conclusion

Understanding and effectively using lists and tuples is crucial for handling data in Python. Lists are versatile, mutable, and suitable for tasks that require frequent changes to the data. Tuples, on the other hand, offer immutability, performance benefits, and are ideal for fixed collections of data. In AI development, both data structures have distinct advantages, and choosing the right one depends on the needs of your application, such as the requirement for flexibility or performance. Mastering these two data structures will provide you with the foundation to build more efficient and organized AI programs.

3.2 Dictionaries and Sets: Fast Lookups and Unique Values

In Python, dictionaries and sets are two highly useful data structures that provide efficient ways to manage collections of data. They serve different purposes, but both are designed to make common operations like lookups, insertions, and deletions fast and efficient. As you develop AI applications, especially when working with large datasets or when speed is a priority, mastering these data structures becomes crucial. In this section, we will explore the fundamentals of dictionaries and sets, their use cases, and how they can be effectively used in AI development.

3.2.1 Dictionaries: Key-Value Pairs for Fast Lookups

A dictionary in Python is an unordered collection of key-value pairs. Each key is unique, and it maps to a specific value. Dictionaries provide a fast way to store and retrieve data based on a key, making them incredibly useful for tasks that require quick lookups. For example, you can use dictionaries to store model configurations, feature mappings, or training parameters.

Basic Syntax of Dictionaries

Dictionaries are created by enclosing key-value pairs within curly braces ({}). The key and value are separated by a colon (:), and each pair is separated by a comma.

```python
# Creating a dictionary
my_dict = {"name": "Alice", "age": 25, "city": "New York"}
```

Accessing Values in a Dictionary

You can retrieve a value from a dictionary by specifying its corresponding key.

```python
print(my_dict["name"])  # Output: Alice
print(my_dict["age"])   # Output: 25
```

If the key doesn't exist in the dictionary, a KeyError will be raised.

Modifying Dictionaries

Dictionaries are mutable, meaning their values can be updated or new key-value pairs can be added.

Updating a value:

```python
my_dict["age"] = 26  # Updating the value for the key "age"
print(my_dict) # Output: {"name": "Alice", "age": 26, "city": "New York"}
```

Adding a new key-value pair:

```
my_dict["job"] = "Engineer"  # Adding a new key-value pair
print(my_dict)   # Output: {"name": "Alice", "age": 26, "city": "New York", "job": "Engineer"}
```

Removing key-value pairs:

You can remove a key-value pair using the del keyword or the pop() method.

```
del my_dict["city"]  # Removing the key "city"
print(my_dict)  # Output: {"name": "Alice", "age": 26, "job": "Engineer"}

# Using pop() to remove and return a value
removed_value = my_dict.pop("job")
print(removed_value)  # Output: Engineer
print(my_dict)  # Output: {"name": "Alice", "age": 26}
```

Dictionaries in AI Applications

Dictionaries are particularly useful in AI when you need to map keys to data values. Here are a few common scenarios:

Mapping features to values: For example, in machine learning models, you might map feature names to their corresponding values.

```
features = {"age": 30, "height": 175, "weight": 70}
```

Storing model parameters: Dictionaries are often used to store hyperparameters or configuration settings for machine learning algorithms.

```
model_params = {"learning_rate": 0.01, "epochs": 100, "batch_size": 32}
```

Storing results of computations: After running an experiment or model evaluation, you might want to store the results in a dictionary.

```
results = {"accuracy": 0.92, "precision": 0.89, "recall": 0.87}
```

Dictionary Methods

keys(): Returns a view of the dictionary's keys.
values(): Returns a view of the dictionary's values.
items(): Returns a view of the dictionary's key-value pairs.
get(): Returns the value for a given key, or None if the key does not exist (instead of raising an error).

```
print(my_dict.keys())  # Output: dict_keys(["name", "age"])
print(my_dict.values())  # Output: dict_values([Alice, 26])
```

3.2.2 Sets: Storing Unique Elements

A set is an unordered collection of unique elements. Unlike dictionaries, sets only store values without any associated keys. Sets are very useful when you want to track unique items and perform operations like union, intersection, or difference on these values. Sets automatically discard duplicate values, making them ideal for tasks such as identifying unique features or filtering out repetitive data.

Basic Syntax of Sets

A set is created by enclosing elements in curly braces ({}). It is important to note that a set cannot contain duplicate values.

```
# Creating a set
my_set = {1, 2, 3, 4, 5}
```

Adding and Removing Elements from a Set

You can add new elements to a set using the add() method, and you can remove elements using the remove() or discard() method.

```
my_set.add(6)  # Adding an element
print(my_set)  # Output: {1, 2, 3, 4, 5, 6}

my_set.remove(3)  # Removing an element
print(my_set)  # Output: {1, 2, 4, 5, 6}
```

```
# Removing an element without raising an error if the element doesn't exist
my_set.discard(10)  # Nothing happens if 10 is not in the set
```

Set Operations

Sets support several powerful operations for working with multiple sets:

Union: Combines two sets and returns a new set with all unique elements.

```
set1 = {1, 2, 3}
set2 = {3, 4, 5}
union_set = set1 | set2  # Union of set1 and set2
print(union_set)  # Output: {1, 2, 3, 4, 5}
```

Intersection: Returns a new set with only the elements that are common to both sets.

```
intersection_set = set1 & set2  # Intersection of set1 and set2
print(intersection_set)  # Output: {3}
```

Difference: Returns a new set with elements that are in the first set but not in the second.

```
difference_set = set1 - set2  # Elements in set1 but not in set2
print(difference_set)  # Output: {1, 2}
```

Symmetric Difference: Returns a new set with elements that are in either set, but not in both.

```
symmetric_difference_set = set1 ^ set2  # Elements in either set1 or set2, but not both
print(symmetric_difference_set)  # Output: {1, 2, 4, 5}
```

Sets in AI Applications

In AI, sets are often used to handle data that requires uniqueness or to filter out repeated data points. Here are a few examples:

Unique Features: When preprocessing data, sets can help eliminate duplicate features or labels.

```
unique_features = {"age", "height", "weight", "income"}
```

Data Preprocessing: Sets are useful for removing duplicates in large datasets, ensuring that each data point is unique.

```
data_points = {("John", 25), ("Alice", 30), ("John", 25)}  # Duplicates are removed
```

Identifying Common Elements: You can use the intersection operation to find common elements between two sets, such as comparing predicted labels with actual labels in machine learning models.

```
predicted_labels = {1, 0, 1, 1}
actual_labels = {1, 1, 0, 0}
common_labels = predicted_labels & actual_labels  # Common values between the two sets
```

3.2.3 Dictionaries vs Sets: When to Use Each?

Use Dictionaries When:

- You need to map a key to a corresponding value.
- Fast lookups, insertions, and deletions are important.
- You need to store metadata about items, such as feature names or model parameters.

Use Sets When:

- You need to store unique elements and avoid duplicates.
- You need to perform set operations such as union, intersection, or difference.
- You want fast membership testing (checking if an item is part of a set).

3.2.4 Conclusion

Both dictionaries and sets are powerful data structures that offer significant advantages in terms of performance and functionality when handling collections of data. Dictionaries allow you to store and quickly retrieve data using key-value pairs, while sets provide a way to manage unique elements and perform efficient set operations. Understanding when and how to use these data structures is essential for building efficient AI applications, whether you're working with model configurations, feature sets, or data processing tasks. By mastering dictionaries and sets, you'll be able to handle a wide variety of data management challenges with ease.

3.3 Working with Strings for Text Data

In the world of artificial intelligence (AI), text data is ubiquitous, and working with it efficiently is essential. Whether you're building a natural language processing (NLP) model, developing a chatbot, or processing user input, you'll need to know how to manipulate and analyze strings (sequences of characters) effectively. Python provides a rich set of tools for string manipulation that makes it an ideal language for working with text data.

In this section, we'll explore how to work with strings in Python, covering everything from basic string operations to advanced techniques for processing and cleaning text data for AI applications.

3.3.1 Basic String Operations

A string in Python is a sequence of characters enclosed in single (') or double (") quotes. Python allows for a wide variety of operations to manipulate and work with strings.

Creating Strings

Strings can be created using either single or double quotes:

```
# Single quotes
my_string1 = 'Hello, AI world!'

# Double quotes
my_string2 = "Python is great for AI."
```

String Concatenation

You can combine strings using the + operator. This is called string concatenation:

```
greeting = "Hello"
name = "Alice"
message = greeting + ", " + name + "!"  # Concatenating strings
print(message)  # Output: Hello, Alice!
```

String Repetition

You can repeat a string multiple times using the * operator:

```
repeat = "AI " * 3
print(repeat)  # Output: AI AI AI
```

String Length

To get the length (number of characters) of a string, you can use the len() function:

```
sentence = "Machine learning is fun."
print(len(sentence))  # Output: 26
```

String Indexing and Slicing

Strings are indexed, which means you can access individual characters by their position. Indexing starts from 0 for the first character and goes up to the length of the string minus 1. You can also use slicing to extract a substring from a string.

```
text = "Hello, world!"
print(text[0])  # Output: H (first character)
print(text[-1]) # Output: ! (last character)

# Slicing the string
substring = text[7:12]  # Extracting "world"
print(substring)  # Output: world
```

3.3.2 String Methods

Python provides many built-in methods to manipulate strings, making them incredibly versatile for text processing. Here are some commonly used string methods:

Changing Case

You can easily convert the case of a string to lowercase, uppercase, or title case:

```
text = "Python is Amazing"

print(text.lower())  # Output: python is amazing
print(text.upper())  # Output: PYTHON IS AMAZING
print(text.title())  # Output: Python Is Amazing
```

Removing Whitespace

Strings often have extra spaces at the beginning or end, especially when processing user input. You can remove leading or trailing spaces using the strip() method:

```
text = "  Hello, AI!  "
print(text.strip())  # Output: "Hello, AI!" (removes the extra spaces)
```

If you only want to remove leading or trailing spaces, you can use lstrip() or rstrip():

```
print(text.lstrip())  # Output: "Hello, AI!  " (removes leading spaces)
print(text.rstrip())  # Output: "  Hello, AI!" (removes trailing spaces)
```

Replacing Substrings

To replace a substring in a string, use the replace() method:

```
sentence = "I love Python!"
modified_sentence = sentence.replace("love", "adore")
print(modified_sentence) # Output: I adore Python!
```

Checking Substring Presence

You can check if a string contains a certain substring using the in operator:

```
text = "Natural language processing is fun!"
```

```
print("language" in text)  # Output: True
print("AI" in text)  # Output: False
```

Splitting Strings

Strings can be split into a list of substrings using the split() method. The default delimiter is any whitespace, but you can specify other delimiters as well.

```
sentence = "Python, AI, and NLP"
words = sentence.split(", ")  # Splitting by comma and space
print(words)  # Output: ['Python', 'AI', 'and', 'NLP']
```

Joining Strings

To join a list of strings into a single string, you can use the join() method:

```
words = ['Python', 'is', 'awesome']
sentence = " ".join(words)  # Joining with a space separator
print(sentence)  # Output: Python is awesome
```

3.3.3 String Formatting

In many AI applications, particularly when dealing with user input or displaying results, you often need to insert variables into strings. Python provides several ways to format strings, including f-strings, format(), and the older percent formatting.

F-strings (Python 3.6 and later)

F-strings are a modern and efficient way to format strings by embedding expressions inside string literals. The expressions are evaluated at runtime and formatted using curly braces {}.

```
name = "Alice"
age = 30
message = f"Hello, {name}. You are {age} years old."
print(message)  # Output: Hello, Alice. You are 30 years old.
format() Method
```

The format() method allows you to insert values into placeholders within the string:

```
name = "Alice"
age = 30
message = "Hello, {}. You are {} years old.".format(name, age)
print(message)  # Output: Hello, Alice. You are 30 years old.
```

You can also specify the order of placeholders:

```
message = "Hello, {1}. You are {0} years old.".format(age, name)
print(message)  # Output: Hello, Alice. You are 30 years old.
```

Percent Formatting (older method)

While not commonly used in modern Python code, you can also format strings using the percent (%) operator:

```
name = "Alice"
age = 30
message = "Hello, %s. You are %d years old." % (name, age)
print(message)  # Output: Hello, Alice. You are 30 years old.
```

3.3.4 Working with Text Data in AI Applications

In AI, text data often needs to be preprocessed, cleaned, and transformed before being fed into models. Here are a few examples of how string manipulation comes in handy when working with text data:

Text Cleaning and Preprocessing

For machine learning and natural language processing (NLP), text data typically needs to be cleaned and prepared. Common tasks include:

- **Removing punctuation**: Stripping out unnecessary characters like commas, periods, and question marks.
- **Converting to lowercase**: Standardizing text to lowercase to ensure consistency.
- **Tokenization**: Splitting text into individual words (or tokens) for analysis.

Example:

```
import string

text = "Hello, AI world! Let's start working."
text_cleaned = text.lower()  # Convert to lowercase
text_cleaned = text_cleaned.translate(str.maketrans("", "", string.punctuation))  # Remove punctuation
print(text_cleaned)  # Output: hello ai world lets start working
```

Word Frequency Count

One common task in NLP is to count the frequency of each word in a text. This can be done using a dictionary and string manipulation:

```
text = "AI is amazing. AI is the future."
words = text.lower().split()
word_count = {}

for word in words:
    word_count[word] = word_count.get(word, 0) + 1

print(word_count)  # Output: {'ai': 2, 'is': 2, 'amazing.': 1, 'the': 1, 'future.': 1}
```

Handling Text Data for NLP Models

In NLP applications, text data often needs to be transformed into a format that machine learning models can work with. Common tasks include:

- **Tokenization**: Breaking down text into individual words or subword units.
- **Removing stopwords**: Filtering out common words (e.g., "the", "and", "is") that don't contribute much meaning.
- **Stemming or Lemmatization**: Reducing words to their base form (e.g., "running" → "run").

Example (removing stopwords):

```
stopwords = {"the", "is", "in", "on", "and"}
text = "The cat is in the house."
words = text.lower().split()
filtered_words = [word for word in words if word not in stopwords]
print(filtered_words)  # Output: ['cat', 'house']
```

3.3.5 Conclusion

Strings are essential for working with text data in Python, especially in AI and natural language processing applications. Whether you're cleaning and preprocessing text, performing tokenization, or formatting output for users, Python's rich set of string methods and operations makes it easy to handle text data efficiently. Mastering string manipulation allows you to process text effectively and prepare it for analysis and machine learning models, enabling you to build powerful AI-driven applications.

3.4 Understanding Stacks, Queues, and Linked Lists

In the world of computer science and AI, understanding data structures is fundamental to efficiently storing, processing, and managing data. Three of the most important and commonly used data structures are stacks, queues, and linked lists. These structures each serve specific purposes and are used to solve different types of problems. In this section, we'll dive into these data structures, explaining how they work, their characteristics, and how to implement them in Python.

3.4.1 Stacks: LIFO (Last In, First Out)

A stack is a collection of elements that follows the LIFO (Last In, First Out) principle. This means that the last element added to the stack is the first one to be removed. You can think of a stack like a stack of plates: the last plate added to the top of the stack is the first one you remove.

Basic Operations in a Stack

The two primary operations associated with stacks are:

Push: Add an item to the top of the stack.
Pop: Remove the item from the top of the stack.

Stacks can also have a peek operation, which allows you to look at the item at the top of the stack without removing it.

Implementing a Stack in Python

Python's list data type can be used to implement a stack. You can use the append() method to push elements onto the stack, and pop() to remove elements from the stack.

```
# Implementing a stack using a list
stack = []

# Pushing items onto the stack
stack.append(10)  # Stack: [10]
stack.append(20)  # Stack: [10, 20]
stack.append(30)  # Stack: [10, 20, 30]

# Popping items from the stack
top = stack.pop()  # Removes 30, Stack: [10, 20]
print(top)  # Output: 30

# Peek at the top item
print(stack[-1])  # Output: 20 (item at the top)
```

Use Cases of Stacks

- **Undo operations**: Stacks are useful in applications like text editors where you can undo the last action by popping from the stack of actions.
- **Expression evaluation**: Stacks are often used for evaluating arithmetic expressions (e.g., using the Reverse Polish Notation).
- **Depth-First Search (DFS):** In graph traversal, stacks are used to explore nodes in a depth-first manner.

3.4.2 Queues: FIFO (First In, First Out)

A queue is a collection of elements that follows the FIFO (First In, First Out) principle. This means that the first element added to the queue is the first one to be removed. A good analogy is a line at a coffee shop: the first person to join the line is the first person to be served.

Basic Operations in a Queue

The two primary operations associated with queues are:

- **Enqueue**: Add an item to the end of the queue.
- **Dequeue**: Remove the item from the front of the queue.

Queues also have a peek operation, which allows you to view the item at the front of the queue without removing it.

Implementing a Queue in Python

Python's collections.deque class provides an efficient way to implement a queue. The append() method adds elements to the queue, and popleft() removes them from the front.

```python
from collections import deque

# Implementing a queue using deque
queue = deque()

# Enqueue items
queue.append(10)  # Queue: [10]
queue.append(20)  # Queue: [10, 20]
queue.append(30)  # Queue: [10, 20, 30]

# Dequeue items
front = queue.popleft()  # Removes 10, Queue: [20, 30]
print(front)  # Output: 10

# Peek at the front item
print(queue[0])  # Output: 20 (item at the front)
```

Use Cases of Queues

- **Job scheduling**: Queues are ideal for managing tasks that need to be processed in the order they arrive, such as print jobs or task queues in operating systems.
- **Breadth-First Search (BFS):** In graph traversal, queues are used to explore nodes in a breadth-first manner.
- **Data streaming**: Queues are often used in scenarios where data is streamed and processed in the order of arrival.

3.4.3 Linked Lists: Dynamic Data Structures

A linked list is a linear data structure consisting of a sequence of elements, where each element (called a node) contains two parts:

- **Data**: The actual value stored in the node.
- **Next**: A reference (or link) to the next node in the sequence.

The key difference between a linked list and an array is that linked lists do not use contiguous memory. Instead, each node in the list points to the next node, and the last node's next reference is set to None (indicating the end of the list).

Types of Linked Lists

Singly Linked List: Each node points to the next node in the sequence.

Doubly Linked List: Each node points to both the next and the previous node in the sequence, allowing traversal in both directions.

Circular Linked List: The last node points back to the first node, forming a circular structure.

Basic Operations in a Linked List

- **Insert**: Add a new node to the list.
- **Delete**: Remove a node from the list.
- **Search**: Find a node with a specific value.
- **Traverse**: Access all nodes in the list.

Implementing a Singly Linked List in Python

Here's a simple implementation of a singly linked list in Python:

```
class Node:
    def __init__(self, data):
        self.data = data
        self.next = None

class LinkedList:
    def __init__(self):
```

```python
        self.head = None

    # Insert a new node at the end
    def append(self, data):
        new_node = Node(data)
        if not self.head:
            self.head = new_node
        else:
            last = self.head
            while last.next:
                last = last.next
            last.next = new_node

    # Print the linked list
    def print_list(self):
        current = self.head
        while current:
            print(current.data, end=" -> ")
            current = current.next
        print("None")

# Create a linked list and add nodes
ll = LinkedList()
ll.append(10)
ll.append(20)
ll.append(30)
ll.print_list()  # Output: 10 -> 20 -> 30 -> None
```

Use Cases of Linked Lists

- **Dynamic memory allocation**: Linked lists are used when the number of elements is unknown in advance, and we want to dynamically allocate and deallocate memory.
- **Implementing other data structures**: Linked lists are foundational for implementing more complex data structures like stacks, queues, and graphs.
- **Efficient insertions and deletions**: Linked lists are useful when you need to frequently insert or delete elements at the beginning or middle of the list, as these operations can be more efficient than with arrays.

Understanding the fundamentals of stacks, queues, and linked lists is crucial for building efficient algorithms and solving complex data management problems in AI. Each of these data structures has its own strengths and is suitable for specific tasks. Whether you're managing tasks in a job scheduler (queue), implementing a depth-first search (stack), or building a dynamic collection of data (linked list), these structures are indispensable tools for solving a wide range of problems in AI development.

By mastering stacks, queues, and linked lists, you will have the ability to choose the right data structure for the right problem, enabling you to write more efficient, readable, and scalable AI applications.

4. Working with Libraries

Python's rich ecosystem of libraries is one of the reasons it's the top choice for AI development. In this chapter, you'll dive into some of the most essential Python libraries for AI, starting with NumPy for numerical computing, Pandas for data manipulation, and Matplotlib and Seaborn for data visualization. You'll learn how to leverage these powerful tools to perform complex mathematical operations, clean and structure data, and visualize trends and patterns in your datasets. By the end of this chapter, you'll be equipped with the practical skills to efficiently work with data, which is a critical step in any AI project.

4.1 Introduction to NumPy: Handling Large Data Efficiently

In the realm of Artificial Intelligence (AI) and data science, handling large datasets efficiently is a key challenge. Whether you're working on machine learning algorithms, neural networks, or any other AI application, the ability to manage and process data in a fast and memory-efficient manner is crucial. This is where NumPy (Numerical Python) comes in.

NumPy is a fundamental package for scientific computing in Python, and it is the go-to library for working with large datasets, numerical data, and arrays in AI projects. With its powerful array structures and a wide range of mathematical functions, NumPy is the backbone of many AI and machine learning tasks.

In this section, we'll introduce you to NumPy, explore how it works, and demonstrate how to use it to handle large data efficiently.

4.1.1 What is NumPy?

NumPy is an open-source Python library used primarily for numerical computations. At the heart of NumPy is the ndarray (n-dimensional array), a fast and flexible container for large datasets. Unlike Python's built-in lists, NumPy arrays are homogeneous, meaning that all elements in an array are of the same type, which allows NumPy to be much faster and more memory-efficient.

Key features of NumPy:

- **Efficient Array Operations**: NumPy arrays allow for efficient element-wise operations, making it faster than Python's built-in lists for numerical computations.

- **Multidimensional Arrays**: NumPy supports n-dimensional arrays (e.g., 1D, 2D, 3D, etc.), which are essential for handling complex datasets, especially in AI.
- **Mathematical Functions**: NumPy includes a variety of mathematical functions, such as linear algebra, statistics, and Fourier transforms, all of which are critical for AI tasks.
- **Integration with Other Libraries**: NumPy is the foundation of many popular libraries in the Python ecosystem, including Pandas (for data manipulation), Matplotlib (for data visualization), and SciPy (for scientific computing).

4.1.2 The Core of NumPy: ndarray (N-Dimensional Array)

The ndarray (n-dimensional array) is the primary object in NumPy. It is a grid of values, all of the same type, indexed by a tuple of non-negative integers. The ndarray allows for fast, efficient, and convenient operations on large datasets, making it ideal for numerical computations in AI.

Creating NumPy Arrays

You can create NumPy arrays in several ways, including converting Python lists, creating arrays from scratch, or reading data from external sources.

```
import numpy as np

# Create an array from a Python list
arr = np.array([1, 2, 3, 4, 5])
print(arr)  # Output: [1 2 3 4 5]

# Create a 2D array (matrix)
arr2d = np.array([[1, 2], [3, 4], [5, 6]])
print(arr2d)
# Output:
# [[1 2]
#  [3 4]
#  [5 6]]

# Create an array of zeros
zeros_arr = np.zeros((3, 3))
print(zeros_arr)
# Output:
# [[0. 0. 0.]
```

```
# [0. 0. 0.]
# [0. 0. 0.]]

# Create an array of ones
ones_arr = np.ones((2, 4))
print(ones_arr)
# Output:
# [[1. 1. 1. 1.]
# [1. 1. 1. 1.]]

# Create a range of values
range_arr = np.arange(0, 10, 2)
print(range_arr)  # Output: [0 2 4 6 8]
```

Key Properties of ndarrays

- **Shape**: The dimensions of the array (e.g., 1D, 2D, 3D).
- **Size**: The total number of elements in the array.
- **Dtype**: The type of the elements in the array (e.g., integer, float).
- **Itemsize**: The size (in bytes) of each element in the array.

```
arr = np.array([1, 2, 3, 4, 5])
print(arr.shape)   # Output: (5,) (1D array with 5 elements)
print(arr.size)     # Output: 5
print(arr.dtype)    # Output: int64 (depends on your system)
print(arr.itemsize) # Output: 8 (depends on the data type)
```

4.1.3 Array Operations: Speed and Efficiency

NumPy arrays are designed to enable fast element-wise operations. This means that you can apply mathematical operations to entire arrays, or even specific rows/columns, without the need for explicit loops. This approach is much faster than using Python's built-in list data type, which is why NumPy is widely used for data manipulation and AI-related tasks.

Element-wise Operations

One of the core features of NumPy is the ability to perform element-wise operations on arrays. For example, adding, subtracting, multiplying, or dividing arrays directly:

```
arr1 = np.array([1, 2, 3])
arr2 = np.array([4, 5, 6])

# Element-wise addition
result = arr1 + arr2
print(result)  # Output: [5 7 9]

# Element-wise multiplication
result = arr1 * arr2
print(result)  # Output: [ 4 10 18]

# Element-wise division
result = arr1 / arr2
print(result)  # Output: [0.25 0.4  0.5 ]
```

Broadcasting: Expanding Arrays for Operations

One of the powerful features of NumPy is broadcasting, which allows you to perform operations between arrays of different shapes. The smaller array is "broadcast" over the larger array, meaning that NumPy automatically adjusts the dimensions of the smaller array to match the larger array for element-wise operations.

Example:

```
arr = np.array([1, 2, 3])
scalar = 10

# Broadcasting the scalar to add to each element of the array
result = arr + scalar
print(result)  # Output: [11 12 13]
```

Matrix Operations

NumPy also excels in handling 2D arrays (matrices) and performing operations like matrix multiplication, transposition, and more. These operations are crucial for AI applications, particularly when working with datasets or neural networks.

```
# Matrix multiplication
arr1 = np.array([[1, 2], [3, 4]])
arr2 = np.array([[5, 6], [7, 8]])

result = np.dot(arr1, arr2)  # Matrix multiplication
print(result)
# Output:
# [[19 22]
#  [43 50]]

# Transposing a matrix
transposed = arr1.T
print(transposed)
# Output:
# [[1 3]
#  [2 4]]
```

4.1.4 Advanced NumPy Functions

Beyond basic operations, NumPy provides a variety of functions that can help you manipulate and process data more efficiently:

Linear Algebra: NumPy has built-in support for common linear algebra operations, such as dot products, matrix decompositions, and solving systems of linear equations.

```
# Solving a system of linear equations (Ax = B)
A = np.array([[3, 1], [1, 2]])
B = np.array([9, 8])

x = np.linalg.solve(A, B)
print(x)  # Output: [2. 3.]
```

Random Numbers: NumPy includes a subpackage called numpy.random that allows you to generate random numbers for simulations, testing, or initializing machine learning models.

```
# Generate random numbers
random_arr = np.random.rand(3, 2)  # 3x2 array of random numbers between 0 and 1
```

```
print(random_arr)
```

Statistical Functions: NumPy provides numerous functions for calculating statistical measures such as the mean, median, variance, and standard deviation.

```
data = np.array([1, 2, 3, 4, 5])

# Calculate mean, median, variance, and standard deviation
mean = np.mean(data)
median = np.median(data)
variance = np.var(data)
std_dev = np.std(data)

print(f"Mean: {mean}, Median: {median}, Variance: {variance}, Standard Deviation: {std_dev}")
```

4.1.5 Why NumPy is Essential for AI

Handling large datasets and performing mathematical operations efficiently is critical when developing AI models. NumPy enables you to:

- **Store large datasets**: Its memory-efficient n-dimensional arrays can hold large datasets in a compact manner.
- **Perform computations faster**: NumPy is implemented in C, making array operations much faster than Python's built-in data types.
- **Work with high-dimensional data**: AI tasks often involve data with multiple features (e.g., 2D matrices for images or 3D arrays for videos). NumPy supports n-dimensional arrays and facilitates efficient computation on such data.
- **Integration with AI frameworks**: Many AI libraries, such as TensorFlow and PyTorch, use NumPy under the hood for their tensor operations, meaning that learning and understanding NumPy lays the foundation for working with more advanced AI libraries.

4.1.6 Conclusion

NumPy is an essential tool for anyone working in data science or AI. It allows you to manage and process large datasets efficiently and perform fast, element-wise mathematical operations. With its powerful ndarray structure and a wealth of built-in functions, NumPy provides the foundation for many AI tasks, from data preprocessing to training complex machine learning models. By mastering NumPy, you'll be able to work with vast amounts of data, perform advanced numerical operations, and significantly accelerate your AI development process.

4.2 Data Manipulation with Pandas

In the world of Data Science and Artificial Intelligence (AI), one of the most important skills is the ability to manipulate and analyze data efficiently. Whether you're building a machine learning model or working with large datasets, manipulating and preparing your data is a crucial step. This is where Pandas comes in.

Pandas is a powerful Python library designed for data manipulation and analysis. It provides data structures like DataFrame and Series that allow you to handle and analyze data in a highly efficient and flexible way. Pandas integrates seamlessly with other libraries like NumPy, making it an indispensable tool for any data-driven project.

In this section, we'll explore the key features of Pandas, and how you can use it for data manipulation in AI and machine learning tasks.

4.2.1 What is Pandas?

Pandas is an open-source library built for data analysis. It provides fast, flexible, and expressive data structures that are designed to work with structured data seamlessly. The two primary data structures in Pandas are:

- **DataFrame**: A two-dimensional, size-mutable, and potentially heterogeneous tabular data structure with labeled axes (rows and columns).
- **Series**: A one-dimensional labeled array capable of holding any data type (integers, strings, floats, etc.).

Pandas excels at loading, cleaning, transforming, and analyzing data in preparation for machine learning models, data exploration, and statistical analysis.

4.2.2 The Core Data Structures: Series and DataFrame

The Series

A Series is essentially a one-dimensional labeled array. Think of it like a column in a spreadsheet or a list of values indexed by labels. A Series can contain a variety of data types, including integers, floats, or even strings.

```python
import pandas as pd

# Creating a Series from a list
data = [10, 20, 30, 40, 50]
series = pd.Series(data)
print(series)
```

Output:

```
0    10
1    20
2    30
3    40
4    50
dtype: int64
```

You can also assign custom labels (index) to a Series:

```python
labels = ['a', 'b', 'c', 'd', 'e']
series = pd.Series(data, index=labels)
print(series)
```

Output:

```
a    10
b    20
c    30
d    40
e    50
dtype: int64
```

The DataFrame

A DataFrame is a two-dimensional, labeled data structure. It can hold various types of data, including numbers, strings, or booleans. DataFrames are similar to tables in databases, or spreadsheets in Excel, where data is stored in rows and columns.

Output:

```
    Name  Age        City
0   Alice  25    New York
1     Bob  30  Los Angeles
2 Charlie  35     Chicago
```

4.2.3 Data Selection and Indexing

Selecting and manipulating data is one of the most important aspects of working with data. Pandas offers several ways to select, filter, and index data efficiently.

Selecting Columns

You can access individual columns in a DataFrame using either dot notation or the column name in square brackets.

```python
# Selecting a single column
print(df['Name'])
```

Output:

```
0      Alice
1        Bob
2    Charlie
Name: Name, dtype: object
```

Selecting Rows

You can select rows using loc[] (label-based indexing) or iloc[] (position-based indexing). The loc[] method allows you to select rows by label, while iloc[] allows you to select rows by index position.

```
# Selecting a specific row by label (index)
print(df.loc[1])  # Selects the row with index 1 (Bob's data)

# Selecting a specific row by position
print(df.iloc[1])  # Selects the row at position 1 (Bob's data)
```

Conditional Selection

Pandas allows you to perform conditional selection to filter data based on specific conditions, similar to querying a database.

```
# Select all rows where Age is greater than 30
print(df[df['Age'] > 30])
```

Output:

```
    Name  Age    City
2  Charlie  35  Chicago
```

4.2.4 Data Manipulation: Transforming and Cleaning Data

In real-world datasets, data often needs to be cleaned, transformed, or reshaped to make it suitable for analysis or machine learning tasks. Pandas provides powerful tools for performing these operations.

Renaming Columns

You can rename columns in a DataFrame using the rename() method.

```
df = df.rename(columns={'Name': 'Full Name', 'Age': 'Age (Years)'})
print(df)
```

Output:

```
   Full Name  Age (Years)        City
0      Alice           25    New York
1        Bob           30  Los Angeles
```

2	Charlie	35	Chicago

Handling Missing Data

Real-world data often contains missing values (NaN). Pandas provides multiple functions for handling missing data, such as filling or dropping missing values.

```python
# Fill missing values with a specified value
df['Age (Years)'] = df['Age (Years)'].fillna(0)

# Drop rows with missing values
df = df.dropna()
```

Data Aggregation and Grouping

Pandas allows you to group data and perform aggregation operations (such as sum, mean, and count) across different categories. The groupby() function is commonly used for this purpose.

```python
# Create a new DataFrame with 'City' and 'Age (Years)' columns
data = {
    'City': ['New York', 'Los Angeles', 'Chicago', 'New York', 'Chicago'],
    'Age (Years)': [25, 30, 35, 40, 45]
}

df = pd.DataFrame(data)

# Group data by 'City' and calculate the average age in each city
city_group = df.groupby('City')['Age (Years)'].mean()
print(city_group)
```

Output:

```
City
Chicago        40.0
Los Angeles    30.0
New York       32.5
```

```
Name: Age (Years), dtype: float64
```

Sorting Data

Pandas makes it easy to sort data by one or more columns using the sort_values()
function.

```
# Sort data by Age (Years) in descending order
df_sorted = df.sort_values('Age (Years)', ascending=False)
print(df_sorted)
```

Output:

```
        City  Age (Years)
4     Chicago          45
3    New York          40
2     Chicago          35
1 Los Angeles          30
0    New York          25
```

4.2.5 Merging and Joining Data

In many real-world applications, data is spread across multiple sources. Pandas allows
you to merge and join data from different DataFrames efficiently, similar to SQL joins.

```
# Create two DataFrames
df1 = pd.DataFrame({
    'ID': [1, 2, 3],
    'Name': ['Alice', 'Bob', 'Charlie']
})

df2 = pd.DataFrame({
    'ID': [1, 2, 3],
    'Age': [25, 30, 35]
})

# Merge DataFrames on the 'ID' column
```

```
merged_df = pd.merge(df1, df2, on='ID')
print(merged_df)
```

Output:

```
   ID    Name  Age
0  1    Alice   25
1  2      Bob   30
2  3  Charlie   35
```

4.2.6 Pandas in AI: Preparing Data for Machine Learning

In AI and machine learning workflows, data preprocessing is a critical task, and Pandas plays a central role in preparing datasets for machine learning models. Some common tasks include:

- Handling missing data
- Encoding categorical variables
- Normalizing or scaling numerical features
- Splitting data into training and testing sets

For example, Pandas can be used to normalize the data by scaling it to a specific range:

```
# Normalize 'Age' column
df['Age Normalized'] = (df['Age'] - df['Age'].min()) / (df['Age'].max() - df['Age'].min())
print(df)
```

4.2.7 Conclusion

Pandas is an essential library for anyone working with data, especially in the fields of data science, machine learning, and AI. It provides fast and flexible tools for data manipulation, cleaning, and transformation, which are crucial steps in any data analysis pipeline. By mastering Pandas, you'll be equipped to efficiently handle large datasets, perform complex data manipulations, and prepare your data for machine learning models and AI applications. Whether you're working on small-scale data tasks or large-scale AI projects, Pandas is an indispensable tool for any data scientist or AI developer.

4.3 Visualizing Data with Matplotlib and Seaborn

Data visualization is one of the most powerful ways to understand and communicate insights from your data. By turning complex datasets into easy-to-understand visual representations, you can uncover patterns, trends, and anomalies that might otherwise go unnoticed. In the world of Artificial Intelligence (AI) and Data Science, visualization tools are essential for data exploration, model interpretation, and presentation.

Two of the most widely used libraries for data visualization in Python are Matplotlib and Seaborn. Both libraries provide excellent tools for creating a wide range of plots, from basic charts to complex visualizations, and are commonly used in data-driven projects like AI and machine learning.

In this section, we will explore how to use Matplotlib and Seaborn to visualize data and gain valuable insights that can inform AI model development and analysis.

4.3.1 Introduction to Matplotlib

Matplotlib is one of the most popular and powerful data visualization libraries in Python. It is capable of creating a wide range of static, animated, and interactive plots. It is extremely flexible and allows you to create high-quality charts for presentations, reports, or publication.

Basic Plotting with Matplotlib

To get started with Matplotlib, you first need to install the library (if it is not already installed). You can do so via pip:

```
pip install matplotlib
```

Once installed, you can import the library and create basic plots. Let's start with a simple line plot.

```
import matplotlib.pyplot as plt

# Data for plotting
x = [1, 2, 3, 4, 5]
y = [10, 20, 25, 30, 40]
```

```
# Create a simple line plot
plt.plot(x, y)
plt.xlabel('X Axis')
plt.ylabel('Y Axis')
plt.title('Basic Line Plot')
plt.show()
```

This will create a simple line plot showing the relationship between the x and y values. You can customize the plot by adding titles, labels, gridlines, and more.

Scatter Plots

A scatter plot is a great way to visualize the relationship between two continuous variables. It helps you identify trends or correlations in your data.

```
x = [1, 2, 3, 4, 5]
y = [5, 10, 15, 20, 25]

plt.scatter(x, y)
plt.xlabel('X Axis')
plt.ylabel('Y Axis')
plt.title('Simple Scatter Plot')
plt.show()
```

Bar Charts

A bar chart is useful when comparing discrete categories or groups. It's especially helpful in visualizing categorical data.

```
categories = ['A', 'B', 'C', 'D']
values = [5, 7, 10, 4]

plt.bar(categories, values)
plt.xlabel('Categories')
plt.ylabel('Values')
plt.title('Bar Chart')
plt.show()
```

4.3.2 Introduction to Seaborn

While Matplotlib is versatile and powerful, it can require a bit more code to produce aesthetically pleasing visualizations. This is where Seaborn comes in. Seaborn is built on top of Matplotlib and provides a higher-level interface for creating attractive, informative visualizations. It is especially useful for statistical data visualization and provides functions for automatically handling various visual features like colors, axes, and labels.

To get started, you need to install Seaborn:

```
pip install seaborn
```

Seaborn's Advantages Over Matplotlib

- **Cleaner syntax**: Seaborn provides a simpler, higher-level API for creating plots.
- **Aesthetic defaults**: Seaborn comes with better default color schemes and themes, which makes plots visually appealing without much customization.
- Statistical plots: Seaborn is particularly designed for creating plots that are common in statistical analysis, such as boxplots, histograms, and violin plots.

Basic Plotting with Seaborn

Let's start by creating a simple scatter plot using Seaborn. Unlike Matplotlib, Seaborn allows you to directly pass data from a DataFrame (Pandas DataFrame) into its functions.

```
import seaborn as sns
import pandas as pd

# Sample data
data = {'x': [1, 2, 3, 4, 5], 'y': [5, 10, 15, 20, 25]}
df = pd.DataFrame(data)

# Scatter plot using Seaborn
sns.scatterplot(x='x', y='y', data=df)
plt.title('Seaborn Scatter Plot')
plt.show()
```

Boxplots with Seaborn

A boxplot is a great way to visualize the distribution of a dataset. It displays the median, quartiles, and potential outliers in the data.

```
# Sample data for boxplot
data = {'Category': ['A', 'B', 'C', 'A', 'B', 'C', 'A', 'B', 'C'],
    'Values': [5, 6, 7, 8, 5, 6, 4, 7, 6]}
df = pd.DataFrame(data)

# Boxplot using Seaborn
sns.boxplot(x='Category', y='Values', data=df)
plt.title('Boxplot Example')
plt.show()
```

Histogram with Seaborn

Histograms are useful for understanding the distribution of continuous data. Seaborn makes it easy to plot histograms.

```
# Sample data for histogram
data = [1, 2, 2, 3, 3, 3, 4, 5, 6, 7, 8, 8, 9]

# Histogram using Seaborn
sns.histplot(data, kde=True)  # kde=True adds a Kernel Density Estimate (KDE)
plt.title('Histogram with Seaborn')
plt.show()
```

4.3.3 Visualizing Relationships with Seaborn Pairplot

When you're dealing with datasets that contain multiple variables, understanding how those variables relate to each other can be difficult. A pairplot is a great way to visualize the relationships between all variables in a dataset.

```
# Sample data for pairplot
data = sns.load_dataset('iris')  # Seaborn has built-in datasets

# Create pairplot
sns.pairplot(data, hue='species')
```

```
plt.title('Pairplot Example')
plt.show()
```

The pairplot creates scatterplots for each pair of variables and displays histograms along the diagonal. In this example, we've used the famous Iris dataset, and the hue parameter colors the points based on the species.

4.3.4 Heatmaps: Visualizing Correlations

Heatmaps are used to visualize matrix-like data, such as correlations between variables. The color intensity represents the magnitude of the values in the matrix, allowing you to easily identify patterns.

```
import numpy as np

# Create a random correlation matrix
data = np.random.rand(10, 10)

# Create a heatmap using Seaborn
sns.heatmap(data, annot=True, cmap='coolwarm')
plt.title('Heatmap Example')
plt.show()
```

Heatmaps are particularly useful in AI for visualizing correlations between features or understanding how different features impact a model.

4.3.5 Customizing Plots in Matplotlib and Seaborn

While both Matplotlib and Seaborn offer great default settings, you might want to customize your plots further to make them more informative or visually appealing. Both libraries allow you to modify various plot elements such as axes, labels, titles, and more.

Matplotlib Customization

```
# Create a line plot with customized elements
plt.plot(x, y, color='green', linewidth=2.5, linestyle='dashed')
plt.xlabel('X Axis', fontsize=12)
plt.ylabel('Y Axis', fontsize=12)
```

```
plt.title('Customized Line Plot', fontsize=14)
plt.grid(True)
plt.show()
```

Seaborn Customization

```
# Customize a scatterplot with a color palette
sns.scatterplot(x='x', y='y', data=df, palette='coolwarm', s=100)
plt.title('Custom Scatter Plot with Color Palette')
plt.show()
```

4.3.6 Conclusion

Effective data visualization is a critical skill for anyone working with data science, AI, and machine learning. Both Matplotlib and Seaborn provide powerful and flexible tools for creating a variety of plots that help you explore and communicate insights from your data. While Matplotlib offers great customization options for general plotting, Seaborn is an excellent choice for statistical data visualization and aesthetically pleasing plots.

By mastering these libraries, you can make your AI projects more intuitive and visually appealing, enabling both you and your audience to gain deeper insights into your data.

4.4 Introduction to SciPy for Scientific Computing

In the realm of scientific computing, one of the key challenges is dealing with large, complex datasets and performing advanced mathematical computations. Whether you're working with data for artificial intelligence (AI), machine learning, or other data-intensive applications, efficient mathematical operations are essential. SciPy, built on top of NumPy, is a Python library that specializes in performing a wide range of mathematical, scientific, and engineering computations.

In this section, we'll explore SciPy, its key features, and how it can be used in AI and machine learning workflows. Whether you're dealing with numerical optimization, integration, signal processing, or statistical analysis, SciPy provides the tools you need to perform these tasks quickly and efficiently.

4.4.1 What is SciPy?

SciPy is an open-source Python library used for scientific and technical computing. It builds on the capabilities of NumPy and provides a collection of algorithms and high-level commands for manipulating and visualizing data. SciPy is widely used by researchers, scientists, and engineers for solving mathematical problems, such as optimization, integration, interpolation, and more.

The core of SciPy consists of several submodules, each designed for a specific kind of scientific computation:

- **scipy.integrate**: Integration routines
- **scipy.optimize**: Optimization algorithms
- **scipy.interpolate**: Interpolation functions
- **scipy.linalg**: Linear algebra routines
- **scipy.signal**: Signal processing functions
- **scipy.spatial**: Spatial algorithms
- **scipy.stats**: Statistical functions

Each of these submodules helps solve different types of problems that are common in fields like data science, engineering, physics, and AI.

4.4.2 Key Features of SciPy

1. Mathematical Functions

SciPy provides a variety of mathematical functions that can be directly applied to arrays, vectors, or matrices. These functions cover a broad range of operations, including basic arithmetic, trigonometric functions, logarithms, and more complex functions like special functions (e.g., Bessel functions).

```
from scipy import math

# Compute the sine of a value
import numpy as np
angle = np.pi / 2  # 90 degrees
print(math.sin(angle))  # Output: 1.0
```

2. Optimization

One of the most widely used features in scientific computing is optimization—finding the best solution for a problem under given constraints. SciPy provides several functions to minimize (or maximize) mathematical functions. The scipy.optimize module includes methods for solving both constrained and unconstrained optimization problems.

For example, you can minimize a simple quadratic function:

```
from scipy.optimize import minimize

# Define a simple quadratic function
def func(x):
    return x**2 + 5*x + 6

# Find the minimum of the function
result = minimize(func, 0)  # Initial guess is 0
print(result.x)  # Output: the value that minimizes the function
```

3. Integration

Another essential aspect of scientific computing is numerical integration, which is used to calculate the area under curves, among other things. SciPy provides tools for both single-variable and multi-variable integration. For example, the scipy.integrate.quad function allows you to perform definite integration on a function.

```
from scipy.integrate import quad

# Define a simple function
def f(x):
    return x**2

# Integrate f(x) from 0 to 1
result, error = quad(f, 0, 1)
print(result)  # Output: the integral value
```

4. Interpolation

Interpolation is the process of estimating values between known data points. SciPy provides the scipy.interpolate module, which can be used for 1-D, 2-D, and even N-D interpolation. The function interpolate.interp1d can be used to interpolate 1-dimensional data.

```
from scipy import interpolate

# Define known data points
x = [1, 2, 3, 4]
y = [2, 4, 6, 8]

# Create an interpolation function
f = interpolate.interp1d(x, y)

# Interpolate a new value
print(f(2.5))  # Output: 5.0 (interpolated between 2 and 3)
```

5. Signal Processing

SciPy's signal processing module (scipy.signal) provides tools for filtering, windowing, and analyzing signals. This is especially useful in fields such as image processing, audio processing, and time-series analysis. You can perform operations like Fourier transforms, convolution, and filtering using SciPy.

For example, you can filter a signal using a low-pass filter:

```
from scipy import signal
import numpy as np

# Create a noisy signal
fs = 100  # Sampling frequency
t = np.linspace(0, 1, fs)  # Time vector
noisy_signal = np.sin(2 * np.pi * 5 * t) + 0.5 * np.random.randn(len(t))

# Design a low-pass filter
b, a = signal.butter(4, 0.1)  # 4th-order filter with cutoff frequency of 0.1

# Apply the filter
filtered_signal = signal.filtfilt(b, a, noisy_signal)

import matplotlib.pyplot as plt
```

```
plt.plot(t, noisy_signal, label='Noisy Signal')
plt.plot(t, filtered_signal, label='Filtered Signal', linewidth=2)
plt.legend()
plt.show()
```

This code generates a noisy signal and applies a low-pass Butterworth filter to remove high-frequency noise.

6. Linear Algebra

The linear algebra capabilities of SciPy are vast and include matrix operations like matrix multiplication, eigenvalues and eigenvectors, QR decomposition, and more. The scipy.linalg submodule provides efficient linear algebra routines.

For example, to compute the determinant of a matrix:

```
from scipy.linalg import det
import numpy as np

# Create a 2x2 matrix
A = np.array([[1, 2], [3, 4]])

# Compute the determinant
det_A = det(A)
print(det_A)  # Output: -2.0
```

7. Statistical Analysis

Statistical analysis is an essential part of AI and machine learning, and SciPy provides a variety of statistical functions in the scipy.stats submodule. You can perform hypothesis testing, probability distributions, and descriptive statistics (mean, variance, standard deviation).

For example, you can perform a t-test to check if two groups have different means:

```
from scipy import stats

# Sample data
```

```
group1 = [23, 21, 18, 25, 30]
group2 = [28, 26, 29, 33, 34]

# Perform a t-test
t_stat, p_value = stats.ttest_ind(group1, group2)
print(f"T-statistic: {t_stat}, P-value: {p_value}")
```

A low p-value (typically below 0.05) suggests that the means of the two groups are significantly different.

4.4.3 SciPy in AI and Machine Learning

SciPy plays a crucial role in the field of AI and machine learning, especially during the preprocessing and model optimization phases.

Optimization for Model Training: SciPy's optimization algorithms can be used to train machine learning models by minimizing a loss function. For example, gradient-based optimization methods can be applied to deep learning or support vector machines.

Numerical Integration for Model Evaluation: When evaluating AI models, particularly in fields like physics-based simulations or finance, numerical integration (provided by SciPy) is often used to estimate complex integrals or probabilities.

Signal Processing for Time-Series Data: In AI applications involving time-series data (such as in speech recognition, financial forecasting, or sensor data analysis), SciPy's signal processing functions are crucial for filtering noise and identifying key features in the data.

Statistical Testing: SciPy's statistical functions allow data scientists to perform hypothesis testing and confidence interval estimation, which are often required during the feature selection process and when interpreting the output of AI models.

4.4.4 Conclusion

SciPy is an essential library for anyone involved in scientific computing, especially for applications that require mathematical optimization, integration, statistical analysis, and signal processing. Whether you're building a machine learning model, analyzing time-series data, or solving complex mathematical problems, SciPy provides the tools you need to get the job done efficiently and accurately.

For AI practitioners, SciPy is invaluable because it allows you to optimize models, process data, and analyze results in a highly effective manner. Combined with libraries like NumPy, Pandas, and Matplotlib, SciPy rounds out the set of tools you'll need for a successful AI development pipeline.

5. Understanding Data: The Fuel for AI

Data is the foundation upon which all AI models are built, and understanding how to work with it is key to developing effective AI applications. In this chapter, you'll explore the importance of data in AI, learning how to collect, clean, and preprocess data to ensure it's ready for analysis and modeling. You'll dive into techniques for handling missing data, normalizing data for consistency, and encoding categorical variables. You'll also discover how to identify the right features to use, a critical step in improving the accuracy and performance of your AI models. By the end of this chapter, you'll have the skills needed to transform raw data into meaningful inputs for machine learning and AI systems.

5.1 What is Data? Structured vs. Unstructured Data

In the world of Artificial Intelligence (AI) and machine learning, understanding the nature of your data is crucial for designing effective models and algorithms. The type and format of data you work with directly influence how you preprocess, analyze, and model it.

Data is essentially raw facts and figures that are collected for analysis, decision-making, or solving specific problems. However, not all data is created equal. It can come in various forms and can be classified into two main categories: structured data and unstructured data.

In this section, we'll explore the concept of data in general and delve into the two most common types of data: structured and unstructured. Understanding the differences between these two will help you choose the right techniques and tools to manipulate, clean, and analyze them, which is essential when building AI and machine learning models.

5.1.1 What is Data?

Data is essentially raw information that, when processed and analyzed, can be turned into valuable knowledge. Data can come from multiple sources: sensors, databases, websites, surveys, and more. It is the foundation for almost every AI model, and understanding how to handle it is the first step toward creating intelligent systems.

In the context of AI, data is used to train algorithms to make predictions, understand patterns, or extract meaningful insights. For example, images are used to train computer vision models, while text is used to train natural language processing (NLP) models. Data quality is critical for accurate models—poor or unclean data can result in faulty predictions or incorrect analyses.

5.1.2 Types of Data: Structured vs. Unstructured

Data is usually categorized into two primary types: structured data and unstructured data. These two types differ in how they are stored, organized, and analyzed.

Structured Data

Structured data is organized and highly predictable. It is data that resides in a fixed format and can be easily entered, stored, and queried in databases. Structured data typically consists of tables (rows and columns) and is stored in formats such as spreadsheets, CSV files, and relational databases like SQL databases. The most common example of structured data is data stored in a table, such as sales transactions, employee records, or financial data.

Characteristics of Structured Data:

- **Organized in rows and columns**: Structured data is stored in a tabular format, where each row represents a record and each column represents a field (variable).
- **Easy to analyze**: Because of its rigid structure, it's easy to perform mathematical operations or use queries (such as SQL) to extract insights.
- **Well-defined types**: The data values in structured data are often consistent and fall into predefined data types (e.g., integer, float, string).
- **Machine-readable**: This type of data is easy for machines to read, interpret, and process efficiently.

In this case, the data is well-organized and each field is clearly defined (such as Age, Name, Department, etc.). You can easily run queries to find specific records, aggregate information, or perform statistical analysis.

Unstructured Data

Unstructured data, on the other hand, lacks a predefined format and is not organized in rows and columns. It often exists in formats like text, images, videos, and audio, and may not have clear boundaries or predictable patterns. Unstructured data is often raw and complex, making it much more difficult to analyze compared to structured data.

This type of data is becoming increasingly important in the world of AI because it makes up a significant portion of the data we work with today, such as user-generated content, social media posts, and multimedia files. To analyze unstructured data effectively, we often need specialized techniques like natural language processing (NLP) for text or computer vision for images and videos.

Characteristics of Unstructured Data:

- **No defined format**: Unstructured data can come in many forms, such as text documents, images, social media posts, audio recordings, etc.
- **Difficult to analyze directly**: Unlike structured data, unstructured data cannot easily be stored in a table or queried in the same way. It requires advanced techniques and tools to extract useful insights.
- **Flexible and diverse**: Unstructured data is more flexible in terms of format but requires more effort to process and transform into a usable form.

Example of Unstructured Data:

Here are some examples of unstructured data:

- **Text data**: Blog posts, emails, tweets, product reviews, research papers, etc.
- **Image data**: Photographs, medical imaging, satellite images, etc.
- **Audio data**: Voice recordings, podcasts, music, etc.
- **Video data**: Movies, surveillance footage, video interviews, etc.

For instance, a tweet could contain a variety of information in an unstructured format like this:

"Had an amazing time at the AI conference today! #AI #MachineLearning"

This tweet combines text with hashtags, mentions, and emojis, making it unstructured. In order to analyze such data, AI algorithms need to extract features like sentiment, topics, or keywords.

5.1.3 Why is Understanding Structured vs. Unstructured Data Important for AI?

In Artificial Intelligence (AI), data is the foundation upon which algorithms are built. However, understanding the distinction between structured and unstructured data is important because:

Different Tools and Techniques: The tools and techniques used to analyze structured data are quite different from those used for unstructured data. For instance, when working with structured data, you might rely heavily on SQL, Pandas (for data manipulation), and Matplotlib (for visualization). On the other hand, analyzing unstructured data might require NLP (for text data), deep learning techniques (for image and video data), or speech recognition tools (for audio data).

Preprocessing Complexity: Structured data can be cleaned and processed relatively easily, while unstructured data requires more advanced preprocessing steps. For example, text data may need to be tokenized, stemmed, and vectorized before it can be used for analysis. Image data may need to be resized, normalized, and augmented for use in deep learning models.

Scalability Challenges: Unstructured data is often much larger in volume than structured data, making it more difficult to store, manage, and process. Techniques like cloud computing, distributed processing, and specialized storage solutions are often required to handle the massive scale of unstructured data in AI applications.

5.1.5 Conclusion

Understanding the differences between structured and unstructured data is a fundamental concept for anyone working in AI and machine learning. While structured data is easier to handle and analyze, unstructured data offers more complex and often richer insights, which are essential for tasks such as sentiment analysis, image recognition, and speech-to-text translation.

As AI continues to evolve, the ability to effectively process both types of data will become increasingly important. With the rise of big data and deep learning, unstructured data is playing a bigger role, and tools are evolving to make it easier to analyze. As an AI practitioner, being familiar with both types of data and the tools available for each will be key to building accurate and effective AI models.

5.2 Loading and Storing Data: CSV, JSON, and Databases

In the realm of Artificial Intelligence (AI) and machine learning, data is the fundamental building block for developing and training models. However, before you can even begin the process of analysis or training, you need to know how to load data into your environment and store it efficiently. The ability to handle data in various formats is essential for any data scientist or AI practitioner.

In this section, we will explore how to load and store data in commonly used formats like CSV, JSON, and databases. Each of these formats serves specific purposes, and understanding when to use each one can help streamline your data preprocessing pipeline.

5.2.1 What is CSV (Comma-Separated Values)?

CSV is one of the simplest and most widely used formats for storing and exchanging data, especially when working with structured data. CSV files are plain text files where each line represents a row of data, and the values are separated by commas (hence the name). Each row in a CSV file can contain one or more data fields, and each field represents an attribute of a record.

For example, a CSV file might look like this:

Employee_ID	Name	Age	Department	Salary
1	John Doe	29	HR	50000
2	Jane Smith	34	Marketing	60000
3	Alice Lee	40	Engineering	70000

Each line represents a record, and each value is separated by a comma. CSV files are extremely easy to create, read, and edit, and they are widely supported by various applications, including spreadsheet tools like Excel and data analysis tools like Pandas.

Advantages of CSV:

- Simple and lightweight: Easy to work with and understand.
- Human-readable: You can open and read CSV files with any text editor.
- Widely used: Most data analysis tools and machine learning libraries support CSV.

Disadvantages of CSV:

- Limited to structured data: Not ideal for storing complex data types like nested objects.
- Lacks metadata: It doesn't provide a mechanism for describing the schema or data types.

Loading CSV Data in Python:

Python provides several libraries for loading data from CSV files. One of the most popular is Pandas, which simplifies the process of reading and writing data to CSV files. Here's an example of how you can load data from a CSV file:

```
import pandas as pd

# Load CSV file into a DataFrame
df = pd.read_csv('data.csv')

# Display the first few rows
print(df.head())
```

This will read the CSV file and load it into a Pandas DataFrame, which is a convenient structure for working with data.

Saving Data to CSV:

You can also save data to a CSV file using Pandas. If you have a DataFrame that you want to write back to a CSV file, you can do it like this:

```
# Save DataFrame to CSV file
df.to_csv('output.csv', index=False)
```

The index=False argument prevents Pandas from writing row numbers (index) into the CSV file.

5.2.2 What is JSON (JavaScript Object Notation)?

While CSV is great for tabular data, it's not ideal for more complex, hierarchical data structures. This is where JSON comes in. JSON is a widely used, human-readable text format for storing and transmitting data, and it is particularly useful for storing nested or hierarchical data. JSON is based on key-value pairs, and data is organized in objects (curly braces {}) or arrays (square brackets []).

A simple JSON object could look like this:

```
{
  "employees": [
    {
      "Employee_ID": 1,
      "Name": "John Doe",
      "Age": 29,
      "Department": "HR",
      "Salary": 50000
    },
    {
      "Employee_ID": 2,
      "Name": "Jane Smith",
      "Age": 34,
      "Department": "Marketing",
      "Salary": 60000
    }
  ]
}
```

In the example above, we have a JSON object with a key called employees, which holds an array of employee records. Each record contains nested data like Name, Age, and Department.

Advantages of JSON:

- **Supports nested data**: JSON can store hierarchical or nested structures, making it ideal for more complex datasets.
- **Human-readable**: It's easy to read and edit JSON files with a text editor.
- **Flexible**: JSON can store different types of data, such as strings, numbers, arrays, and objects.

Disadvantages of JSON:

- **Larger size**: JSON files can be larger than CSV files because they store more metadata and structure.
- **Not ideal for flat, tabular data**: For simple structured data, CSV is more efficient.

Loading JSON Data in Python:

You can load data from a JSON file using Python's built-in json module or Pandas. Here's how to load JSON data using json:

```python
import json

# Open and load the JSON file
with open('data.json', 'r') as file:
    data = json.load(file)

# Print the loaded data
print(data)
```

If you have a more structured JSON file and want to load it into a Pandas DataFrame, you can do it like this:

```python
import pandas as pd

# Load JSON file into a DataFrame
df = pd.read_json('data.json')

# Display the first few rows
print(df.head())
```

Saving Data to JSON:

You can also save data to a JSON file in Python. For example:

```python
import json

# Data to be saved in JSON format
data = {
    "employees": [
        {"Employee_ID": 1, "Name": "John Doe", "Age": 29, "Department": "HR", "Salary": 50000},
        {"Employee_ID": 2, "Name": "Jane Smith", "Age": 34, "Department": "Marketing", "Salary": 60000}
    ]
}
```

```
# Write data to JSON file
with open('output.json', 'w') as file:
    json.dump(data, file, indent=4)
```

The indent=4 argument makes the JSON output more readable by adding indentation.

5.2.3 Storing and Accessing Data in Databases

As data grows, it becomes increasingly impractical to store it in flat files like CSV or JSON. This is where databases come in. Databases allow you to efficiently store, query, and manage large volumes of data. There are two main types of databases: relational databases (RDBMS) and NoSQL databases.

Relational Databases (RDBMS)

Relational databases, such as MySQL, PostgreSQL, and SQLite, store data in tables with rows and columns. They use SQL (Structured Query Language) to query and manipulate data. If you're dealing with highly structured data that can fit neatly into tables, a relational database is a great choice.

Advantages of RDBMS:

- **ACID-compliant**: Guarantees data consistency and reliability.
- **Supports complex queries**: You can perform complex joins, groupings, and aggregations with SQL.

Loading Data into a Relational Database:

You can use libraries such as SQLAlchemy or SQLite in Python to interact with relational databases. Here's an example of how to connect to a SQLite database and load data:

```
import sqlite3
import pandas as pd

# Connect to SQLite database (or create it if it doesn't exist)
conn = sqlite3.connect('database.db')

# Load CSV data into a DataFrame
```

```
df = pd.read_csv('data.csv')

# Store DataFrame into SQL database
df.to_sql('employees', conn, if_exists='replace', index=False)

# Query the data back
query = "SELECT * FROM employees"
result = pd.read_sql(query, conn)
print(result)
```

NoSQL Databases

For unstructured or semi-structured data, NoSQL databases like MongoDB, Cassandra, and Firebase are better suited. NoSQL databases are more flexible with data formats and can easily handle nested structures or large volumes of diverse data types.

Advantages of NoSQL:

- **Scalability**: Can handle huge volumes of data.
- **Flexible schema**: Can store structured and unstructured data in the same database.

5.2.4 Conclusion

Understanding how to load and store data in various formats is a fundamental skill for working with AI and machine learning. Whether you're working with simple CSV files for structured data, JSON for more complex and hierarchical data, or databases for large datasets, knowing how to manipulate and store data effectively is key to building efficient AI models.

The choice of data storage format depends on the nature of the data and the requirements of your project. While CSV and JSON are simple and lightweight, databases are more suited for scaling up to large datasets. Mastering these tools will significantly improve your ability to work with data and build powerful AI applications.

5.3 Data Cleaning: Handling Missing and Corrupt Data

One of the most crucial steps in any data science or AI project is data cleaning. Data is often messy, incomplete, or inconsistent, which can significantly hinder the performance of machine learning models. Cleaning and preprocessing the data ensures that it is in a suitable format for analysis and modeling. A significant part of data cleaning is dealing with missing and corrupt data, which can distort the insights drawn from the data and lead to inaccurate predictions.

In this section, we will explore techniques for handling missing and corrupt data, which are common issues in most real-world datasets. By mastering data cleaning techniques, you can ensure the quality of your data, which is essential for building reliable and effective AI models.

5.3.1 Why is Data Cleaning Important?

Data cleaning is essential because AI and machine learning models rely on high-quality data to make accurate predictions. If the data is incomplete or contains errors, it can lead to biased results, overfitting, or a lack of generalization, which ultimately degrades the performance of the model. In fact, dirty data—such as missing or corrupt values—can have a greater impact on model accuracy than the model's complexity.

Real-world datasets almost always contain some degree of imperfection. It's a natural part of the data collection process. As a data scientist or AI practitioner, you need to be able to detect, handle, and correct these imperfections. Missing and corrupt data are particularly troublesome, and knowing how to deal with them will make your AI models more robust and reliable.

5.3.2 Understanding Missing Data

Missing data refers to the absence of a value where one is expected. Missing data can occur for various reasons, such as incomplete surveys, sensor failures, or data entry errors. Missing values can manifest in different ways, such as blank cells, null values, or placeholders like "NA" or "None."

Handling missing data appropriately is essential because models cannot process or use incomplete data without appropriate strategies in place.

Types of Missing Data:

- **MCAR (Missing Completely at Random):** The missingness of data is unrelated to any other values in the dataset. For example, if a person accidentally skips a question on a survey, the data is missing completely at random.
- **MAR (Missing at Random):** The missing data may depend on other observed data but not the missing values themselves. For example, survey respondents in a particular age group might be less likely to answer certain questions.
- **MNAR (Missing Not at Random):** The missingness is related to the unobserved data itself. For example, if older individuals are more likely to leave a particular question unanswered, then the missingness is dependent on the unobserved age.

Strategies for Handling Missing Data:

Remove Missing Data: If the dataset has very few missing values, it may be acceptable to simply drop the rows or columns containing missing values. This can be done using Pandas' dropna() function:

```
import pandas as pd

# Remove rows with any missing data
df_cleaned = df.dropna()
```

This method is simple but can lead to a significant loss of data if many rows or columns are missing values.

Impute Missing Data: If removing missing data is not ideal because it would lead to a large loss of information, another option is to impute the missing values. Imputation is the process of filling in missing values with a reasonable guess, based on the existing data. Common imputation strategies include:

Mean/Median/Mode Imputation: Replacing missing numerical data with the mean (average), median, or mode (most frequent value) of that column.

```
# Impute missing numerical values with the column mean
df['column_name'].fillna(df['column_name'].mean(), inplace=True)
```

Forward or Backward Fill: Replacing missing values with the previous (forward fill) or next (backward fill) value in the column.

```
# Forward fill missing values
df.fillna(method='ffill', inplace=True)
```

Using Machine Learning Models: In some cases, you may want to use machine learning models to predict the missing values based on the existing data. For example, you could use regression or k-nearest neighbors (KNN) to estimate the missing values.

Flag Missing Data: Another approach is to create an additional column that flags whether a value is missing. This can be particularly useful when the presence or absence of a value is important and may contain information.

```
# Create a new column to flag missing data
df['column_name_missing'] = df['column_name'].isnull()
```

5.3.3 Dealing with Corrupt Data

Corrupt data refers to data that is incorrectly formatted, inconsistent, or contains errors that cannot be processed by the machine learning model. Examples of corrupt data include invalid entries, inconsistencies in numerical ranges, and data that doesn't conform to the expected type.

Corrupt data can arise from a variety of sources, such as:

- Data entry mistakes (e.g., typing errors).
- Problems during data conversion (e.g., encoding issues).
- Inconsistent units or scales (e.g., mixing pounds with kilograms).

Strategies for Handling Corrupt Data:

Identify and Fix Formatting Issues: If the dataset contains data with inconsistent formats (e.g., dates represented in different formats like YYYY-MM-DD and DD/MM/YYYY), the data needs to be normalized. In Pandas, you can use the to_datetime() function to convert date columns into a consistent format:

```
# Convert date column to datetime format
df['date_column'] = pd.to_datetime(df['date_column'], errors='coerce')
```

The errors='coerce' argument will turn invalid date entries into NaT (Not a Time), which can then be handled as missing data.

Handling Outliers: Outliers are extreme values that fall far outside the expected range. These can be considered "corrupt" data, or they could represent rare but valid observations. Identifying and handling outliers is an essential part of data cleaning.

Remove Outliers: You can identify outliers using statistical methods (e.g., Z-scores or IQR) and then remove them if they are deemed to be errors.

Transform Data: In some cases, outliers can be handled by applying a transformation to the data, such as using logarithmic or square root transformations to reduce their impact.

Fixing Inconsistent Entries: For categorical data, inconsistencies such as typos, misspellings, or different naming conventions can cause issues. You can clean this type of data by:

Standardizing categories: Make sure categories follow a consistent format (e.g., "Male" and "male" should be treated as the same).

```
# Standardize categories
df['gender'] = df['gender'].str.lower()
```

Replacing inconsistent entries: If certain entries are clearly incorrect or outside the acceptable range, you can replace or impute them.

```
# Replace incorrect data values
df['age'] = df['age'].replace(-1, df['age'].median())
```

5.3.4 Detecting and Removing Duplicates

In some cases, your dataset may contain duplicate records, which can skew results and affect the accuracy of the model. You can detect and remove duplicates in Pandas using the drop_duplicates() function:

```
# Remove duplicate rows
df_cleaned = df.drop_duplicates()
```

You can also use keep to specify whether to retain the first or last occurrence of the duplicate row.

5.3.5 Conclusion

Data cleaning is an essential process that prepares your dataset for analysis and modeling. Handling missing and corrupt data is one of the most important aspects of data cleaning, and there are many strategies available to address these issues. By learning how to identify and deal with missing values, outliers, inconsistencies, and duplicates, you can ensure that your data is ready for machine learning algorithms, ultimately improving the accuracy and robustness of your AI models.

In the next steps, remember to not only focus on cleaning the data but also to continuously monitor and update your cleaning procedures as you work with different datasets, since each dataset may require unique handling based on its characteristics. Properly cleaned and preprocessed data is the foundation of successful AI projects!

5.4 Feature Engineering for AI

In the world of Artificial Intelligence (AI) and machine learning, the quality and structure of the data you work with play a critical role in the performance of your models. Feature engineering is the process of transforming raw data into meaningful features (input variables) that help machine learning algorithms make better predictions. It is one of the most important steps in building an effective machine learning model.

This section explores the concept of feature engineering, why it's crucial for building robust AI models, and various techniques to generate new features, select the best ones, and handle categorical, numerical, and time series data.

5.4.1 What is Feature Engineering?

Feature engineering is the process of selecting, modifying, and creating new features from raw data to improve the performance of a machine learning model. The goal is to create data representations that allow the model to better recognize patterns and make more accurate predictions.

In machine learning, the quality of the features you provide to the model is often more important than the complexity of the model itself. Even a simple algorithm, like linear regression or decision trees, can perform exceptionally well with well-engineered features, while complex algorithms may fail to produce good results without proper features.

Feature engineering is highly domain-specific. What works well for one type of data or problem may not work well for another. As such, effective feature engineering requires both domain expertise and a deep understanding of the data you're working with.

5.4.2 Why Feature Engineering Matters for AI?

Machine learning algorithms rely on the features they receive to identify patterns and make predictions. The better the features, the better the model's performance. Well-engineered features can significantly improve the predictive power of a model, while poorly chosen features can lead to overfitting, underfitting, or a lack of generalization.

Here are some reasons why feature engineering is important:

- **Improves Model Performance**: The right features can lead to better accuracy and faster convergence in machine learning models.
- **Reduces the Complexity of the Model**: By selecting the most informative features, you can reduce the complexity of the model and improve its interpretability.
- **Captures Hidden Relationships**: Some relationships within the data might not be obvious at first. Feature engineering helps expose hidden patterns and correlations.
- **Prevents Overfitting**: Feature engineering helps avoid overfitting by creating features that capture the underlying trends in the data, rather than just noise or random fluctuations.

5.4.3 Types of Features and Feature Engineering Techniques

Feature engineering involves a wide range of techniques to create the best features for a machine learning model. These techniques depend on the type of data you're working with (numerical, categorical, time series, etc.) and the task you're trying to accomplish.

1. Numerical Feature Engineering

Numerical features are continuous variables, such as age, salary, or temperature. Common feature engineering techniques for numerical features include:

Scaling and Normalization: Many machine learning algorithms, especially those based on distance metrics (e.g., KNN, SVM), perform better when features are on the same scale. Scaling ensures that each feature contributes equally to the model.

Min-Max Scaling: Rescales features to a fixed range, often between 0 and 1.

from sklearn.preprocessing import MinMaxScaler

```
scaler = MinMaxScaler()
df['scaled_feature'] = scaler.fit_transform(df[['numerical_feature']])
```

Standardization: Centers the data around 0 with a standard deviation of 1.

```
from sklearn.preprocessing import StandardScaler

scaler = StandardScaler()
df['standardized_feature'] = scaler.fit_transform(df[['numerical_feature']])
```

Binning: Divides numerical data into bins or categories. For example, you could bin age into ranges (e.g., 0–18, 19–35, etc.).

```
bins = [0, 18, 35, 50, 100]
labels = ['0-18', '19-35', '36-50', '50+']
df['age_group'] = pd.cut(df['age'], bins=bins, labels=labels)
```

Log Transformation: Applied to skewed data to reduce the influence of outliers and make the data more normally distributed.

```
import numpy as np
df['log_feature'] = np.log(df['numerical_feature'] + 1)
```

Polynomial Features: You can create new features by adding polynomial combinations of existing numerical features to capture non-linear relationships between features.

```
from sklearn.preprocessing import PolynomialFeatures
poly = PolynomialFeatures(degree=2)
df_poly = poly.fit_transform(df[['feature1', 'feature2']])
```

2. Categorical Feature Engineering

Categorical features are variables that take on a limited, fixed number of values, such as "red", "green", or "blue" for colors or "low", "medium", "high" for a rating.

Techniques for handling categorical data include:

One-Hot Encoding: Converts categorical variables into binary columns, where each category becomes a separate column with values of 0 or 1.

```
df_encoded = pd.get_dummies(df['category_column'])
```

Label Encoding: Converts each category to a unique integer value.

```
from sklearn.preprocessing import LabelEncoder
encoder = LabelEncoder()
df['encoded_feature'] = encoder.fit_transform(df['category_column'])
```

Frequency Encoding: Replaces each category with the frequency of that category in the dataset. This technique can be particularly useful when dealing with high-cardinality features.

```
freq_encoding = df['category_column'].value_counts()
df['encoded_feature'] = df['category_column'].map(freq_encoding)
```

Target Encoding: Replaces categorical values with the average target value for each category. This technique is useful when working with categorical features that have a direct correlation to the target variable.

```
mean_target = df.groupby('category_column')['target'].mean()
df['encoded_feature'] = df['category_column'].map(mean_target)
```

3. Time Series Feature Engineering

For time-dependent data, such as stock prices or sensor readings over time, feature engineering helps capture temporal patterns and trends. Techniques for time series feature engineering include:

Extracting Date and Time Components: You can extract useful features such as the year, month, day, hour, or weekday from a datetime feature.

```
df['year'] = df['timestamp'].dt.year
df['month'] = df['timestamp'].dt.month
df['weekday'] = df['timestamp'].dt.weekday
```

Lag Features: Create features based on the previous time steps to capture temporal dependencies (e.g., using the previous day's value to predict the current day's value).

```
df['lag_1'] = df['target'].shift(1)
```

Rolling Window Statistics: Calculate rolling statistics such as the moving average or moving standard deviation over a sliding window of time.

```
df['rolling_mean'] = df['target'].rolling(window=5).mean()
```

4. Text Feature Engineering

For text-based data (e.g., customer reviews, tweets, or news articles), converting the text into numeric features is essential. Common techniques for text feature engineering include:

Bag of Words: Represents text data as a matrix of word frequencies.

```
from sklearn.feature_extraction.text import CountVectorizer
vectorizer = CountVectorizer()
X = vectorizer.fit_transform(df['text_column'])
```

TF-IDF (Term Frequency-Inverse Document Frequency): A more sophisticated version of Bag of Words that takes into account the importance of words in relation to the entire corpus.

```
from sklearn.feature_extraction.text import TfidfVectorizer
tfidf = TfidfVectorizer()
X = tfidf.fit_transform(df['text_column'])
```

5.4.4 Feature Selection: Choosing the Best Features

After creating or modifying features, the next step is selecting the most informative features for the model. Too many features can lead to overfitting, while too few features may not capture enough information for the model to perform well.

Common feature selection techniques include:

- **Correlation Matrix**: Identifying highly correlated features and removing one of the features to avoid multicollinearity.
- **Recursive Feature Elimination (RFE):** Iteratively builds models and removes the least important features based on their contribution to the model's performance.
- **Tree-based Methods**: Algorithms like Random Forest or XGBoost can be used to calculate feature importance and identify the most significant features.

5.4.5 Conclusion

Feature engineering is one of the most important tasks in the machine learning workflow. It involves creating new features, transforming raw data, and selecting the most relevant features to enhance the predictive power of AI models. Mastering feature engineering techniques helps improve model performance, increase interpretability, and prevent overfitting, ultimately leading to more accurate and reliable AI models.

By applying the right feature engineering methods to different types of data—whether numerical, categorical, time series, or text—you'll be better equipped to tackle a wide range of AI challenges.

6. Introduction to Machine Learning

Machine learning is at the heart of AI, enabling computers to learn from data and make decisions without explicit programming. In this chapter, you'll get a beginner-friendly introduction to the core concepts of machine learning, including the difference between supervised and unsupervised learning. You'll explore how algorithms use training data to create models that can predict, classify, and identify patterns. You'll also gain an understanding of common machine learning tasks, such as regression and classification, and how these tasks are applied in real-world AI applications. By the end of this chapter, you'll be ready to dive deeper into machine learning algorithms and start building your own models.

6.1 What is Machine Learning? Supervised vs. Unsupervised Learning

Machine learning (ML) is a subfield of artificial intelligence (AI) that focuses on enabling computers to learn from data and make predictions or decisions without explicit programming. Rather than being programmed to perform specific tasks, a machine learning model learns from patterns in data and improves its performance over time. The more data it processes, the better its ability to make accurate predictions or classifications.

Machine learning is transforming industries, from healthcare and finance to marketing and robotics, by automating decision-making processes and uncovering insights from vast amounts of data. This section introduces the fundamental concepts of machine learning and explains the key types of learning: supervised learning and unsupervised learning.

6.1.1 What is Machine Learning?

Machine learning involves developing algorithms that allow systems to recognize patterns, adapt to new data, and make predictions. It is based on the idea that systems can learn from data, identify trends, and make decisions with minimal human intervention. Machine learning models are often categorized based on how they learn and the type of data they work with.

ML models rely on data to "train" or learn. The process of training a model involves providing it with a set of input data (features) along with the correct outputs (labels) or targets (in supervised learning). The model adjusts its internal parameters or structure to minimize the difference between its predictions and the actual outputs, improving its accuracy.

The primary goal of machine learning is to generalize well from training data to unseen data, ensuring that the model can make correct predictions on new data outside the training set.

6.1.2 Types of Machine Learning

Machine learning can be divided into different types, based on how the learning process works and how the data is provided. The two primary categories are supervised learning and unsupervised learning. Let's explore both:

1. Supervised Learning

In supervised learning, the algorithm learns from labeled data, meaning that both the input features and the correct output labels are provided during the training process. The goal of supervised learning is for the model to learn the mapping between inputs (features) and outputs (labels) so that it can predict the output for new, unseen data.

Supervised learning is called "supervised" because the algorithm is guided (or supervised) by the correct answers, and it tries to minimize the error between its predictions and the true labels.

Key Characteristics of Supervised Learning:

- **Labeled Data**: Each training example consists of an input vector (features) paired with the correct output (label).
- **Goal**: The model learns to predict the label of new data based on patterns in the training data.
- **Applications**: Supervised learning is used for tasks such as classification (e.g., identifying emails as spam or not) and regression (e.g., predicting house prices based on features like location and square footage).

Examples of Supervised Learning Algorithms:

- **Linear Regression**: Predicts a continuous output (e.g., predicting salary based on experience).

- **Logistic Regression**: Used for binary classification problems (e.g., predicting whether a customer will buy a product or not).
- **Decision Trees**: Build models by splitting the data into subsets based on feature values (used for both classification and regression).
- **Random Forest**: An ensemble method based on decision trees that improves accuracy by averaging multiple models.
- **Support Vector Machines (SVM):** A classifier that finds the optimal hyperplane to separate different classes in the data.
- **Neural Networks**: A series of algorithms that attempt to recognize underlying relationships in a set of data through a process that mimics the way the human brain operates.

Supervised Learning Example:

Let's say you have a dataset of emails, where each email is labeled as either spam or not spam. You can train a model using the labeled data by providing it with features (such as the text content, sender, and subject) and the label (spam or not). The model learns to identify patterns that correlate with spam emails, and after training, it can predict whether new, unseen emails are spam or not.

2. Unsupervised Learning

In unsupervised learning, the algorithm learns from unlabeled data. There are no predefined labels or target outputs, so the goal is to explore the structure and patterns within the data. The model tries to find inherent structures or relationships in the data, such as groupings or clusters, without the guidance of labeled outputs.

Unsupervised learning is useful for tasks where the goal is to explore the data and discover hidden patterns, rather than predict a specific output.

Key Characteristics of Unsupervised Learning:

- **Unlabeled Data**: Only the input data is available; there are no corresponding output labels.
- **Goal**: The model tries to organize the data into groups (clustering) or reduce the number of features (dimensionality reduction).
- **Applications**: Unsupervised learning is used for clustering (e.g., grouping customers based on purchasing behavior) and anomaly detection (e.g., identifying fraud in transactions).

Examples of Unsupervised Learning Algorithms:

- **K-Means Clustering**: Divides the dataset into a specified number of clusters by minimizing the distance between data points and the centroid of each cluster.
- **Hierarchical Clustering**: Builds a hierarchy of clusters, where each data point is initially its own cluster, and clusters are merged based on similarity.
- **Principal Component Analysis (PCA):** A dimensionality reduction technique that transforms the data into a lower-dimensional space while retaining the most important variance in the data.
- **Autoencoders**: A type of neural network used for dimensionality reduction and feature learning.

Unsupervised Learning Example:

Consider a shopping website that collects data on customer behavior but doesn't know what kinds of customers exist. With unsupervised learning, you can apply clustering techniques, like K-means, to group customers into segments based on patterns in their shopping behavior (e.g., frequent buyers, bargain hunters, etc.). These insights can then inform targeted marketing strategies.

6.1.3 Semi-Supervised and Reinforcement Learning

While supervised and unsupervised learning cover most ML applications, there are also other types of machine learning that fall in between or serve unique purposes:

Semi-Supervised Learning: A hybrid approach where the model is trained using a small amount of labeled data and a large amount of unlabeled data. This approach is used when labeling data is expensive or time-consuming. Semi-supervised learning takes advantage of both labeled and unlabeled data to improve model accuracy.

Reinforcement Learning: In reinforcement learning, an agent learns by interacting with an environment and receiving feedback in the form of rewards or penalties. The agent takes actions based on its experiences and aims to maximize cumulative rewards. Reinforcement learning is used in applications such as robotics, gaming, and self-driving cars.

6.1.4 Conclusion

Machine learning is a powerful tool for making predictions and uncovering hidden patterns from data. Supervised learning and unsupervised learning are two fundamental types of machine learning, each with distinct methods and applications.

Supervised learning excels in problems where labeled data is available, such as classification and regression tasks.

Unsupervised learning is useful for discovering hidden structures and relationships within data, such as clustering and dimensionality reduction.

By understanding the difference between these types of learning, you can better apply machine learning algorithms to solve real-world problems, whether you're predicting outcomes, grouping similar items, or uncovering complex patterns in large datasets. As you dive deeper into machine learning, you'll learn how to apply these methods to build AI models that make intelligent decisions and predictions.

6.2 Understanding Training Data and Labels

In machine learning, data is the fundamental building block upon which models are trained. The quality, quantity, and type of data play a significant role in the performance of machine learning algorithms. Training data and labels are critical elements of this data, particularly in supervised learning, where the model learns by example.

This section explains the concepts of training data and labels, their importance in the training process, and how to handle them effectively. Understanding these concepts is essential for building accurate and reliable machine learning models.

6.2.1 What is Training Data?

Training data refers to the dataset used to train a machine learning model. It consists of input features (also called predictors or independent variables) and the corresponding labels (also called targets or dependent variables in supervised learning). During the training process, the model learns to identify patterns in the data so it can make accurate predictions when exposed to new, unseen data.

In supervised learning, the training data is critical because the algorithm uses this data to adjust its internal parameters and learn from it. The goal is for the model to recognize relationships between the input features and the labels, which will then allow it to make predictions on new data.

Training data can be of many different types, including:

Structured Data: This refers to data that is organized in a tabular format (e.g., spreadsheets or databases) with rows and columns. Each row represents an instance or example, and each column represents a feature or variable.

Unstructured Data: This refers to data that is not organized in a predefined manner, such as text, images, and audio. Models working with unstructured data often require additional preprocessing techniques to convert them into a usable format.

For example, if you're building a model to predict house prices, your training data might consist of features such as square footage, number of bedrooms, and location, and the labels (or targets) would be the price of the house.

6.2.2 What are Labels?

In supervised learning, labels are the correct answers or outputs associated with each training instance. These labels are used to guide the model in learning the relationship between the input features and the output.

For example, in a classification task, the labels indicate the class or category that each input belongs to. In a regression task, the labels are continuous values that represent the output the model is trying to predict.

Examples of Labels:

Classification (Categorical Labels):

- In a spam email classification task, the label might be "spam" or "not spam."
- In a medical diagnosis model, the label might be "disease" or "no disease."

Regression (Continuous Labels):

- In a house price prediction task, the label might be the actual price of the house (a continuous value, e.g., $500,000).
- In a stock price prediction task, the label might be the stock price at a future time.

The labels are the target outputs the model is attempting to predict. In supervised learning, the algorithm compares its predictions to these labels to evaluate its accuracy and improve over time.

6.2.3 The Role of Labels in Supervised Learning

The labels guide the learning process in supervised learning. Here's a breakdown of how labels influence the training process:

Learning the Relationship: The model uses the labeled data to learn the underlying relationship between the input features and the labels. For example, in a classification problem, the model will learn which features (e.g., the presence of certain words in an email) are indicative of spam or non-spam emails.

Error Calculation: During training, the model makes predictions based on the input features, and these predictions are compared to the actual labels. The difference between the predicted value and the true label is called the error (or loss). The model uses this error to adjust its internal parameters to improve future predictions.

Model Evaluation: Once the model is trained, it is evaluated based on how well it can predict labels for new, unseen data. The more accurately the model can predict labels, the better it has learned from the training data.

6.2.4 The Importance of High-Quality Training Data

The quality of the training data directly affects the performance of the machine learning model. Good quality data ensures that the model can learn accurate patterns and relationships, while poor-quality data can lead to poor performance. Here are some factors to consider:

Data Relevance: The training data must be relevant to the problem the model is trying to solve. If the training data doesn't reflect the real-world conditions the model will encounter, the model will likely fail to generalize well.

Data Consistency: The data should be consistent in format and structure. Inconsistent data, such as missing values, mismatched data types, or duplicate entries, can confuse the model and reduce its ability to learn.

Data Volume: The more data you have, the better the model can learn. Having a large and diverse dataset helps the model generalize better and avoid overfitting (when the model learns patterns specific to the training data but fails to generalize to new data).

Data Labeling Accuracy: The accuracy of the labels is crucial for supervised learning. If the labels are incorrect or inconsistent, the model will learn incorrect patterns and produce inaccurate predictions.

6.2.5 Types of Labels

The labels you work with can be of various types, depending on the task you're trying to solve. Below are the two primary categories of labels:

1. Categorical Labels (Classification Tasks)

In classification tasks, the labels are categorical, meaning that they represent distinct classes or categories. The model is tasked with predicting the category that each data point belongs to.

Examples of classification tasks and labels:

- **Image Classification**: Predicting whether an image contains a cat or a dog (labels: "cat", "dog").
- **Email Classification**: Predicting whether an email is spam or not (labels: "spam", "not spam").
- **Medical Diagnosis**: Predicting whether a patient has a disease or not (labels: "disease", "no disease").

In classification, the labels are typically discrete values. The model is trained to output one of these categories.

2. Continuous Labels (Regression Tasks)

In regression tasks, the labels are continuous numerical values. The goal of the model is to predict a numeric value based on input features.

Examples of regression tasks and labels:

- **House Price Prediction**: Predicting the price of a house given its features like square footage and location (label: continuous price, e.g., $500,000).

- **Stock Price Prediction**: Predicting the future stock price of a company (label: continuous price value).
- **Temperature Forecasting**: Predicting the temperature on a given day (label: continuous temperature value in degrees Celsius).

In regression, the model outputs a continuous value that can vary within a given range.

6.2.6 Handling Imbalanced Data and Labels

In some machine learning tasks, especially classification, the dataset may contain an unequal distribution of classes. This situation is called class imbalance, and it can cause the model to favor the majority class, leading to poor performance on the minority class.

For example, in a fraud detection task, the number of fraudulent transactions may be much smaller than the number of legitimate transactions. If the model is trained on imbalanced data, it may become biased toward predicting legitimate transactions and fail to detect fraudulent ones.

To address class imbalance, several techniques can be applied:

- **Resampling**: Either oversampling the minority class or undersampling the majority class to balance the class distribution.
- **Synthetic Data Generation**: Using techniques like SMOTE (Synthetic Minority Over-sampling Technique) to generate synthetic samples for the minority class.
- **Cost-sensitive Learning**: Assigning higher weights to the minority class to penalize the model more for misclassifying minority class examples.

6.2.7 Conclusion

Understanding training data and labels is crucial for building successful machine learning models. Training data is used to teach the model the relationships between input features and labels, while labels are the target outputs the model aims to predict. The quality and accuracy of both the data and labels have a direct impact on the model's ability to generalize and make correct predictions.

When preparing your data for machine learning, it is essential to ensure the data is relevant, consistent, and properly labeled. Additionally, understanding the types of tasks (classification vs. regression) and the nature of your labels will guide your model selection and evaluation process. By effectively managing training data and labels, you can build models that learn efficiently and make accurate predictions on real-world data.

6.3 Key ML Algorithms Overview

Machine learning (ML) is powered by a diverse set of algorithms that are used to identify patterns and make predictions from data. These algorithms vary in their complexity and use cases, but each has specific strengths and applications. Understanding the key ML algorithms is essential for selecting the right approach to solve a given problem.

This section provides an overview of some of the most commonly used machine learning algorithms, categorized into supervised and unsupervised learning. We will explore the characteristics, use cases, and advantages of each algorithm to give you a foundational understanding of how they work and where they can be applied.

6.3.1 Supervised Learning Algorithms

Supervised learning algorithms are used when the training data contains input-output pairs, meaning the model is provided with both the features (inputs) and the corresponding labels (outputs). The goal is for the algorithm to learn the relationship between these inputs and outputs so that it can predict the labels for new, unseen data.

1. Linear Regression

Linear regression is one of the simplest and most commonly used algorithms in supervised learning for regression tasks. It predicts a continuous target variable based on the linear relationship between the input features and the target.

How it works: Linear regression tries to find the line of best fit through the data points. The line is determined by minimizing the sum of the squared differences between the observed values and the predicted values (least squares).

Use cases: Predicting house prices based on features like size, location, and age, or predicting sales revenue based on advertising spend.

Advantages: Simple to understand and implement, interpretable model (easy to explain the influence of each feature on the outcome), and computationally efficient.

2. Logistic Regression

Logistic regression is used for classification problems, where the goal is to predict a binary outcome (i.e., two possible classes, such as "yes/no" or "spam/not spam"). It estimates the probability that a given input belongs to a certain class using the logistic function (also known as the sigmoid function), which maps any real-valued number into the range [0, 1].

How it works: The algorithm uses the input features to calculate a weighted sum of them and applies the logistic function to predict the probability of the target class.

Use cases: Classifying emails as spam or non-spam, diagnosing whether a patient has a particular disease, predicting whether a customer will churn.

Advantages: Simple, fast, and interpretable. Good for binary classification tasks and can handle linear decision boundaries.

3. Decision Trees

A decision tree is a supervised learning algorithm that is used for both classification and regression tasks. It splits the data into subsets based on feature values to make decisions at each branch. The tree's leaves contain the final predictions or outcomes.

How it works: The decision tree uses a greedy approach to split the data into subsets that maximize the information gain or minimize the impurity (e.g., Gini impurity or entropy) at each node.

Use cases: Credit scoring, customer segmentation, medical diagnosis, predicting equipment failure.

Advantages: Easy to understand and interpret, handles both numerical and categorical data, can model non-linear relationships.

4. Random Forest

Random forest is an ensemble method based on decision trees. It combines the predictions of multiple decision trees to improve accuracy and reduce overfitting. The algorithm works by training several decision trees on different subsets of the training data and averaging the results (for regression) or using majority voting (for classification).

How it works: Each tree is trained on a random sample of the data with replacement (bootstrap sampling), and during the tree-building process, only a random subset of features is considered for each split.

Use cases: Predicting customer churn, fraud detection, and image classification.

Advantages: More accurate than individual decision trees, reduces overfitting, works well with both small and large datasets.

5. Support Vector Machines (SVM)

Support Vector Machines (SVM) are powerful algorithms used for classification and regression tasks. SVM tries to find the hyperplane that best separates the data points of different classes with the maximum margin.

How it works: SVM searches for the optimal hyperplane that separates the classes in the feature space. It uses the support vectors, which are the data points closest to the decision boundary, to define the hyperplane.

Use cases: Face recognition, text classification (e.g., sentiment analysis), and bioinformatics.

Advantages: Effective in high-dimensional spaces, robust to overfitting (especially with a high number of features), can model non-linear decision boundaries using the kernel trick.

6.3.2 Unsupervised Learning Algorithms

Unsupervised learning algorithms are used when the data does not have labels. The goal in unsupervised learning is to identify hidden patterns or intrinsic structures in the data, such as grouping similar instances or reducing the number of features.

1. K-Means Clustering

K-Means clustering is one of the most widely used clustering algorithms. It partitions data into k distinct clusters based on feature similarity.

How it works: The algorithm initializes k centroids, assigns data points to the nearest centroid, and then updates the centroids based on the mean of the assigned data points. The process repeats until convergence.

Use cases: Market segmentation, customer clustering, image compression, and anomaly detection.

Advantages: Simple to understand and implement, works well for large datasets, computationally efficient.

2. Hierarchical Clustering

Hierarchical clustering creates a tree-like structure (called a dendrogram) of clusters by either successively merging clusters (agglomerative approach) or splitting clusters (divisive approach).

How it works: The agglomerative approach starts with each data point as its own cluster and iteratively merges the closest pairs of clusters until all data points are in one cluster. The divisive approach starts with one cluster and recursively splits it.

Use cases: Document clustering, biological taxonomies, and organizing hierarchical data.

Advantages: Produces a dendrogram that can be useful for understanding the hierarchical structure of the data, does not require the number of clusters to be specified in advance.

3. Principal Component Analysis (PCA)

Principal Component Analysis (PCA) is a dimensionality reduction technique that transforms high-dimensional data into a lower-dimensional space while retaining as much variance as possible.

How it works: PCA identifies the principal components (directions of maximum variance) in the data and projects the data onto these components, reducing the number of features.

Use cases: Reducing the dimensionality of data for visualization, noise reduction, and preprocessing for other machine learning models.

Advantages: Helps with overfitting by reducing the number of features, computationally efficient, often improves model performance.

4. Autoencoders

Autoencoders are a type of neural network used for unsupervised learning that learn efficient codings of the input data. They are primarily used for dimensionality reduction and anomaly detection.

How it works: An autoencoder consists of two parts: an encoder that maps the input data to a lower-dimensional latent space, and a decoder that reconstructs the original data from the latent representation.

Use cases: Image compression, anomaly detection, feature extraction.

Advantages: Can learn non-linear relationships, useful for reducing the complexity of high-dimensional data.

6.3.3 Conclusion

Machine learning algorithms are powerful tools for solving a wide range of problems, from predicting house prices and diagnosing diseases to segmenting customers and detecting fraud. Understanding the key algorithms in both supervised and unsupervised learning helps you make informed decisions about which model to use for your task.

Supervised learning algorithms like linear regression, logistic regression, decision trees, and support vector machines are great for prediction tasks when labeled data is available.

Unsupervised learning algorithms like K-means clustering, hierarchical clustering, PCA, and autoencoders excel at discovering hidden patterns and reducing dimensionality when working with unlabeled data.

Each algorithm has its strengths and weaknesses, and selecting the right one depends on the problem at hand, the nature of the data, and the computational resources available. As you gain experience with machine learning, you'll become more adept at choosing the most appropriate algorithm for your tasks and optimizing it for better performance.

6.4 Building Your First AI Model

Building your first AI model is an exciting and essential milestone in your journey toward mastering artificial intelligence. Whether you're working on a simple regression problem or a classification task, constructing an AI model allows you to understand how algorithms learn from data and make predictions. In this section, we will take you step-by-step through the process of building a machine learning model, from preparing your data to evaluating your model's performance.

Let's break down the key stages involved in building your first AI model:

6.4.1 Step 1: Defining the Problem

Before diving into coding and algorithm selection, it's essential to clearly define the problem you're trying to solve. Are you working on a regression problem (predicting a continuous output), a classification problem (predicting discrete categories), or something else? Understanding the nature of the problem will guide you in selecting the right algorithm and preparing the data accordingly.

For example:

- If you are predicting house prices based on features such as size and location, you have a regression problem.
- If you are predicting whether an email is spam or not, you have a binary classification problem.

6.4.2 Step 2: Gathering and Preparing Data

The quality of your data plays a crucial role in the performance of your model. For supervised learning, you need a dataset that contains both input features (the variables used to make predictions) and labels (the outcomes you want to predict).

Data Gathering: You can collect data from various sources such as public datasets, your own data, or APIs that provide real-time information. Some popular sources include:

Kaggle Datasets

UCI Machine Learning Repository

Public APIs (e.g., weather data, stock data)

Data Preparation: Once you have the dataset, the next step is to clean and preprocess the data. This involves:

- **Handling missing values**: Decide whether to drop missing values, replace them with a specific value (e.g., the mean or median), or use imputation techniques.

- **Normalizing and scaling**: If your features are on different scales, consider scaling them so they all have a similar range. This is particularly important for algorithms like KNN and SVM.
- **Encoding categorical variables**: Convert categorical data (e.g., country names, product categories) into numerical format using techniques such as one-hot encoding or label encoding.

For example, if you're working with a dataset of housing prices, you might have features like square footage, number of bedrooms, and neighborhood. You'll need to ensure that these features are clean, standardized, and ready for training.

6.4.3 Step 3: Splitting the Data

Once you have cleaned and prepared the data, it's important to split it into two distinct sets:

- **Training Set**: This is the portion of the data used to train the model. Typically, you will use 70-80% of your data for training.
- **Testing Set**: This set is used to evaluate the model's performance and generalization ability. It's crucial that the testing set is completely unseen during the training process (i.e., the model should not have access to this data while learning).

Splitting the data ensures that your model is evaluated on data it hasn't seen before, which simulates real-world performance where the model encounters new data.

```
from sklearn.model_selection import train_test_split

# Split the data into training and testing sets
X_train, X_test, y_train, y_test = train_test_split(X, y, test_size=0.2, random_state=42)
```

In the code above, X represents the input features, and y represents the labels (target variables). train_test_split will split the dataset into 80% for training and 20% for testing.

6.4.4 Step 4: Choosing the Algorithm

Now that the data is prepared and split, the next step is to choose the appropriate machine learning algorithm. For your first AI model, we recommend starting with a simple algorithm, such as linear regression for regression tasks or logistic regression for binary classification problems. These algorithms are easy to implement and understand, making them excellent starting points.

If you are unsure which algorithm to choose, you can start by trying a few different models and evaluating their performance. More complex models like decision trees, random forests, and support vector machines can be explored as you advance.

For example, let's use Logistic Regression for a binary classification problem like predicting whether a customer will buy a product or not:

```
from sklearn.linear_model import LogisticRegression

# Initialize the model
model = LogisticRegression()

# Train the model using the training data
model.fit(X_train, y_train)
```

6.4.5 Step 5: Training the Model

Once you have selected the model, you can train it using your training dataset. The fit() function in most machine learning libraries (like Scikit-learn) is used to train the model. During the training phase, the algorithm learns the underlying patterns and relationships between the features and the labels.

Here's the code for training a logistic regression model:

model.fit(X_train, y_train)

During training, the algorithm will try to minimize the error between its predictions and the actual labels in the training data, adjusting its internal parameters (weights) accordingly.

6.4.6 Step 6: Evaluating the Model

After training your model, it's important to assess its performance using the testing data that was not seen during training. This helps you understand how well your model generalizes to new, unseen data.

Common evaluation metrics include:

Accuracy: The proportion of correct predictions. Useful for classification tasks.

Mean Squared Error (MSE): Measures the average squared difference between predicted and actual values. Used in regression tasks.

Precision, Recall, F1-Score: Useful in imbalanced datasets, especially for binary classification tasks.

Here's how you can evaluate your logistic regression model's accuracy:

```
from sklearn.metrics import accuracy_score

# Make predictions on the test data
y_pred = model.predict(X_test)

# Calculate the accuracy
accuracy = accuracy_score(y_test, y_pred)
print(f'Accuracy: {accuracy * 100:.2f}%')
```

If you are working with a regression task, you might use Mean Squared Error (MSE) instead:

```
from sklearn.metrics import mean_squared_error

# Make predictions on the test data
y_pred = model.predict(X_test)

# Calculate the Mean Squared Error
mse = mean_squared_error(y_test, y_pred)
print(f'Mean Squared Error: {mse:.2f}')
```

6.4.7 Step 7: Improving Your Model

If your model's performance isn't satisfactory, there are several techniques you can use to improve it:

- **Feature Engineering**: Adding new features or modifying existing ones can improve the model's predictive power. This includes transformations like polynomial features or creating interaction terms between variables.

- **Hyperparameter Tuning**: Most machine learning algorithms have hyperparameters (e.g., learning rate, number of trees in a random forest) that affect their performance. You can fine-tune these hyperparameters using methods like Grid Search or Random Search.
- **Using More Complex Models**: If simpler models do not perform well, you can try more complex models like decision trees, random forests, or neural networks.

6.4.8 Step 8: Deploying the Model

Once your model has been trained and evaluated, the final step is to deploy it in a production environment. This allows the model to make predictions on new, incoming data in real-time or batch mode.

You can deploy your model using various frameworks such as:

- Flask or Django for web-based APIs.
- TensorFlow Serving or FastAPI for deploying machine learning models in production.

To deploy a model, you would save the trained model using a method like pickle or joblib, and then load it in your application to make predictions.

Example of saving and loading a model with joblib:

```
import joblib

# Save the model
joblib.dump(model, 'model.pkl')

# Load the model
loaded_model = joblib.load('model.pkl')
```

6.4.9 Conclusion

Building your first AI model involves several key steps: defining the problem, gathering and preparing the data, selecting the right algorithm, training the model, evaluating its performance, and deploying it. By following these steps and applying best practices, you can create models that learn from data and make predictions to solve real-world problems.

As you gain experience, you will learn how to optimize your models, handle complex data, and experiment with more advanced algorithms. But no matter how advanced you become, the core principles of building a machine learning model remain the same: understand the problem, clean your data, choose the right algorithm, train the model, evaluate it, and deploy it effectively.

Happy building!

7. Getting Started with Scikit-Learn

Scikit-Learn is one of the most powerful and widely used libraries for machine learning in Python. In this chapter, you'll learn how to use Scikit-Learn to implement your first machine learning models. You'll start by exploring how to load datasets, prepare data for training, and split it into training and testing sets. You'll dive into basic machine learning algorithms, such as linear regression for prediction and logistic regression for classification. Through hands-on examples, you'll understand how to train, test, and evaluate your models using performance metrics like accuracy, precision, and recall. By the end of this chapter, you'll be confident in applying Scikit-Learn to solve real-world machine learning problems.

7.1 Introduction to Scikit-Learn

Scikit-learn is one of the most popular and versatile libraries for machine learning in Python. It provides simple and efficient tools for data analysis and modeling, making it an essential library for both beginners and experienced machine learning practitioners. Scikit-learn is built on top of other core scientific Python libraries like NumPy, SciPy, and matplotlib, which means it integrates seamlessly with the broader Python ecosystem.

In this section, we'll introduce you to Scikit-learn, its core functionalities, and how to get started using it to build your machine learning models.

7.1.1 What is Scikit-Learn?

Scikit-learn is an open-source machine learning library that provides a wide range of algorithms for classification, regression, clustering, and dimensionality reduction. It also offers utilities for data preprocessing, model selection, evaluation, and model deployment.

Some of the core features of Scikit-learn include:

- **Classification**: Algorithms to classify data into categories, such as Logistic Regression, Support Vector Machines (SVM), Random Forest, and k-Nearest Neighbors (k-NN).
- **Regression**: Algorithms to predict continuous values, such as Linear Regression, Decision Trees, and SVR.
- **Clustering**: Unsupervised learning algorithms that group similar data points together, like K-Means, DBSCAN, and Hierarchical Clustering.

- **Dimensionality Reduction**: Techniques to reduce the number of features while retaining important information, such as Principal Component Analysis (PCA) and t-SNE.
- **Model Evaluation**: Utilities like cross-validation, confusion matrices, and metrics like accuracy, precision, and recall.
- **Preprocessing**: Tools for scaling, encoding categorical variables, and handling missing values.

One of the reasons Scikit-learn is so popular is its consistent API and easy-to-understand syntax, which makes it beginner-friendly. It's also highly optimized and well-documented, which allows you to get up to speed quickly and efficiently build machine learning models.

7.1.2 Key Features of Scikit-Learn

Let's dive into some of the main features of Scikit-learn and see how they make it so useful for machine learning tasks:

1. Algorithms for Supervised Learning

Scikit-learn includes many well-known algorithms for both regression and classification tasks. Some of the popular algorithms provided by Scikit-learn include:

- **Linear and Logistic Regression**: For predicting continuous and binary outcomes.
- **Decision Trees**: For creating decision rules based on data features.
- **Random Forest**: An ensemble method for improving the performance of decision trees.
- **Support Vector Machines (SVM):** For classification and regression tasks with high-dimensional data.
- **k-Nearest Neighbors (k-NN):** A simple yet powerful algorithm used for classification based on proximity.

These algorithms are ready to be used right out of the box, and they all follow a simple pattern of fit() for training and predict() for making predictions.

2. Algorithms for Unsupervised Learning

Scikit-learn also provides tools for unsupervised learning, where the data is not labeled, and the goal is to find hidden patterns or groupings within the data. Some unsupervised algorithms include:

- **K-Means Clustering**: A popular method for partitioning data into clusters.
- **DBSCAN**: A density-based clustering algorithm that can find arbitrarily shaped clusters.
- **Principal Component Analysis (PCA):** A method for reducing the dimensionality of data.
- **Gaussian Mixture Models (GMM):** A probabilistic model for clustering and density estimation.

3. Model Evaluation and Selection

Scikit-learn offers a variety of utilities for evaluating and selecting models:

- **Cross-Validation**: Split your data into several subsets and evaluate the model on each subset to get a more robust performance estimate.
- **Grid Search**: Find the best hyperparameters for your model by trying multiple combinations.
- **Metrics**: Scikit-learn includes many metrics like accuracy, precision, recall, F1-score, and mean squared error (MSE), making it easy to measure how well your model is performing.

4. Preprocessing Data

Data preprocessing is a crucial step in the machine learning pipeline, and Scikit-learn provides several tools for this task, including:

- **StandardScaler**: Normalize or standardize the features so they all have the same scale.
- **LabelEncoder**: Convert categorical labels into numerical values.
- **OneHotEncoder**: Convert categorical features into binary vectors.
- **Imputer**: Handle missing values by filling them with a specified value, such as the mean or median.

5. Pipelines

Pipelines in Scikit-learn allow you to combine multiple steps of a machine learning workflow (e.g., preprocessing, feature extraction, model training) into a single object. This helps streamline the process and ensures that the same transformations are applied to the training and testing data.

```
from sklearn.pipeline import Pipeline
```

```python
from sklearn.preprocessing import StandardScaler
from sklearn.svm import SVC

# Create a pipeline with scaling and classification
pipeline = Pipeline([
    ('scaler', StandardScaler()),
    ('classifier', SVC())
])

# Train the model
pipeline.fit(X_train, y_train)

# Make predictions
y_pred = pipeline.predict(X_test)
```

Using pipelines ensures that your model is more maintainable and that data transformations are applied consistently.

7.1.3 Installing Scikit-Learn

To get started with Scikit-learn, you need to install it in your Python environment. If you're using Anaconda, Scikit-learn can be easily installed with the following command:

```
conda install scikit-learn
```

Alternatively, you can install Scikit-learn using pip, which is the Python package installer:

```
pip install scikit-learn
```

After installation, you can import the necessary classes and functions from Scikit-learn and start building your machine learning models.

7.1.4 Basic Workflow with Scikit-Learn

Building a machine learning model using Scikit-learn typically follows a standard workflow. Here's a brief overview of the steps involved:

Import the necessary libraries and datasets: You can load datasets from Scikit-learn's collection or use your own data.

```
from sklearn.datasets import load_iris
from sklearn.model_selection import train_test_split
from sklearn.linear_model import LogisticRegression
```

Preprocess the data: This may include handling missing values, encoding categorical features, and scaling numeric features.

Split the data into training and testing sets: This ensures that your model can be trained on one subset of the data and evaluated on another.

```
X_train, X_test, y_train, y_test = train_test_split(X, y, test_size=0.3, random_state=42)
```

Choose and train the model: Select an algorithm from Scikit-learn and use the fit() method to train the model on your data.

```
model = LogisticRegression()
model.fit(X_train, y_train)
```

Evaluate the model: Use various metrics (e.g., accuracy, precision) to assess how well the model performs on the test set.

```
from sklearn.metrics import accuracy_score
y_pred = model.predict(X_test)
accuracy = accuracy_score(y_test, y_pred)
print(f'Accuracy: {accuracy * 100:.2f}%')
```

7.1.5 Conclusion

Scikit-learn is a powerful and user-friendly library that simplifies the process of building machine learning models in Python. With its comprehensive set of algorithms, preprocessing tools, and evaluation metrics, Scikit-learn enables you to tackle a wide range of machine learning tasks with ease.

Whether you're building a simple model for a classification problem or experimenting with more advanced techniques, Scikit-learn's consistent API and extensive documentation make it an excellent choice for learning and applying machine learning algorithms.

By the end of this section, you should have a solid understanding of the core features of Scikit-learn and how to use it to build your own machine learning models. In the next sections, we will dive deeper into specific algorithms and techniques, guiding you through hands-on examples and applications of machine learning. Happy coding!

7.2 Implementing Linear Regression

Linear Regression is one of the simplest and most widely used algorithms in machine learning. It's a supervised learning algorithm that establishes a relationship between a dependent (target) variable and one or more independent (predictor) variables by fitting a linear equation to the observed data.

In this section, we will explore how to implement Linear Regression using Scikit-learn and guide you through the steps involved, from preparing the data to evaluating the model's performance.

7.2.1 What is Linear Regression?

Linear regression aims to model the relationship between a target variable (dependent variable) and one or more predictor variables (independent variables). The relationship is represented by a straight line, making it a linear model.

For a single predictor variable (univariate linear regression), the model is defined by the equation:

$$y = \beta_0 + \beta_1 \cdot X$$

Where:

- y is the predicted value (dependent variable).

- X is the input feature (independent variable).

- β_0 is the y-intercept (constant term).

- β_1 is the slope (coefficient) of the line.

In multiple linear regression, the model extends to multiple predictor variables, where the relationship is defined by the equation:

$$y = \beta_0 + \beta_1 \cdot X_1 + \beta_2 \cdot X_2 + \cdots + \beta_n \cdot X_n$$

Where:

- $X_1, X_2, \ldots, X_n$ are multiple independent variables.

- $\beta_0, \beta_1, \ldots, \beta_n$ are the coefficients that the model learns during training.

Linear regression is typically used for predicting continuous values, such as forecasting sales, predicting housing prices, or estimating a person's weight based on their height.

7.2.2 Steps to Implement Linear Regression with Scikit-learn

Let's go through the key steps to implement a Linear Regression model using Scikit-learn.

Step 1: Importing Necessary Libraries

Before we can implement Linear Regression, we need to import the necessary libraries:

```python
# Importing necessary libraries
import numpy as np
import pandas as pd
from sklearn.model_selection import train_test_split
from sklearn.linear_model import LinearRegression
from sklearn.metrics import mean_squared_error, r2_score
import matplotlib.pyplot as plt
```

Here:

- NumPy is used for numerical operations.
- Pandas helps in handling datasets.
- Scikit-learn provides the tools to create the Linear Regression model and evaluate its performance.
- Matplotlib is used for visualization.

Step 2: Loading the Dataset

Next, we need to load a dataset for training and testing the model. For simplicity, let's use the Boston housing dataset, which is commonly used for linear regression tasks. This dataset contains various features (e.g., number of rooms, crime rate, etc.) and the target variable (house prices).

```python
from sklearn.datasets import load_boston

# Load the Boston housing dataset
data = load_boston()

# Convert the data into a Pandas DataFrame
df = pd.DataFrame(data.data, columns=data.feature_names)
df['Price'] = data.target

# Display the first few rows of the dataset
print(df.head())
```

In this dataset:

- df contains features such as crime rate, average number of rooms, property tax rate, etc.
- The target variable is Price, which represents the median value of homes in thousands of dollars.

Step 3: Splitting the Data into Training and Testing Sets

Once we have the dataset, we need to split it into two parts: one for training the model and one for testing the model's performance. This allows us to train on one subset of data and evaluate the model on another, unseen subset.

```
# Features (X) and target (y)
X = df.drop('Price', axis=1)
y = df['Price']

# Split the data into training and testing sets (80% training, 20% testing)
X_train, X_test, y_train, y_test = train_test_split(X, y, test_size=0.2, random_state=42)
```

Here, we use train_test_split from Scikit-learn to divide the data. 80% of the data will be used for training, and 20% will be used for testing.

Step 4: Initializing and Training the Model

Now, we're ready to initialize the Linear Regression model and train it using the training data.

```
# Create a Linear Regression model
model = LinearRegression()

# Train the model using the training data
model.fit(X_train, y_train)
```

In the code above:

- The LinearRegression() function initializes the model.
- The fit() method is used to train the model using the training data.
- During training, the model learns the optimal coefficients (slopes) for each feature to minimize the error between the predicted and actual target values.

Step 5: Making Predictions

After training the model, we can use it to make predictions on the test data.

```
# Use the trained model to make predictions on the test set
y_pred = model.predict(X_test)
```

The predict() method generates predictions for the target variable based on the input features from the test set.

Step 6: Evaluating the Model

Once the model has made predictions, we need to evaluate its performance. Two common evaluation metrics for regression tasks are Mean Squared Error (MSE) and R-squared (R^2).

Mean Squared Error (MSE): Measures the average squared difference between the predicted and actual values. A lower MSE indicates a better fit.

R-squared (R^2): Represents how well the model explains the variance in the target variable. An R^2 of 1 means the model perfectly fits the data, while an R^2 of 0 means the model is no better than simply predicting the mean value.

```
# Calculate the Mean Squared Error (MSE)
mse = mean_squared_error(y_test, y_pred)
print(f'Mean Squared Error (MSE): {mse:.2f}')

# Calculate the R-squared value
r2 = r2_score(y_test, y_pred)
print(f'R-squared: {r2:.2f}')
```

Step 7: Visualizing the Results

Finally, it's often helpful to visualize the results of the linear regression model. A simple scatter plot of the predicted vs. actual values can provide insight into how well the model performs.

```
# Plotting the predicted vs actual values
plt.scatter(y_test, y_pred)
plt.xlabel('Actual Prices')
plt.ylabel('Predicted Prices')
plt.title('Actual vs Predicted Prices')
plt.show()
```

This scatter plot will give you a clear picture of how close the predicted prices are to the actual prices. The closer the points are to a 45-degree line (where predicted = actual), the better the model is.

7.2.3 Conclusion

In this section, we've successfully implemented a Linear Regression model using Scikit-learn. We:

- Loaded a dataset.
- Split the data into training and testing sets.
- Trained the model and made predictions.
- Evaluated the model using Mean Squared Error and R-squared.
- Visualized the results to assess the performance of our model.

Linear Regression is a powerful and simple algorithm that can be used for predicting continuous variables. It's easy to implement with Scikit-learn, and it provides an excellent introduction to the world of machine learning.

As you move forward, you can experiment with different datasets, explore multiple linear regression, and dive deeper into more complex algorithms.

7.3 Classification with Decision Trees and Logistic Regression

Classification is one of the most fundamental tasks in machine learning, where the goal is to predict the category or class label of a data point. For example, we may want to classify emails as spam or not spam, or predict whether a patient has a certain disease based on medical features.

In this section, we'll cover two popular algorithms for classification: Decision Trees and Logistic Regression. Both are widely used, but they approach classification differently. We will explore their strengths, how they work, and how to implement them using Scikit-learn.

7.3.1 What is a Decision Tree?

A Decision Tree is a non-linear model that makes predictions based on a series of rules derived from the features in the dataset. It splits the data into smaller subsets based on the feature values, creating a tree-like structure where each internal node represents a feature and each leaf node represents a class label.

How Decision Trees Work:

- **Root Node**: The first feature used to split the data.
- **Internal Nodes**: Subsequent features that divide the data further.
- **Leaf Nodes**: Final predicted class labels.

The splits are made in such a way that each subset of data at each level of the tree is as pure as possible with respect to the target class. This is usually done by calculating metrics such as Gini impurity or Entropy.

Advantages of Decision Trees:

- Easy to interpret and visualize.
- Can handle both numerical and categorical data.
- Can model non-linear relationships.
- Disadvantages of Decision Trees:
- Prone to overfitting, especially with very deep trees.
- Sensitive to small changes in the data (instability).

7.3.2 What is Logistic Regression?

Logistic Regression is a linear model used for binary classification tasks (though it can be extended to multi-class classification). Unlike linear regression, which predicts continuous values, logistic regression predicts the probability of a data point belonging to a particular class. The output is then mapped to a binary outcome (0 or 1) using the sigmoid function.

The equation for logistic regression is:

$$P(y = 1|X) = \frac{1}{1 + e^{-(\beta_0 + \beta_1 X_1 + \beta_2 X_2 + \cdots + \beta_n X_n)}}$$

Where:

- $P(y = 1|X)$ is the probability of the target being 1 (class 1).

- $\beta_0, \beta_1, \ldots, \beta_n$ are the learned model parameters.

- $X_1, X_2, \ldots, X_n$ are the input features.

Logistic regression is commonly used in problems like email spam detection, disease diagnosis, and customer churn prediction.

Advantages of Logistic Regression:

- Simple and easy to implement.
- Provides probabilities, which gives a sense of the certainty of predictions.
- Less prone to overfitting compared to decision trees.

Disadvantages of Logistic Regression:

- Assumes a linear relationship between the features and the log-odds of the target variable.
- Limited in its ability to capture complex relationships.

7.3.3 Steps to Implement Decision Trees and Logistic Regression with Scikit-learn

Let's go through the steps to implement both Decision Trees and Logistic Regression for a classification problem using Scikit-learn. We will use the Iris dataset, a well-known dataset that contains features of flowers (sepal length, sepal width, petal length, and petal width) and the corresponding species (Setosa, Versicolor, or Virginica).

Step 1: Importing Necessary Libraries

```
# Import necessary libraries
import numpy as np
import pandas as pd
from sklearn.datasets import load_iris
from sklearn.model_selection import train_test_split
from sklearn.tree import DecisionTreeClassifier
from sklearn.linear_model import LogisticRegression
from sklearn.metrics import accuracy_score, confusion_matrix, classification_report
import matplotlib.pyplot as plt
```

Step 2: Loading the Dataset

We will load the Iris dataset from Scikit-learn, which is included in the library:

```
# Load the Iris dataset
iris = load_iris()
X = iris.data  # Features (sepal length, sepal width, petal length, petal width)
y = iris.target  # Target (species of the flower)
```

Step 3: Splitting the Dataset

We split the dataset into training and testing sets to train and evaluate the model:

```
# Split the data into training and testing sets (80% training, 20% testing)
X_train, X_test, y_train, y_test = train_test_split(X, y, test_size=0.2, random_state=42)
```

Step 4: Implementing Decision Tree Classifier

Now, let's implement the Decision Tree Classifier:

```
# Initialize the Decision Tree Classifier
dt_model = DecisionTreeClassifier(random_state=42)

# Train the model
dt_model.fit(X_train, y_train)

# Make predictions
y_pred_dt = dt_model.predict(X_test)

# Evaluate the model
print("Decision Tree Accuracy:", accuracy_score(y_test, y_pred_dt))
print("Confusion Matrix:\n", confusion_matrix(y_test, y_pred_dt))
print("Classification Report:\n", classification_report(y_test, y_pred_dt))
```

Here:

- We use the DecisionTreeClassifier from Scikit-learn to create the decision tree model.
- The fit() method trains the model, and predict() is used to generate predictions.
- accuracy_score(), confusion_matrix(), and classification_report() help evaluate the model's performance.

Step 5: Implementing Logistic Regression

Next, let's implement Logistic Regression:

```
# Initialize the Logistic Regression model
log_reg_model = LogisticRegression(max_iter=200)

# Train the model
log_reg_model.fit(X_train, y_train)

# Make predictions
y_pred_lr = log_reg_model.predict(X_test)

# Evaluate the model
print("Logistic Regression Accuracy:", accuracy_score(y_test, y_pred_lr))
print("Confusion Matrix:\n", confusion_matrix(y_test, y_pred_lr))
print("Classification Report:\n", classification_report(y_test, y_pred_lr))
```

Here:

- We use the LogisticRegression from Scikit-learn to initialize the model.
- The max_iter=200 argument ensures that the model converges (we may increase the iterations for large datasets).
- The evaluation steps are the same as with the decision tree.

Step 6: Visualizing Decision Tree

One of the great features of decision trees is that they are highly interpretable. We can visualize the decision tree using Scikit-learn's built-in plotting functions.

```
from sklearn.tree import plot_tree

# Visualize the trained Decision Tree
plt.figure(figsize=(12,8))
plot_tree(dt_model,          filled=True,          feature_names=iris.feature_names,
class_names=iris.target_names)
plt.show()
```

This plot will show the splits, the features used at each decision node, and the predicted class at each leaf node.

7.3.4 Conclusion

In this section, we've implemented two widely used classification algorithms: Decision Trees and Logistic Regression, using the Iris dataset. We have:

- Implemented and trained a Decision Tree Classifier and a Logistic Regression model using Scikit-learn.
- Evaluated both models using accuracy, confusion matrix, and classification report.
- Visualized the decision tree to gain insights into how the model makes predictions.
- Key Takeaways:
- Decision Trees are highly interpretable and work well when the relationship between features and target is non-linear.
- Logistic Regression is a simple linear model suited for binary and multi-class classification problems.
- Both models have their strengths and weaknesses, and choosing the right one depends on the nature of the problem and the data.

As you progress in your machine learning journey, you'll likely explore more sophisticated algorithms and techniques, but understanding these fundamental classifiers will serve as a strong foundation.

7.4 Evaluating Model Performance

Evaluating the performance of a machine learning model is crucial to understanding how well it generalizes to new, unseen data. The process involves assessing how accurately the model makes predictions on test data, comparing the predictions against actual results, and using various evaluation metrics to quantify the model's effectiveness.

In this section, we'll focus on the key evaluation metrics used in machine learning, particularly for classification and regression problems. We will also explore how to interpret the results and how to improve model performance.

7.4.1 Why Evaluate Model Performance?

The goal of evaluating a model is to ensure that it not only performs well on the training data but also generalizes well to new data (i.e., unseen data). This helps prevent overfitting, where a model performs very well on training data but poorly on test data. Proper evaluation ensures that the model is both accurate and robust.

Evaluation is also essential for:

```
# Initialize the Logistic Regression model
log_reg_model = LogisticRegression(max_iter=200)

# Train the model
log_reg_model.fit(X_train, y_train)

# Make predictions
y_pred_lr = log_reg_model.predict(X_test)

# Evaluate the model
print("Logistic Regression Accuracy:", accuracy_score(y_test, y_pred_lr))
print("Confusion Matrix:\n", confusion_matrix(y_test, y_pred_lr))
print("Classification Report:\n", classification_report(y_test, y_pred_lr))
```

Here:

- We use the LogisticRegression from Scikit-learn to initialize the model.
- The max_iter=200 argument ensures that the model converges (we may increase the iterations for large datasets).
- The evaluation steps are the same as with the decision tree.

Step 6: Visualizing Decision Tree

One of the great features of decision trees is that they are highly interpretable. We can visualize the decision tree using Scikit-learn's built-in plotting functions.

```
from sklearn.tree import plot_tree

# Visualize the trained Decision Tree
plt.figure(figsize=(12,8))
plot_tree(dt_model,          filled=True,          feature_names=iris.feature_names,
class_names=iris.target_names)
plt.show()
```

This plot will show the splits, the features used at each decision node, and the predicted class at each leaf node.

7.3.4 Conclusion

In this section, we've implemented two widely used classification algorithms: Decision Trees and Logistic Regression, using the Iris dataset. We have:

- Implemented and trained a Decision Tree Classifier and a Logistic Regression model using Scikit-learn.
- Evaluated both models using accuracy, confusion matrix, and classification report.
- Visualized the decision tree to gain insights into how the model makes predictions.
- Key Takeaways:
- Decision Trees are highly interpretable and work well when the relationship between features and target is non-linear.
- Logistic Regression is a simple linear model suited for binary and multi-class classification problems.
- Both models have their strengths and weaknesses, and choosing the right one depends on the nature of the problem and the data.

As you progress in your machine learning journey, you'll likely explore more sophisticated algorithms and techniques, but understanding these fundamental classifiers will serve as a strong foundation.

7.4 Evaluating Model Performance

Evaluating the performance of a machine learning model is crucial to understanding how well it generalizes to new, unseen data. The process involves assessing how accurately the model makes predictions on test data, comparing the predictions against actual results, and using various evaluation metrics to quantify the model's effectiveness.

In this section, we'll focus on the key evaluation metrics used in machine learning, particularly for classification and regression problems. We will also explore how to interpret the results and how to improve model performance.

7.4.1 Why Evaluate Model Performance?

The goal of evaluating a model is to ensure that it not only performs well on the training data but also generalizes well to new data (i.e., unseen data). This helps prevent overfitting, where a model performs very well on training data but poorly on test data. Proper evaluation ensures that the model is both accurate and robust.

Evaluation is also essential for:

- Comparing different models to choose the best one for a given task.
- Identifying whether the model requires further tuning or adjustments.
- Understanding where and how the model might fail.

7.4.2 Key Evaluation Metrics for Classification

For classification problems, such as predicting whether an email is spam or not, or identifying a type of flower in the Iris dataset, we have several key metrics to measure how well the model performs. Some of the most common metrics include:

Accuracy

Accuracy is the simplest and most widely used metric. It measures the proportion of correct predictions made by the model.

$$\text{Accuracy} = \frac{\text{Number of Correct Predictions}}{\text{Total Number of Predictions}}$$

Accuracy works well when the classes are balanced, meaning that each class has a similar number of instances. However, it can be misleading when there is a significant class imbalance.

Confusion Matrix

A confusion matrix provides a more detailed view of the model's performance. It shows the true positives (TP), true negatives (TN), false positives (FP), and false negatives (FN), which represent the model's correct and incorrect classifications.

A confusion matrix looks like this:

	Predicted: No	Predicted: Yes
Actual: No	TN	FP
Actual: Yes	FN	TP

Using this matrix, you can calculate other metrics such as precision, recall, and F1-score.

Precision

Precision measures the accuracy of the positive predictions made by the model. It answers the question: "Of all the instances predicted as positive, how many were actually positive?"

$$\text{Precision} = \frac{TP}{TP + FP}$$

Recall (Sensitivity)

Recall measures the ability of the model to identify all relevant instances. It answers the question: "Of all the actual positive instances, how many did the model correctly identify?"

$$\text{Recall} = \frac{TP}{TP + FN}$$

F1-Score

The F1-score is the harmonic mean of precision and recall. It is a more balanced metric, especially useful when there is an uneven class distribution or when false positives and false negatives have different costs.

$$\text{F1-Score} = \frac{2 \times \text{Precision} \times \text{Recall}}{\text{Precision} + \text{Recall}}$$

ROC Curve and AUC (Area Under the Curve)

The Receiver Operating Characteristic (ROC) curve plots the true positive rate (recall) against the false positive rate (1 - specificity). The area under the ROC curve (AUC) represents the model's ability to distinguish between classes. AUC ranges from 0 to 1, with 1 being perfect and 0.5 indicating a random model.

7.4.3 Key Evaluation Metrics for Regression

For regression problems, where the goal is to predict a continuous value (e.g., predicting house prices), different metrics are used to assess model performance.

Mean Absolute Error (MAE)

The Mean Absolute Error (MAE) measures the average of the absolute differences between the predicted values and the actual values. It's easy to interpret because it provides the average error in the same units as the target variable.

$$\text{MAE} = \frac{1}{n} \sum_{i=1}^{n} |y_i - \hat{y}_i|$$

Where:

- y_i is the actual value,

- $\hat{y}_i$ is the predicted value,

- n is the total number of data points.

Mean Squared Error (MSE)

The Mean Squared Error (MSE) is the average of the squared differences between predicted and actual values. MSE penalizes larger errors more than MAE due to the squaring of differences, making it more sensitive to outliers.

$$\text{MSE} = \frac{1}{n} \sum_{i=1}^{n} (y_i - \hat{y}_i)^2$$

Root Mean Squared Error (RMSE)

The Root Mean Squared Error (RMSE) is the square root of the MSE. It also penalizes larger errors more than MAE and provides the error in the same units as the target variable, making it easier to interpret.

$$\text{RMSE} = \sqrt{\frac{1}{n} \sum_{i=1}^{n} (y_i - \hat{y}_i)^2}$$

R-Squared (R²)

The R-squared metric provides an indication of how well the model explains the variance in the target variable. R^2 ranges from 0 to 1, where a value of 1 means the model perfectly predicts the target, and 0 means the model does not explain any of the variance.

$$R^2 = 1 - \frac{\sum (y_i - \hat{y}_i)^2}{\sum (y_i - \bar{y})^2}$$

Where:

- y_i is the actual value,

- $\hat{y}_i$ is the predicted value,

- $\bar{y}$ is the mean of the actual values.

7.4.4 Model Evaluation in Practice: Scikit-learn Implementation

Let's demonstrate how to evaluate a model using Scikit-learn with the Iris dataset for classification.

```
from sklearn.model_selection import train_test_split
from sklearn.tree import DecisionTreeClassifier
from sklearn.metrics import accuracy_score, confusion_matrix, classification_report,
roc_auc_score

# Split the dataset into training and testing sets
X_train, X_test, y_train, y_test = train_test_split(X, y, test_size=0.2, random_state=42)

# Initialize the model (Decision Tree Classifier in this case)
model = DecisionTreeClassifier(random_state=42)
```

```
# Train the model
model.fit(X_train, y_train)

# Make predictions
y_pred = model.predict(X_test)

# Evaluate the model
print("Accuracy:", accuracy_score(y_test, y_pred))
print("Confusion Matrix:\n", confusion_matrix(y_test, y_pred))
print("Classification Report:\n", classification_report(y_test, y_pred))

# If it's a binary classification, evaluate AUC
y_prob = model.predict_proba(X_test)[:, 1]  # Probabilities of the positive class
print("AUC:", roc_auc_score(y_test, y_prob))
```

In this example:

- We use accuracy_score to evaluate the overall performance of the model.
- The confusion_matrix provides a breakdown of correct and incorrect predictions.
- The classification_report gives a detailed overview of precision, recall, and F1-score for each class.
- roc_auc_score measures the model's ability to distinguish between classes, especially useful for binary classification.

7.4.5 Conclusion

Model evaluation is a vital step in the machine learning workflow. By using appropriate metrics, you can assess how well your model performs and determine if it's ready for deployment. For classification tasks, metrics like accuracy, precision, recall, F1-score, and the confusion matrix provide a comprehensive view of the model's performance. For regression tasks, metrics like MAE, MSE, RMSE, and R^2 give insight into the model's error and its ability to explain the variance in the target variable.

Understanding and interpreting these evaluation metrics helps you improve the model and ensure its effectiveness on new data. As you progress in machine learning, mastering model evaluation will be a critical skill in building robust and reliable AI systems.

8. Neural Networks Basics with TensorFlow & PyTorch

Neural networks are the backbone of deep learning, the advanced branch of machine learning that powers technologies like image recognition, voice assistants, and self-driving cars. In this chapter, you'll get an introduction to artificial neural networks (ANNs) and explore how they mimic the human brain to recognize patterns and make predictions. You'll learn how to implement simple neural networks using TensorFlow and PyTorch, two of the most popular deep learning frameworks. With hands-on examples, you'll build your first neural network model, train it on data, and evaluate its performance. By the end of this chapter, you'll have the foundational knowledge needed to explore more complex deep learning models and apply them to a variety of AI tasks.

8.1 What are Neural Networks?

Neural networks are a core component of artificial intelligence (AI), specifically within the realm of deep learning. They are computational models inspired by the way the human brain processes information, designed to recognize patterns, classify data, and make predictions. A neural network is made up of layers of interconnected nodes, or neurons, each performing specific tasks, and when trained properly, they are capable of solving complex tasks like image recognition, speech processing, and even playing games.

In this section, we'll explore what neural networks are, how they work, their components, and why they are so powerful for many AI applications.

8.1.1 Inspiration from the Human Brain

Neural networks were inspired by biological neurons, the building blocks of the human brain. In the brain, neurons transmit information through electrical impulses, passing signals to each other across synapses. Similarly, in a neural network, artificial neurons (also called nodes or units) are connected in layers and transmit information through weighted connections.

While the human brain consists of billions of neurons and synapses, artificial neural networks are much simpler, typically involving hundreds or thousands of neurons. Despite their simplicity, neural networks are still able to learn from data, identify patterns, and make intelligent decisions.

8.1.2 Basic Structure of a Neural Network

A typical neural network consists of three primary layers:

Input Layer: This layer takes in the raw data. Each neuron in the input layer corresponds to a feature in the data. For example, if you're training a neural network to classify images, each pixel in an image would be represented by a neuron in the input layer.

Hidden Layers: These are layers between the input and output layers. Neural networks can have one or more hidden layers, and each layer contains multiple neurons. The neurons in these hidden layers perform various computations on the input data. The more hidden layers a neural network has, the "deeper" it is, which is why the term deep learning is used when referring to neural networks with many hidden layers. Hidden layers allow the network to capture more complex patterns and hierarchical features in the data.

Output Layer: The final layer in the neural network produces the output. This could be a classification label (for classification problems), a continuous value (for regression problems), or any other result based on the task.

Each connection between neurons has a weight, which determines how much influence one neuron has on another. The strength of these weights is adjusted during training to optimize the model's performance.

8.1.3 How Neural Networks Work

Neural networks learn by adjusting the weights of the connections between neurons based on the data they process. Here's a high-level overview of how they work:

1. Forward Propagation

In the forward propagation step, data is passed through the network from the input layer to the output layer. Each neuron processes the data by applying a mathematical function to the weighted sum of its inputs. This sum is then passed through an activation function (more on this shortly), which determines the neuron's output.

For example, for a given input, the neural network performs the following steps:

- Multiply the input by a weight.
- Add a bias term (optional).

- Apply an activation function to produce the output of the neuron.

This process is repeated for each layer in the network until the final output is produced.

2. Activation Functions

Activation functions play a crucial role in neural networks. They introduce non-linearity into the model, allowing it to learn complex patterns. Without activation functions, neural networks would essentially be linear models, unable to capture the complexity of real-world data.

Some commonly used activation functions include:

- **Sigmoid**: Squashes the output between 0 and 1, often used in binary classification tasks.
- **ReLU (Rectified Linear Unit):** A simple function that outputs 0 for negative inputs and the input itself for positive inputs. It helps with faster training.
- **Tanh (Hyperbolic Tangent):** Squashes the output between -1 and 1. It's useful for certain types of data.
- **Softmax**: Used in the output layer for multi-class classification, converting raw scores into probabilities that sum to 1.

3. Backpropagation

After forward propagation, the network needs to learn from the errors in its predictions. This is where backpropagation comes into play. Backpropagation is a process where the network adjusts its weights by propagating the error back through the network, using a method called gradient descent to minimize the error.

The steps in backpropagation include:

- Calculate the error (the difference between the predicted output and the true output).
- Propagate this error backward through the network, adjusting the weights of the neurons in the process.
- Update the weights using an optimization algorithm like gradient descent to minimize the error.

This process repeats iteratively, refining the weights each time, until the network's performance reaches an acceptable level.

8.1.4 Types of Neural Networks

There are several different types of neural networks, each suited for different types of problems. Some of the most commonly used include:

1. Feedforward Neural Networks (FNN)

Feedforward Neural Networks are the simplest type of neural network. In this architecture, the data moves in one direction, from input to output, without any feedback loops. These networks are typically used for basic classification and regression tasks.

2. Convolutional Neural Networks (CNN)

Convolutional Neural Networks are particularly effective for image-related tasks. They use convolutional layers to automatically learn spatial hierarchies of features (such as edges, textures, and objects) from raw images. CNNs are widely used in image classification, object detection, and computer vision tasks.

3. Recurrent Neural Networks (RNN)

Recurrent Neural Networks are designed to handle sequential data, such as time series or natural language. They have feedback loops that allow information to persist across time steps, making them suitable for tasks like language modeling, speech recognition, and video analysis.

4. Generative Adversarial Networks (GAN)

Generative Adversarial Networks consist of two networks: a generator that creates fake data and a discriminator that tries to distinguish between real and fake data. GANs are widely used in image generation, data augmentation, and deepfake creation.

8.1.5 Why Neural Networks Are Powerful

Neural networks are powerful because they have the capacity to:

- **Model complex relationships**: Neural networks, especially deep ones, can learn complex patterns in data that are difficult to model using traditional algorithms.

- **Handle unstructured data**: Neural networks are effective at processing unstructured data types such as images, audio, and text, which are challenging for other algorithms.
- **Automatically extract features**: In many cases, neural networks can automatically learn relevant features from raw data (e.g., CNNs automatically extract features from images), reducing the need for manual feature engineering.
- **Improve with more data**: Neural networks generally improve in performance as they are exposed to more data, making them highly scalable for large datasets.

8.1.6 Challenges of Neural Networks

Despite their power, neural networks do face certain challenges:

- **Overfitting**: Neural networks can easily overfit to training data, especially with very deep networks, leading to poor performance on new, unseen data.
- **Require large amounts of data**: Training a neural network often requires large amounts of data to produce good results.
- **Computationally expensive**: Deep learning models are computationally expensive to train and require powerful hardware, such as Graphics Processing Units (GPUs).
- **Interpretability**: Neural networks are often referred to as "black-box" models because their decision-making process can be difficult to interpret, especially for deep models with many layers.

8.1.7 Conclusion

Neural networks are a powerful tool in artificial intelligence, capable of solving complex problems across a wide range of fields, from computer vision to natural language processing. By mimicking the way the human brain processes information, neural networks can learn from vast amounts of data, making them essential for modern AI applications. However, they come with their own set of challenges, such as the need for large datasets and computational resources. Understanding neural networks is a crucial step in mastering AI, as they form the backbone of many advanced techniques and algorithms in machine learning.

8.2 Introduction to TensorFlow

TensorFlow is one of the most popular and powerful open-source libraries used for building and training machine learning (ML) models, particularly in the fields of deep learning and artificial intelligence (AI). Developed by Google Brain, TensorFlow provides a comprehensive ecosystem of tools, libraries, and community resources that simplify the process of developing AI and machine learning models, making it accessible to both beginners and experienced researchers.

In this section, we will provide an introduction to TensorFlow, its architecture, key features, and why it is widely used for building neural networks and other machine learning models.

8.2.1 What is TensorFlow?

TensorFlow is an end-to-end open-source platform for machine learning that was initially developed by the Google Brain team for research and production at Google. It has since evolved into a comprehensive framework for building both simple and complex ML models, especially neural networks. TensorFlow is designed to enable the easy deployment of machine learning models across various platforms, such as desktops, mobile devices, and cloud servers.

The name "TensorFlow" comes from the idea of a tensor, which is a mathematical object that generalizes matrices and vectors, and flow, which refers to the computational graph that defines the flow of data in the system.

In a nutshell, TensorFlow is a flexible and powerful framework that allows developers and data scientists to create machine learning models from scratch, fine-tune pre-existing models, and deploy them efficiently across different environments.

8.2.2 Key Features of TensorFlow

TensorFlow offers a range of features that make it highly effective for building machine learning and deep learning models:

1. Tensor Computation

TensorFlow is built around the concept of tensors. A tensor is a multi-dimensional array or matrix, and TensorFlow uses these tensors to represent data. The name "TensorFlow" reflects its ability to represent data as tensors and perform mathematical computations on them.

A key strength of TensorFlow is its efficient handling of these high-dimensional tensors. It can perform a variety of operations on these tensors, such as matrix multiplication, addition, and more, which are essential for building machine learning models.

2. Computational Graph

TensorFlow models are built using a computational graph, a series of operations that define the flow of data and the relationships between different computations. Each operation in the graph (e.g., a multiplication or an addition) is represented as a node, and the edges between the nodes represent the flow of data.

The computational graph is flexible because it can be executed on multiple hardware platforms, such as CPUs, GPUs, and TPUs (Tensor Processing Units), without modifying the model.

3. Automatic Differentiation

TensorFlow offers automatic differentiation, which is an essential feature for training machine learning models. The core of the training process involves computing gradients of the loss function with respect to model parameters, and TensorFlow automatically computes these gradients using backpropagation. This helps update the weights of the model during training, enabling it to learn from the data.

4. Scalability and Flexibility

TensorFlow is designed to scale to large datasets and can be run on multiple devices, including local machines, clusters, and cloud platforms. TensorFlow provides tools like TensorFlow Serving for deploying models to production, TensorFlow Lite for running models on mobile and embedded devices, and TensorFlow.js for deploying models in the browser.

Additionally, TensorFlow can be integrated with a wide variety of programming languages, and it is compatible with various hardware accelerators, such as GPUs and TPUs, making it highly efficient for training large-scale models.

5. High-Level APIs: Keras

TensorFlow includes high-level APIs like Keras, which simplifies the process of building neural networks and deep learning models. Keras allows users to quickly prototype and experiment with different architectures, such as feedforward networks, convolutional networks (CNNs), and recurrent networks (RNNs). With Keras, TensorFlow is more accessible to beginners, as it abstracts away much of the complexity involved in model creation.

6. Pre-Trained Models and Model Sharing

TensorFlow provides access to many pre-trained models via the TensorFlow Hub, allowing developers to quickly use powerful models that have already been trained on large datasets (e.g., image classification models trained on ImageNet). This enables fast prototyping and transfer learning, where a model trained on one dataset can be fine-tuned to perform well on a different but related dataset.

8.2.3 TensorFlow Components and Architecture

TensorFlow is made up of several components that collectively make it a powerful machine learning framework. Here are the key components of TensorFlow:

1. TensorFlow Core

TensorFlow Core provides the foundational building blocks for creating and training models. It offers low-level control over model design, such as defining the structure of computational graphs and performing tensor operations.

2. Keras (High-Level API)

As mentioned earlier, Keras is an API that simplifies the process of creating deep learning models. It is fully integrated with TensorFlow and provides an easy-to-use interface for building neural networks. Keras offers predefined layers, activation functions, optimizers, and loss functions to help you quickly build your models.

3. TensorFlow Estimators

Estimators are a high-level API that simplifies model training and deployment. They are wrappers around machine learning algorithms and provide easy-to-use interfaces for model training, evaluation, and inference. Estimators support both distributed training and model export, making them ideal for production environments.

4. TensorFlow Datasets

TensorFlow Datasets (TFDS) provides a collection of ready-to-use datasets for various machine learning tasks, including image classification, text processing, and more. These datasets can be directly imported into your model for training, which saves time and effort.

5. TensorFlow Extended (TFX)

TensorFlow Extended (TFX) is a production-ready machine learning platform designed to help deploy and manage machine learning pipelines. It provides tools for model validation, monitoring, and managing data throughout the machine learning lifecycle.

8.2.4 Why Use TensorFlow?

TensorFlow is widely adopted for machine learning and deep learning projects due to several key reasons:

1. Comprehensive Ecosystem

TensorFlow provides an end-to-end ecosystem for building, training, and deploying machine learning models. Whether you're just starting out or need to scale a model to production, TensorFlow has the tools and resources to meet your needs.

2. Strong Community Support

As one of the most popular machine learning frameworks, TensorFlow has a large, active community of developers and researchers. This means that you can easily find tutorials, documentation, and pre-trained models to help with your projects.

3. Performance and Scalability

TensorFlow offers excellent performance, especially when running on hardware accelerators like GPUs and TPUs. It also scales well across multiple devices and platforms, making it ideal for large-scale training and real-time applications.

4. Flexibility

TensorFlow is flexible enough to support a wide range of machine learning models and applications, from simple linear regression to deep neural networks, reinforcement learning, and more. Its flexibility allows you to experiment with different architectures and optimization techniques.

5. TensorFlow Lite and TensorFlow.js

TensorFlow also supports TensorFlow Lite, which enables you to run models on mobile and embedded devices, and TensorFlow.js, which allows you to run models directly in the web browser using JavaScript.

8.2.5 Getting Started with TensorFlow

To get started with TensorFlow, you need to install the library. TensorFlow can be installed using pip, Python's package manager:

```
pip install tensorflow
```

Once installed, you can start building neural networks, training models, and making predictions. Here is a simple example of building a neural network with Keras in TensorFlow:

```python
import tensorflow as tf
from tensorflow.keras.models import Sequential
from tensorflow.keras.layers import Dense

# Load a dataset (e.g., MNIST)
(X_train, y_train), (X_test, y_test) = tf.keras.datasets.mnist.load_data()

# Preprocess the data (normalize pixel values)
X_train, X_test = X_train / 255.0, X_test / 255.0

# Build a simple neural network model
model = Sequential([
    Dense(128, activation='relu', input_shape=(784,)),
    Dense(10, activation='softmax')
])

# Compile the model
model.compile(optimizer='adam',                loss='sparse_categorical_crossentropy',
metrics=['accuracy'])

# Train the model
model.fit(X_train, y_train, epochs=5)
```

```
# Evaluate the model on test data
model.evaluate(X_test, y_test)
```

This example demonstrates how easy it is to create a simple neural network for digit classification using TensorFlow and Keras. The dataset used here is the famous MNIST dataset, which contains handwritten digits.

8.2.6 Conclusion

TensorFlow is a powerful, flexible, and scalable framework for building machine learning and deep learning models. Whether you are a beginner or an experienced AI practitioner, TensorFlow offers a range of tools and libraries to help you efficiently develop, train, and deploy AI models. With its strong community support, comprehensive ecosystem, and support for a variety of hardware platforms, TensorFlow is one of the best choices for machine learning and deep learning projects. By understanding TensorFlow, you open the door to building state-of-the-art AI models for a wide range of applications, from image classification to natural language processing and beyond.

8.3 Introduction to PyTorch

PyTorch is an open-source deep learning framework developed by Facebook's AI Research lab (FAIR). It has quickly gained popularity in the machine learning community due to its flexibility, ease of use, and dynamic computational graph, making it an excellent choice for both research and production applications. With its user-friendly interface, dynamic nature, and strong support for GPU acceleration, PyTorch has become a go-to framework for deep learning practitioners and researchers.

In this section, we will introduce you to PyTorch, explore its core features, its differences from TensorFlow, and why it has become a favorite for many AI developers.

8.3.1 What is PyTorch?

PyTorch is a deep learning framework that provides powerful tools for developing machine learning models with a focus on deep neural networks. At its core, PyTorch provides the following key features:

Dynamic Computational Graph: Unlike TensorFlow (which originally used static computation graphs), PyTorch uses a dynamic computational graph, also known as define-by-run. This means that the graph is built on the fly as operations are performed. This dynamic nature allows for more flexibility, particularly for models that require variable input sizes, such as Recurrent Neural Networks (RNNs) or models with conditional branches.

Tensor Library: PyTorch provides a tensor library that is similar to NumPy but with additional support for GPU computation. Tensors are multi-dimensional arrays that are the foundation of PyTorch operations and represent the data fed into neural networks.

Autograd: PyTorch has built-in automatic differentiation capabilities via Autograd, a system that automatically calculates gradients for backpropagation during the training process. This simplifies the model training process and ensures that the weights of the network are updated correctly.

GPU Acceleration: PyTorch supports CUDA, which allows users to run computations on NVIDIA GPUs, making the training of large models and processing of large datasets faster and more efficient.

8.3.2 Key Features of PyTorch

Let's dive deeper into the features that make PyTorch stand out:

1. Tensors

Tensors are the core data structure in PyTorch. They are similar to NumPy arrays but with added capabilities for GPU acceleration. Tensors can represent scalar values, vectors, matrices, and multi-dimensional arrays, and they can be created and manipulated using a variety of operations. PyTorch makes it easy to move data to GPUs for faster computation by using the .to() method or .cuda().

For example:

```
import torch
# Create a tensor
tensor = torch.tensor([1.0, 2.0, 3.0])
print(tensor)

# Move tensor to GPU (if available)
```

```
tensor = tensor.cuda() if torch.cuda.is_available() else tensor
```

2. Dynamic Computational Graph (Define-by-Run)

One of the most powerful features of PyTorch is its dynamic computational graph. In traditional frameworks like TensorFlow (prior to version 2.0), the computational graph is built once before the model is run, which can be limiting for certain types of models. With PyTorch's dynamic graph, the structure of the network is created during execution, which makes it easier to modify and debug.

In PyTorch, each operation (like matrix multiplication or addition) creates a new node in the graph, and these nodes are executed immediately. This allows for quick prototyping and experimentation, which is a major advantage for researchers who need to test new ideas quickly.

3. Autograd and Backpropagation

Autograd is PyTorch's automatic differentiation engine, which records operations performed on tensors in a dynamic graph and calculates the gradients required for backpropagation. PyTorch's autograd module tracks the history of operations on tensors, so that gradients can be computed efficiently during the backward pass.

For example:

```
x = torch.tensor([1.0, 2.0, 3.0], requires_grad=True)
y = x * 2
z = y.mean()
z.backward()

# Get gradients
print(x.grad)
```

In this example, PyTorch will calculate the gradient of z with respect to x after calling z.backward().

4. Neural Networks with nn.Module

PyTorch provides the torch.nn module for building and training neural networks. All models in PyTorch are subclassed from the nn.Module class, which provides built-in methods for defining layers, forwarding data through the model, and calculating loss. This makes it easy to define both simple and complex models.

For example, here's a simple feedforward neural network:

```python
import torch
import torch.nn as nn
import torch.optim as optim

class SimpleNN(nn.Module):
    def __init__(self):
        super(SimpleNN, self).__init__()
        self.fc1 = nn.Linear(784, 128)  # Fully connected layer
        self.fc2 = nn.Linear(128, 10)   # Output layer

    def forward(self, x):
        x = torch.relu(self.fc1(x))  # Apply ReLU activation
        x = self.fc2(x)             # Output layer
        return x

# Instantiate the model
model = SimpleNN()

# Loss and optimizer
criterion = nn.CrossEntropyLoss()
optimizer = optim.SGD(model.parameters(), lr=0.01)
```

In this example, the SimpleNN class defines a neural network with one hidden layer and an output layer. The forward method defines the forward pass of the model, which applies a ReLU activation to the output of the first layer and passes it through the second layer.

5. GPU Support

PyTorch makes it simple to use GPUs for model training and inference, which can significantly speed up the process, especially for large datasets and deep neural networks. Tensors in PyTorch can be easily moved to and from the GPU using the .cuda() or .to(device) methods.

```python
# Move model to GPU
```

```
model = model.cuda()

# Move data to GPU
data = data.cuda()
```

Using the GPU, PyTorch can achieve parallel processing, which makes training much faster.

6. TorchVision and TorchText

PyTorch comes with a set of specialized libraries for handling image and text data:

TorchVision: A library for computer vision tasks that includes utilities for image transformations, loading popular datasets (e.g., ImageNet, CIFAR-10), and pre-trained models like ResNet and VGG.

TorchText: A library for natural language processing (NLP) that provides tools for text processing, tokenization, and working with popular NLP datasets (e.g., IMDB, AG News).

These libraries make it easy to work with structured datasets, saving time and effort in data preprocessing and augmentation.

8.3.3 Why Choose PyTorch?

There are several reasons why PyTorch has become one of the most popular deep learning frameworks, particularly in research:

1. Flexibility and Ease of Use

The dynamic nature of PyTorch makes it incredibly flexible. Unlike static frameworks like TensorFlow 1.x, PyTorch allows you to modify the model during runtime, which is useful for models with variable inputs or complex architectures. This flexibility makes it a great choice for researchers who need to experiment with different algorithms and architectures.

2. Better Debugging and Development

Since PyTorch is based on a dynamic computational graph, it allows for easier debugging, as the graph is built as operations are executed. This means that traditional debugging tools (such as Python's built-in debugger, pdb) work seamlessly with PyTorch. The real-time feedback you get when running models makes it easier to catch errors and iterate quickly.

3. Strong Community and Research Support

PyTorch has gained significant traction in the research community, and many cutting-edge research papers and models are implemented in PyTorch. The PyTorch community is large, vibrant, and continuously growing, meaning that you have access to numerous resources, tutorials, and pre-trained models.

4. Seamless Transition to Production

While PyTorch has been historically considered a research-focused framework, it has evolved to better support production environments. PyTorch now offers tools like TorchServe for serving models in production and TorchScript for optimizing models for deployment. TorchScript allows you to export a PyTorch model to a serialized format that can be run in a non-Python environment, making it suitable for mobile or embedded systems.

8.3.4 Getting Started with PyTorch

To get started with PyTorch, you can easily install it using pip:

```
pip install torch torchvision
```

Here's a simple example of defining a neural network model and training it:

```
import torch
import torch.nn as nn
import torch.optim as optim
from torch.utils.data import DataLoader
from torchvision import datasets, transforms

# Define a simple model
class SimpleNN(nn.Module):
    def __init__(self):
        super(SimpleNN, self).__init__()
        self.fc1 = nn.Linear(28*28, 128)
        self.fc2 = nn.Linear(128, 10)
```

```
    def forward(self, x):
        x = torch.relu(self.fc1(x))
        x = self.fc2(x)
        return x

# Data transformation and loading
transform = transforms.Compose([transforms.ToTensor(), transforms.Normalize((0.5,),
(0.5,))])
train_data      =      datasets.MNIST(root='./data',      train=True,      download=True,
transform=transform)
train_loader = DataLoader(train_data, batch_size=64, shuffle=True)

# Instantiate the model, loss function, and optimizer
model = SimpleNN()
criterion = nn.CrossEntropyLoss()
optimizer = optim.SGD(model.parameters(), lr=0.01)

# Training loop
for epoch in range(10):
    for images, labels in train_loader:
        optimizer.zero_grad()
        outputs = model(images.view(-1, 28*28))
        loss = criterion(outputs, labels)
        loss.backward()
        optimizer.step()
    print(f'Epoch {epoch+1}, Loss: {loss.item()}')
```

8.3.5 Conclusion

PyTorch is a powerful and flexible deep learning framework that has become a favorite among researchers, data scientists, and engineers. Its dynamic nature, ease of use, and extensive support for GPU acceleration make it ideal for rapid prototyping and experimentation. Whether you are building a simple neural network or working on cutting-edge research, PyTorch provides the tools you need to implement efficient, scalable, and flexible AI models.

8.4 Building a Simple Neural Network

In this section, we will build a simple neural network using PyTorch to understand how the basic building blocks of deep learning come together. This example will focus on creating a feedforward neural network, training it on the MNIST dataset, and evaluating its performance. We'll walk through each component of the neural network, explaining its purpose, and how to implement it with PyTorch.

A feedforward neural network (FNN) is one of the simplest types of neural networks where the information flows in one direction from input to output through hidden layers. For this example, we will use the MNIST dataset, which consists of images of handwritten digits (0-9), and our goal will be to classify these images.

8.4.1 Understanding the MNIST Dataset

The MNIST dataset consists of 60,000 training images and 10,000 test images of handwritten digits, each 28x28 pixels in grayscale. The goal is to train a neural network to recognize these digits and assign the correct label (0 through 9) to each image. The MNIST dataset is often used as a benchmark for testing the performance of machine learning models.

The dataset is available in PyTorch's torchvision library, making it easy to load and work with.

8.4.2 Defining the Neural Network Architecture

Our neural network will consist of three layers:

- **Input Layer**: The input layer will consist of 28 * 28 = 784 nodes (since each image is 28x28 pixels).
- **Hidden Layer**: We will use one hidden layer with 128 nodes. This layer applies non-linearity to the data, enabling the network to learn more complex patterns.
- **Output Layer**: The output layer will have 10 nodes, corresponding to the 10 possible classes (digits 0-9).

Each layer will be fully connected, meaning that every node in one layer is connected to every node in the next layer. We will also use the ReLU activation function for the hidden layer to introduce non-linearity, and Softmax for the output layer to convert the network's raw output into probabilities.

Here's how to define the model in PyTorch:

```python
import torch
import torch.nn as nn

class SimpleNN(nn.Module):
    def __init__(self):
        super(SimpleNN, self).__init__()

        # Input layer to hidden layer
        self.fc1 = nn.Linear(28 * 28, 128)  # 28x28 input image size to 128 hidden units

        # Hidden layer to output layer
        self.fc2 = nn.Linear(128, 10)       # 128 hidden units to 10 output classes

    def forward(self, x):
        # Flatten the input images into 1D vector
        x = x.view(-1, 28 * 28)  # Flatten 28x28 images to 784-dimensional vectors

        # Apply the first fully connected layer and ReLU activation
        x = torch.relu(self.fc1(x))

        # Apply the second fully connected layer (no activation function here as Softmax
will be applied in loss function)
        x = self.fc2(x)

        return x
```

8.4.3 Explanation of the Model

nn.Linear(28 * 28, 128): This defines a fully connected layer (also called a dense layer) that takes in 784 features (28x28 pixels flattened) and outputs 128 values, which will be passed to the hidden layer.

torch.relu(self.fc1(x)): This applies the ReLU activation function to the output of the first fully connected layer, introducing non-linearity.

self.fc2(x): The second fully connected layer, which reduces the output from 128 to 10 values, one for each possible digit (0-9).

Softmax activation: While we don't apply the Softmax activation explicitly in the model, the CrossEntropyLoss function we will use later in PyTorch does this for us automatically.

8.4.4 Preparing the Data

We'll use PyTorch's torchvision library to load the MNIST dataset and apply necessary transformations, such as converting the images to PyTorch tensors and normalizing the pixel values.

```python
import torch
import torchvision
import torchvision.transforms as transforms
from torch.utils.data import DataLoader

# Define transformations: convert to tensor and normalize pixel values to be between -1 and 1
transform = transforms.Compose([
    transforms.ToTensor(),
    transforms.Normalize((0.5,), (0.5,))  # Normalize to [0,1]
])

# Load the MNIST dataset (train and test)
trainset = torchvision.datasets.MNIST(root='./data', train=True, download=True, transform=transform)
testset = torchvision.datasets.MNIST(root='./data', train=False, download=True, transform=transform)

# Create DataLoader objects for batching and shuffling
trainloader = DataLoader(trainset, batch_size=64, shuffle=True)
testloader = DataLoader(testset, batch_size=64, shuffle=False)
```

8.4.5 Defining the Loss Function and Optimizer

To train the model, we need a loss function that will measure how well our model is performing. For classification tasks, CrossEntropyLoss is commonly used. It combines both Softmax and Negative Log Likelihood Loss, so we don't need to apply Softmax in the model itself.

Additionally, we need an optimizer that will adjust the model's weights based on the gradients calculated during backpropagation. We will use Stochastic Gradient Descent (SGD) as the optimizer for this example.

```python
import torch.optim as optim

# Instantiate the model
model = SimpleNN()

# Loss function: Cross Entropy Loss (includes Softmax)
criterion = nn.CrossEntropyLoss()

# Optimizer: Stochastic Gradient Descent (SGD) with learning rate of 0.01
optimizer = optim.SGD(model.parameters(), lr=0.01)
```

8.4.6 Training the Model

Now that we have defined the model, the loss function, and the optimizer, it's time to train the model. In the training loop, we will iterate over the dataset, perform a forward pass, compute the loss, perform backpropagation to compute gradients, and update the model's weights.

```python
# Training loop
num_epochs = 5
for epoch in range(num_epochs):
    running_loss = 0.0
    for images, labels in trainloader:
        # Zero the gradients from previous step
        optimizer.zero_grad()

        # Forward pass: compute predicted outputs by passing inputs to the model
        outputs = model(images)

        # Compute the loss
        loss = criterion(outputs, labels)

        # Backward pass: compute gradients of the loss with respect to model parameters
        loss.backward()
```

```
    # Update the weights using the optimizer
    optimizer.step()

    # Print statistics
    running_loss += loss.item()

print(f"Epoch {epoch+1}/{num_epochs}, Loss: {running_loss / len(trainloader)}")
```

In each epoch:

- The model computes predictions based on input images.
- The loss function computes how far the predictions are from the true labels.
- The gradients are calculated and used to update the model's weights.
- The average loss for the epoch is printed to monitor the model's progress.

8.4.7 Evaluating the Model

After training, we can evaluate the model's performance on the test set. We will pass the test images through the network and calculate the accuracy of the model by comparing its predictions with the true labels.

```
# Evaluation loop
correct = 0
total = 0
with torch.no_grad():  # No need to compute gradients during evaluation
    for images, labels in testloader:
        outputs = model(images)
        _, predicted = torch.max(outputs, 1)  # Get predicted class
        total += labels.size(0)
        correct += (predicted == labels).sum().item()

accuracy = 100 * correct / total
print(f"Accuracy on test set: {accuracy}%")
```

This code calculates the accuracy by comparing the predicted labels to the true labels for all test samples.

8.4.8 Conclusion

In this section, we built a simple feedforward neural network to classify handwritten digits from the MNIST dataset using PyTorch. We walked through each step: defining the model architecture, preparing the data, choosing a loss function and optimizer, training the model, and evaluating its performance.

By using PyTorch's flexible, easy-to-understand API, we were able to implement a basic neural network in just a few lines of code. This is just the beginning, and as you move forward, you can explore more complex architectures, including Convolutional Neural Networks (CNNs), Recurrent Neural Networks (RNNs), and more.

9. Building a Simple Chatbot

Chatbots are one of the most popular applications of Artificial Intelligence, revolutionizing customer service, virtual assistants, and user interactions across industries. In this chapter, you'll learn how to build a simple rule-based chatbot using Python and basic Natural Language Processing (NLP) techniques. You'll explore how to process and understand text input, match it to predefined responses, and enhance the chatbot's functionality by integrating basic machine learning to improve its responses over time. With practical examples, you'll also discover how to handle user queries, store conversation history, and deploy the chatbot for real-world use. By the end of this chapter, you'll have the skills to create and customize your own AI-driven chatbot.

9.1 Introduction to Natural Language Processing (NLP)

Natural Language Processing (NLP) is a specialized subfield of Artificial Intelligence (AI) that focuses on the interaction between computers and human languages. It involves the development of algorithms and models that allow machines to understand, interpret, and generate human language in a way that is meaningful. NLP enables machines to process and analyze large amounts of natural language data—such as text and speech—helping them perform tasks such as language translation, sentiment analysis, text generation, and more.

Language is inherently complex, involving nuances, context, tone, idioms, and ambiguities that make it challenging for computers to fully grasp. NLP aims to bridge this gap by teaching machines how to process and understand human language.

Why is NLP Important?

The increasing amount of textual data generated daily—whether in the form of social media posts, news articles, customer reviews, research papers, or conversations—has led to the growing importance of NLP in various industries. Organizations use NLP to extract valuable insights from unstructured data, which can help inform decisions, improve customer experiences, and streamline operations.

Here are some common applications of NLP:

Sentiment Analysis: NLP is used to determine the sentiment behind a piece of text, such as whether a review is positive, negative, or neutral. This is particularly useful in businesses to gauge customer feedback.

Text Classification: NLP is widely used for classifying text into predefined categories. Examples include spam detection, news categorization, and topic modeling.

Machine Translation: NLP plays a key role in translating text from one language to another. Google Translate, for instance, uses advanced NLP techniques to deliver translations across a wide range of languages.

Speech Recognition: Converting spoken language into written text is another significant application of NLP, found in voice assistants like Siri, Google Assistant, and Alexa.

Chatbots and Virtual Assistants: NLP helps power chatbots that can understand and respond to customer queries, providing automated customer support.

Named Entity Recognition (NER): NLP is used to identify and classify entities in a text (e.g., names of people, places, organizations) for various tasks, such as extracting structured data from unstructured sources.

Challenges in NLP

Despite its potential, NLP is riddled with challenges. Some of the primary hurdles include:

Ambiguity: Words can have multiple meanings depending on context. For example, the word "bank" can refer to a financial institution, the side of a river, or a place for storing something. Resolving this ambiguity is crucial for effective NLP systems.

Context Understanding: Understanding the context of a word or sentence is essential for accurate interpretation. For example, the meaning of "I went to the bank to fish" differs greatly from "I went to the bank to deposit money."

Sarcasm and Idioms: Sarcasm and idiomatic expressions are often difficult for machines to interpret. "Break a leg" may seem nonsensical, but it's understood as wishing someone good luck in human communication.

Language Variations: NLP systems need to handle the diversity in language, including different dialects, regionalisms, informal language, and slang.

Data Quality: Since much of NLP relies on massive datasets, ensuring the quality and accuracy of the data is vital to the success of any NLP model.

Components of NLP

NLP involves multiple components and techniques, each working together to process and understand human language. These components include:

Tokenization: Tokenization is the process of splitting a piece of text into smaller units called tokens (which can be words, phrases, or even characters). This is the first step in most NLP tasks.

Part-of-Speech Tagging: This involves identifying the grammatical structure of sentences. For example, tagging words as nouns, verbs, adjectives, etc., helps to understand the sentence's meaning.

Named Entity Recognition (NER): NER identifies entities (such as names, locations, and dates) within text. For example, in the sentence "Barack Obama was born in Hawaii," NER would identify "Barack Obama" as a person and "Hawaii" as a location.

Lemmatization and Stemming: These techniques reduce words to their root form. Lemmatization returns the base or dictionary form of a word (e.g., "better" becomes "good"), while stemming removes suffixes to arrive at the root form (e.g., "running" becomes "run").

Dependency Parsing: This technique analyzes the grammatical structure of a sentence and establishes relationships between words, helping the machine understand how words depend on one another.

Word Embeddings: Word embeddings represent words as dense vectors of numbers, allowing words with similar meanings to have similar representations in the vector space. Common word embeddings include Word2Vec, GloVe, and FastText.

Text Generation: Text generation involves creating new text based on patterns learned from a training dataset. Models like GPT-3 and LSTM networks excel at this task and can generate human-like text.

NLP Techniques and Tools

To implement NLP models, various techniques and tools are employed. Some of the most popular NLP techniques include:

Machine Learning: Machine learning algorithms, such as decision trees, SVMs, and random forests, can be used for NLP tasks like classification and sentiment analysis.

Deep Learning: Deep learning, particularly Recurrent Neural Networks (RNNs) and Long Short-Term Memory (LSTM) networks, has greatly advanced the field of NLP, especially for tasks like language translation, text generation, and speech recognition.

Transfer Learning: Models like BERT (Bidirectional Encoder Representations from Transformers) and GPT (Generative Pre-trained Transformer) use transfer learning to leverage pre-trained models and fine-tune them for specific NLP tasks.

Python Libraries for NLP

Python has become the go-to language for NLP due to its simplicity and the vast array of libraries available to facilitate NLP tasks. Some of the most commonly used libraries for NLP include:

NLTK (Natural Language Toolkit): One of the most popular Python libraries for NLP, NLTK provides easy-to-use interfaces for tokenization, part-of-speech tagging, stemming, and more. It's perfect for beginners and educational purposes.

spaCy: spaCy is a modern NLP library designed for performance and scalability. It includes pre-trained models for tasks like part-of-speech tagging, named entity recognition, and dependency parsing.

TextBlob: TextBlob simplifies many NLP tasks and offers a convenient API for tasks like part-of-speech tagging, sentiment analysis, and translation.

Transformers (by Hugging Face): This library provides access to state-of-the-art pre-trained models like BERT, GPT-2, T5, and others. It allows for easy fine-tuning and deployment of models on custom NLP tasks.

Gensim: Gensim specializes in topic modeling and document similarity, with tools for working with word embeddings and large text corpora.

The Future of NLP

The field of NLP has seen significant progress in recent years, thanks to advances in deep learning, massive datasets, and powerful computing resources. NLP models, especially those based on transformers (like BERT and GPT-3), are now achieving human-level performance on a variety of tasks.

Looking ahead, we expect further breakthroughs in NLP, particularly in areas such as:

- **Multilingual NLP**: Advances in NLP will enable better understanding and translation across multiple languages, breaking down language barriers.
- **Conversational AI**: NLP will continue to improve virtual assistants and chatbots, making them more intuitive and capable of handling complex queries.
- **Text Summarization**: Automated summarization of large documents and articles is expected to become more accurate and widely used.
- **Bias and Fairness**: Addressing biases in NLP models and ensuring fairness in automated decision-making processes will be crucial for responsible AI development.

In summary, NLP is a rapidly evolving field that bridges the gap between human language and machine understanding. With applications in every industry, from customer service to healthcare, NLP continues to revolutionize the way we interact with computers. As the field advances, it holds the potential to unlock even more sophisticated applications that will transform our daily lives.

9.2 Tokenization and Text Preprocessing

Tokenization and text preprocessing are essential steps in any Natural Language Processing (NLP) pipeline. Before feeding text data into machine learning models, it must be transformed into a format that the algorithms can process. Tokenization and preprocessing help break down raw text data into meaningful structures, making it easier for models to understand the underlying patterns and relationships. In this section, we'll explore the concepts of tokenization and text preprocessing and their importance in preparing textual data for analysis.

What is Tokenization?

Tokenization is the process of splitting text into smaller units called tokens. These tokens can be words, subwords, sentences, or characters. The goal of tokenization is to break down a text into its constituent parts, which are easier to analyze and process.

Tokenization serves as the first step in almost all NLP tasks, such as text classification, sentiment analysis, or machine translation.

There are different types of tokenization methods:

Word Tokenization: This is the most common form of tokenization, where the text is split into individual words.

Example: The sentence "I love programming" would be tokenized into the list: ["I", "love", "programming"].

Subword Tokenization: Some models, such as BERT and GPT, use subword tokenization to break down words into smaller meaningful components (subwords), which helps to deal with out-of-vocabulary words.

Example: The word "unhappiness" could be tokenized into: ["un", "happiness"].

Character Tokenization: In character tokenization, each character is treated as a token. This approach is often used when working with languages with complex morphology or when trying to handle rare words or misspellings.

Example: The word "love" could be tokenized into: ["l", "o", "v", "e"].

Sentence Tokenization: This involves breaking text into individual sentences, which is useful in tasks like summarization or machine translation.

Example: The text "I love programming. Python is great." would be tokenized into: ["I love programming.", "Python is great."].

Importance of Tokenization

Tokenization plays a pivotal role in simplifying the text data and converting it into a format that machine learning models can effectively process. Here's why tokenization is important:

Converts Text into Structured Data: Tokenization transforms unstructured text into a sequence of tokens, which are easier to manipulate programmatically.

Enables Model Understanding: By splitting text into tokens, models can recognize and learn patterns in the data. For instance, identifying how certain words or phrases appear together can reveal sentiment, topic, or intent.

Facilitates Feature Extraction: Tokenization allows the extraction of relevant features such as word frequencies, named entities, and n-grams, which can be used in downstream tasks like classification or clustering.

Improves Handling of Unknown Words: By using subword or character tokenization, models can handle out-of-vocabulary (OOV) words, which occur when an unseen word appears in the input.

Text Preprocessing: Preparing Raw Text for NLP

Text preprocessing involves cleaning and transforming raw text data into a structured form that is more suitable for analysis. Preprocessing steps help remove noise, standardize the text, and enhance the quality of the input data for NLP models. Below are some common preprocessing techniques:

1. Lowercasing

One of the simplest and most effective text preprocessing steps is converting all text to lowercase. This helps standardize the data by ensuring that words like "Apple" and "apple" are treated the same. This is particularly important in tasks like text classification, where the model should focus on the content of the text, not on case differences.

Example:

```
Input: "I Love Python"
Output: "i love python"
```

2. Removing Punctuation

Punctuation marks, such as commas, periods, and question marks, may not add meaningful value to certain NLP tasks, especially when we are working with text classification or sentiment analysis. Removing punctuation helps to clean up the text and focus on the important words.

Example:

```
Input: "Hello, world! How are you?"
Output: "Hello world How are you"
```

3. Removing Stopwords

Stopwords are common words like "and", "the", "in", "on", and "for" that occur frequently in text but don't carry much meaningful information. These words are often removed in text preprocessing to reduce the complexity of the text and improve model performance. However, the decision to remove stopwords depends on the specific NLP task; in some cases, stopwords may be important (e.g., in machine translation).

Example:

```
Input: "I love programming in Python"
Output: "love programming Python"
```

4. Lemmatization and Stemming

Both lemmatization and stemming are techniques used to reduce words to their base or root form. The goal is to standardize variations of a word (e.g., "running", "runner", "ran") so that they all represent the same concept.

Stemming is a simpler, heuristic approach that cuts off prefixes or suffixes to return a word's root form, sometimes resulting in non-existent words.

Example: "running" -> "run"

Lemmatization is a more sophisticated method that reduces a word to its base or dictionary form (lemma) using linguistic knowledge. It ensures that the output word is meaningful.

Example: "running" -> "run", "better" -> "good"

5. Removing Special Characters and Numbers

In some cases, special characters (e.g., @, #, $) and numbers may not be useful for text analysis, especially in tasks like text classification. Removing them can help focus on the important words in the text. However, in certain applications (e.g., sentiment analysis of social media posts or financial data analysis), these characters may carry significant meaning, so this step should be applied carefully.

Example:

Input: "I love #Python programming at 10 PM!"
Output: "I love Python programming at PM"

6. Tokenization (As Discussed Earlier)

After performing basic text cleaning steps, the next stage is tokenization, where the text is split into individual units, such as words, subwords, or characters. Tokenization helps structure the text into a format that is easier for machine learning models to handle.

Example: Tokenization and Preprocessing in Python

Let's look at a simple Python example using the NLTK library to perform tokenization and preprocessing:

```
import nltk
from nltk.corpus import stopwords
from nltk.stem import WordNetLemmatizer
import string

# Download necessary NLTK datasets
nltk.download('punkt')
nltk.download('stopwords')
nltk.download('wordnet')

# Sample text
text = "I love programming in Python! It is amazing."

# 1. Convert to lowercase
text = text.lower()

# 2. Remove punctuation
text = text.translate(str.maketrans("", "", string.punctuation))

# 3. Tokenization
```

```
tokens = nltk.word_tokenize(text)

# 4. Remove stopwords
stop_words = set(stopwords.words('english'))
tokens = [word for word in tokens if word not in stop_words]

# 5. Lemmatization
lemmatizer = WordNetLemmatizer()
tokens = [lemmatizer.lemmatize(word) for word in tokens]

# Final processed tokens
print(tokens)
```

Output:

```
['love', 'programming', 'python', 'amazing']
```

In this example:

- The text is first converted to lowercase.
- Punctuation is removed.
- The text is tokenized into individual words.
- Stopwords like "in" and "is" are removed.
- Lemmatization is applied to reduce words to their root forms.

Tokenization and text preprocessing are fundamental steps in preparing text for NLP tasks. Tokenization breaks down raw text into manageable pieces, while preprocessing cleans and standardizes the data to improve the performance of NLP models. By applying techniques like lowercasing, stopword removal, stemming, and lemmatization, we can create cleaner, more efficient text data that allows machine learning models to make better predictions and classifications.

In the next sections, we'll explore how to use tokenized and preprocessed text data in various NLP tasks like text classification, sentiment analysis, and more!

9.3 Implementing a Rule-Based Chatbot

A rule-based chatbot is a simple form of a conversational agent that responds to user inputs based on predefined rules or patterns. Unlike more sophisticated chatbots that use machine learning or deep learning to generate responses, rule-based chatbots rely on logic and specific patterns that map user input to a predefined set of responses. These types of chatbots are typically easy to implement and provide valuable functionalities, such as answering frequently asked questions (FAQs), providing customer support, or assisting with simple tasks.

In this section, we'll walk through the process of building a simple rule-based chatbot in Python. We'll cover key components such as pattern matching, defining rules, and using Python libraries like nltk and re to implement the chatbot. By the end of this guide, you will have a basic rule-based chatbot that can be expanded for more complex tasks.

What is a Rule-Based Chatbot?

A rule-based chatbot operates based on a set of predefined rules that match user inputs with specific responses. These rules can be designed using simple pattern matching techniques, where the chatbot looks for specific keywords, phrases, or syntactic structures in the user's message to determine an appropriate response.

Rule-based chatbots are limited by the rules they are programmed with, meaning they can only respond to queries they have been specifically trained for. They cannot handle out-of-scope or unexpected questions, making them ideal for specific, structured tasks but not for complex conversations.

For example, if a user asks a rule-based chatbot "What is your name?", the chatbot will respond with a predefined answer such as "My name is Chatbot." However, if the user asks a question outside of the predefined rules, such as "How are you?", the chatbot might not be able to handle that query unless explicitly defined in its rules.

Step-by-Step Guide to Building a Simple Rule-Based Chatbot

We'll implement a basic rule-based chatbot that can respond to a set of predefined questions. We will use Python libraries such as nltk for natural language processing (NLP) and re for regular expression-based pattern matching.

1. Install Necessary Libraries

Before we start implementing the chatbot, let's make sure we have the necessary libraries installed. The primary libraries we'll be using include nltk and re. You can install nltk using the following command:

```
pip install nltk
```

We also need to download some necessary NLTK resources like stopwords and punkt for tokenization and pattern matching:

```
import nltk
nltk.download('punkt')
nltk.download('stopwords')
```

2. Define Predefined Responses

The core of our chatbot will be a set of rules that match specific patterns and return predefined responses. To keep things simple, we'll create a dictionary of patterns and corresponding responses.

```
import nltk
from nltk.chat.util import Chat, reflections

# Define a set of rules
patterns = [
    (r"hi|hello|hey", ["Hello!", "Hi there!", "Hey! How can I help you?"]),
    (r"what is your name?", ["My name is Chatbot."]),
    (r"how are you?", ["I'm doing well, thank you!", "I'm great! How can I assist you today?"]),
    (r"bye|exit|quit", ["Goodbye!", "See you later!", "Bye! Have a great day!"]),
    (r"what is (.*)?", ["Sorry, I don't know about that."]),
]

# Define the chatbot function
def chatbot():
    print("Welcome to Chatbot! Type 'quit' to exit.")
    chat = Chat(patterns, reflections)
    chat.converse()
```

In this example, we've created a set of patterns that the chatbot will recognize. These patterns are simple regular expressions (regex) that match user inputs like greetings or questions about the chatbot's name. For instance:

- If the user types "Hi", "hello", or "hey", the chatbot will respond with a friendly greeting like "Hello!" or "Hi there!".
- If the user asks "What is your name?", the chatbot will respond with "My name is Chatbot".
- If the user types "How are you?", the chatbot will reply with "I'm doing well, thank you!".
- We also added a quit pattern so the user can exit the chatbot with the commands "bye", "exit", or "quit".

3. Use the nltk.chat.util.Chat Class

To facilitate pattern matching and chatbot interactions, we use the Chat class from NLTK's chat.util module. The Chat class takes two parameters:

- **patterns**: A list of pairs where the first element is a regular expression and the second element is a list of possible responses.
- **reflections**: A dictionary of common conversational patterns (like turning "I am" into "you are").

The reflections dictionary is built-in to NLTK and helps the chatbot understand certain responses in different forms. For example, when the user says "I am feeling great", the chatbot will transform that to "You are feeling great".

The chat.converse() method starts an interactive session with the user. The chatbot waits for input, tries to match it to one of the patterns, and responds with a random response from the list of responses.

4. Running the Chatbot

Now that we have our chatbot function defined, we can run the chatbot by calling the chatbot() function:

```
# Run the chatbot
chatbot()
```

Once the function is executed, the chatbot will prompt the user to type something. The chatbot will then check the input against its predefined patterns and return a matching response. If the user types something that doesn't match any predefined pattern, the chatbot will use a fallback response such as "Sorry, I don't understand."

Here's an example interaction:

```
Welcome to Chatbot! Type 'quit' to exit.
> hi
Hello!
> How are you?
I'm doing well, thank you!
> what is your name?
My name is Chatbot.
> exit
Goodbye!
```

5. Enhancing the Chatbot

While this chatbot is simple and rule-based, you can enhance it by adding more complex patterns, keywords, and responses. Here are a few ideas for improvements:

- **Handling Synonyms**: You can use more general patterns or add synonyms to match a wider range of user inputs. For instance, the chatbot could recognize different ways of asking about the time, such as "What time is it?" or "Can you tell me the time?"
- **Complex Regex Matching**: Use more complex regular expressions to handle varied sentence structures. For instance, you could recognize questions like "Can you help me?" or "How can I contact support?".
- **More Dynamic Responses**: Instead of using static predefined responses, the chatbot could generate dynamic responses using templates or access data (e.g., pulling in the current weather or time).
- **Integrating APIs**: You could integrate external APIs into the chatbot. For example, you could use an API to fetch the current weather when the user asks about it, or a news API to deliver the latest headlines.

Limitations of Rule-Based Chatbots

Rule-based chatbots, while useful for specific, simple tasks, have some key limitations:

- **Limited Scope**: Rule-based chatbots can only respond to queries they have been explicitly programmed to handle. They don't learn from new inputs and can't adapt to unforeseen questions.
- **Rigid Responses**: Since responses are predefined, rule-based chatbots can lack flexibility and might offer repetitive or overly simple responses.
- **Handling Ambiguity**: Rule-based chatbots struggle with ambiguous queries. For example, if a user asks a vague question like "Tell me about your services," the chatbot may not know how to respond unless specific rules for that query exist.

Despite these limitations, rule-based chatbots are still valuable for customer service, answering FAQs, and handling basic tasks.

In this section, we've created a simple rule-based chatbot using Python and the nltk library. This type of chatbot is useful for straightforward tasks and is easy to implement, but it is limited in its ability to handle complex or ambiguous queries. While rule-based chatbots are not as flexible as machine learning-based chatbots, they serve as a great starting point for building conversational agents.

You can expand this chatbot by adding more complex patterns, integrating external data sources, or even combining it with more advanced techniques such as machine learning or natural language understanding (NLU) to make the chatbot smarter and more dynamic.

9.4 Enhancing the Chatbot with Machine Learning

In the previous section, we built a basic rule-based chatbot using predefined patterns and responses. While this type of chatbot can handle simple tasks like answering frequently asked questions (FAQs), it has several limitations, including a lack of flexibility and the inability to learn from new data. To overcome these limitations and make the chatbot more intelligent, we can enhance it with machine learning techniques.

Machine learning allows the chatbot to learn from historical data, adapt to new user inputs, and generate more relevant, context-aware responses. In this section, we will explore how to enhance a rule-based chatbot by incorporating machine learning techniques, such as intent classification, to allow the bot to better understand and respond to user queries.

What is Intent Classification?

Intent classification is a crucial component of a machine learning-based chatbot. In essence, intent classification involves determining the underlying goal or purpose of a user's query. For example:

```
User Input: "What is the weather today?"
Intent: Request for weather information.
User Input: "I need help with my order."
Intent: Request for customer support.
```

In a machine learning-enhanced chatbot, instead of relying on simple keyword matching, the chatbot uses a machine learning model to classify user queries into predefined intents. Once the intent is identified, the chatbot can trigger the appropriate response or action.

Step-by-Step Guide to Enhancing the Chatbot with Machine Learning

We'll go through the process of building an intent-based chatbot that uses Natural Language Processing (NLP) and machine learning to classify user intents and generate responses. For this, we'll use scikit-learn for building the machine learning model and nltk for text preprocessing and feature extraction.

1. Install Necessary Libraries

First, we need to install the necessary libraries:

```
pip install nltk scikit-learn
```

We will be using scikit-learn for the machine learning part and nltk for text preprocessing.

2. Define Intents and Responses

For this example, let's define some intents that our chatbot should recognize. Each intent will have associated phrases (user queries) and corresponding responses.

```
intents = [
    {
        "intent": "greeting",
        "patterns": ["hi", "hello", "hey", "howdy", "good morning"],
```

```
        "responses": ["Hello!", "Hi there!", "Hey! How can I help you?"]
    },
    {
        "intent": "goodbye",
        "patterns": ["bye", "exit", "quit", "see you later"],
        "responses": ["Goodbye!", "See you later!", "Take care!"]
    },
    {
        "intent": "weather",
        "patterns": ["weather", "temperature", "forecast", "what's the weather like", "how is
the weather"],
        "responses": ["The weather is great today!", "It's sunny and warm."]
    },
    {
        "intent": "help",
        "patterns": ["help", "assist", "support", "can you help me", "I need help"],
        "responses": ["Sure! How can I assist you?", "I'm here to help you!"]
    },
]
```

Here, each intent has:

- **A list of patterns**: These are user inputs that represent the specific intent.
- **A list of responses**: These are the predefined responses that the chatbot will choose from when the corresponding intent is detected.

3. Text Preprocessing and Feature Extraction

Before training a machine learning model, we need to preprocess the user inputs (patterns) and convert them into a format suitable for classification. We will use nltk to tokenize the text and scikit-learn's TfidfVectorizer to convert the text into numerical features.

```
import nltk
from sklearn.feature_extraction.text import TfidfVectorizer
from sklearn.preprocessing import LabelEncoder
import numpy as np
import random
```

```
# Download NLTK data
nltk.download('punkt')

# Prepare the dataset
patterns = []
intents_labels = []
responses = []

# Loop through the intents and create lists of patterns and labels
for intent in intents:
    for pattern in intent["patterns"]:
        patterns.append(pattern)
        intents_labels.append(intent["intent"])

# Create a TF-IDF vectorizer to convert the text into numeric features
vectorizer = TfidfVectorizer(stop_words='english')
X = vectorizer.fit_transform(patterns).toarray()

# Encode the labels (intent labels)
label_encoder = LabelEncoder()
y = label_encoder.fit_transform(intents_labels)
```

TfidfVectorizer converts the patterns (text) into numerical features using the TF-IDF method, which captures the importance of words based on their frequency across the text.
LabelEncoder is used to encode the intents as numeric labels.

4. Train a Machine Learning Model

Now that the data is ready, we can use a machine learning classifier to train the model. For simplicity, we will use Logistic Regression, which is effective for text classification tasks.

```
from sklearn.linear_model import LogisticRegression

# Train a Logistic Regression model
model = LogisticRegression(max_iter=200)
model.fit(X, y)
```

This will train a logistic regression model on the feature vectors (X) and their corresponding labels (y).

5. Define a Function to Predict Intents

Once the model is trained, we need to define a function that will take user input, preprocess it, and classify it into one of the intents.

```
def classify_intent(user_input):
    # Preprocess user input and convert it to features
    input_features = vectorizer.transform([user_input]).toarray()

    # Predict the intent label
    predicted_label = model.predict(input_features)[0]

    # Get the predicted intent name
    intent_name = label_encoder.inverse_transform([predicted_label])[0]

    # Get the response based on the predicted intent
    intent_responses = [intent["responses"] for intent in intents if intent["intent"] ==
intent_name][0]
    return random.choice(intent_responses)
```

In this function:

- The user input is transformed into features using the same TfidfVectorizer.
- The machine learning model predicts the intent label.
- The chatbot then selects a response from the predefined responses corresponding to that intent.

6. Chatbot Interaction

Now that we've trained the chatbot, we can interact with it. Let's define a function to run the chatbot and allow the user to enter queries.

```
def chatbot():
    print("Welcome to the ML-enhanced Chatbot! Type 'quit' to exit.")
    while True:
        user_input = input("You: ")
```

```
        if user_input.lower() == 'quit':
            print("Goodbye!")
            break

        response = classify_intent(user_input)
        print("Chatbot: " + response)

# Run the chatbot
chatbot()
```

Example Interaction

```
Welcome to the ML-enhanced Chatbot! Type 'quit' to exit.
You: hi
Chatbot: Hello!

You: what's the weather like
Chatbot: The weather is great today!

You: I need help
Chatbot: I'm here to help you!

You: exit
Goodbye!
```

In this interaction, the chatbot classifies the user's query using the machine learning model and provides an appropriate response.

Enhancements and Improvements

Now that we've created a basic intent-based chatbot with machine learning, there are many ways to enhance and improve it:

- **Handling Synonyms**: You can expand your training dataset to include synonyms and variations of queries to improve intent classification.
- **Adding More Intents**: You can add more intents, such as booking a ticket, answering FAQs, or providing customer support for different services.

- **Entity Recognition**: In addition to intent classification, you can add named entity recognition (NER) to extract specific details (such as dates, locations, or names) from user queries.
- **Advanced Models**: For more complex conversations, you can experiment with deep learning models such as RNNs (Recurrent Neural Networks) or Transformers (e.g., BERT, GPT-3) for better performance and context understanding.

Enhancing a rule-based chatbot with machine learning techniques, such as intent classification, allows the bot to become much more powerful and adaptable. By training a model to classify user queries into predefined intents, the chatbot can handle a wide range of user inputs and provide more accurate and context-aware responses. While this approach improves flexibility, there's still plenty of room for further development, such as adding more intents, improving data preprocessing, and using more advanced machine learning techniques.

10. Image Recognition with AI

Image recognition is one of the most exciting and impactful areas of AI, enabling machines to interpret and classify visual data. In this chapter, you'll learn the fundamentals of computer vision and how to build an image recognition model using Python and popular machine learning libraries. You'll start by exploring how to preprocess images, convert them into formats suitable for training, and apply machine learning techniques to recognize objects within images. Using libraries like TensorFlow and Keras, you'll implement a convolutional neural network (CNN), a powerful model for image classification tasks. By the end of this chapter, you'll be able to build your own image recognition system capable of identifying and classifying images with high accuracy.

10.1 Introduction to Computer Vision

Computer Vision (CV) is a field of artificial intelligence (AI) that focuses on enabling machines to interpret, understand, and analyze visual information from the world, in much the same way that humans do. The goal of computer vision is to develop algorithms that allow computers to process and understand images and videos, detect objects, recognize faces, and perform tasks that typically require human vision.

This field has a wide range of applications, including self-driving cars, medical image analysis, facial recognition, surveillance, augmented reality (AR), robotics, and much more. Essentially, computer vision aims to simulate human vision and make decisions based on visual inputs, helping machines interpret the world in visual terms.

How Does Computer Vision Work?

At its core, computer vision involves the following basic steps:

Image Acquisition: The first step in any computer vision task is obtaining images or videos. These can be from cameras, scanners, or other imaging devices.

Preprocessing: Raw images are often noisy and require preprocessing to enhance features. Common preprocessing tasks include:

- Resizing images to a standard dimension.
- Grayscale conversion (converting color images to black-and-white).
- Noise reduction (removing irrelevant background information).

Feature Extraction: Once images are preprocessed, the next step is to extract meaningful features from them. This might involve identifying edges, contours, textures, or patterns within an image that are important for analysis.

Object Detection and Recognition: After extracting features, the system detects specific objects in an image (e.g., faces, cars, trees) and classifies them into categories. Techniques like Haar cascades, HOG (Histogram of Oriented Gradients), and deep learning approaches like Convolutional Neural Networks (CNNs) are commonly used for this.

Decision Making: After detecting and recognizing objects, the final step involves making a decision or taking an action. For example, a computer vision system in a self-driving car might identify pedestrians and stop the vehicle, or an image classification system might label an image as "cat" or "dog."

Key Techniques and Algorithms in Computer Vision

Some of the fundamental algorithms and techniques used in computer vision include:

Convolutional Neural Networks (CNNs): CNNs are a class of deep learning algorithms specifically designed to work with visual data. These networks have proven highly effective in tasks such as image classification, object detection, and facial recognition. CNNs use layers of convolutions (filters) that automatically detect features like edges, textures, and shapes in an image.

Object Detection: This task involves identifying and locating objects in an image. Popular models for object detection include:

YOLO (You Only Look Once): A real-time object detection system that can detect multiple objects in images and videos.

Faster R-CNN: An advanced CNN model that performs both object detection and classification.

Image Segmentation: Segmentation divides an image into smaller regions (or segments) to make it easier to analyze. The goal is to partition the image into parts that are meaningful and easier to understand. Semantic segmentation assigns a class to each pixel in an image, while instance segmentation differentiates between different instances of the same object in an image.

Feature Matching: In some applications, like facial recognition, the system needs to match features from one image to another. Techniques like SIFT (Scale-Invariant Feature Transform) and SURF (Speeded Up Robust Features) are used to detect distinctive keypoints and match them between images.

Optical Character Recognition (OCR): OCR enables a system to read and understand text from scanned documents or images. This technology is widely used in document scanning, number plate recognition, and digitizing handwritten text.

Image Classification: Image classification involves categorizing an image into one of several predefined classes. This can be done using traditional machine learning models or, more commonly today, deep learning techniques like CNNs.

Face Recognition: Face recognition identifies and verifies individuals based on their facial features. It's used in security systems, social media tagging, and biometric identification.

Applications of Computer Vision

Autonomous Vehicles: Self-driving cars rely heavily on computer vision to interpret their surroundings. CV algorithms process data from cameras, LiDAR, and radar to detect pedestrians, vehicles, road signs, traffic lights, and obstacles. This allows the car to make decisions in real-time, such as stopping at a red light or avoiding a pedestrian.

Medical Imaging: Computer vision is used in the medical field to analyze images like X-rays, MRIs, and CT scans. Algorithms can detect abnormalities such as tumors or fractures, aiding in diagnosis and providing valuable insights for doctors.

Facial Recognition: This is one of the most widespread applications of computer vision. It's used in security systems for identifying and verifying individuals. Facial recognition is also used in social media to automatically tag friends in photos.

Retail and eCommerce: Retailers are using computer vision to enhance the shopping experience. For example, Amazon Go stores use CV to track products that customers pick up, enabling a checkout-free shopping experience. Similarly, computer vision is used for visual search, where users can upload a picture to find similar products online.

Agriculture: CV is used in agriculture for tasks like monitoring crop health, detecting pests, and automating harvesting. Drones equipped with cameras can capture high-resolution images of fields, and CV algorithms analyze the data to provide farmers with insights into crop conditions.

Robotics: Robots use computer vision for navigation and interaction with their environment. In manufacturing, robots rely on CV to identify parts, assemble products, or inspect quality.

Surveillance and Security: CV systems are used in surveillance cameras to detect suspicious activity, track movements, and recognize faces in real-time, providing enhanced security in public and private spaces.

Augmented Reality (AR): AR applications, such as Pokémon GO or Snapchat filters, use computer vision to overlay digital information on real-world objects. Computer vision allows these applications to detect and track surfaces, faces, or environments in real-time.

Challenges in Computer Vision

While computer vision has come a long way in recent years, it still faces several challenges:

Data Quality: For computer vision models to work effectively, they need large amounts of high-quality labeled data. Data collection and annotation can be expensive and time-consuming.

Complexity of Real-World Scenarios: In the real world, images can be noisy, blurred, or contain multiple overlapping objects, making it difficult for computer vision models to detect and recognize them accurately.

Lighting and Environmental Conditions: Variations in lighting, shadows, and weather conditions can affect the performance of computer vision models, making them less reliable in dynamic environments.

Generalization: Computer vision models trained on one set of images may not generalize well to other datasets, especially if they come from different environments or contain diverse objects.

Future of Computer Vision

As technology advances, the field of computer vision is rapidly evolving. Several exciting trends are shaping the future of CV:

Deep Learning Revolution: Deep learning, particularly Convolutional Neural Networks (CNNs), has significantly improved the accuracy of computer vision systems. With the rise of more powerful GPUs and large-scale datasets, deep learning models will continue to improve.

Edge Computing: Edge computing enables real-time processing of visual data on devices (such as smartphones, drones, or cameras) without relying on cloud servers. This will help reduce latency and allow for faster decision-making in real-time applications.

AI and Automation: The integration of AI into computer vision systems is driving the automation of various tasks, such as manufacturing, healthcare, and agriculture. AI-driven CV systems will continue to streamline workflows, increase efficiency, and reduce human intervention.

Explainability and Interpretability: As computer vision models become more complex, there will be a greater need for transparency and explainability in decision-making. Understanding why a model makes certain predictions will be crucial, especially in applications like healthcare or autonomous driving.

Computer vision is a fascinating and rapidly growing field within AI that enables machines to interpret and analyze visual information. From self-driving cars to medical imaging, computer vision has already made significant strides in transforming industries. By leveraging powerful algorithms like Convolutional Neural Networks and advancements in deep learning, computer vision will continue to advance, offering exciting possibilities for the future. However, challenges remain, including the need for large datasets, improving generalization, and ensuring reliability in real-world conditions. As technology advances, computer vision will undoubtedly become an integral part of our daily lives, shaping the way we interact with the world.

10.2 Loading and Processing Images in Python

In computer vision, one of the first steps in analyzing visual data is loading and processing images. Python offers a variety of libraries to handle image loading, manipulation, and preprocessing, making it an ideal language for computer vision tasks. In this section, we'll explore how to load images, perform basic processing tasks like resizing, conversion, and transformation, and prepare images for more advanced computer vision applications such as object detection, facial recognition, and classification.

We'll primarily use libraries such as OpenCV, Pillow (PIL), and Matplotlib to load and process images in Python.

1. Loading Images in Python

The first step in any computer vision task is to load images into memory. Let's start by using two commonly used libraries for this purpose:

1.1 Using OpenCV

OpenCV (Open Source Computer Vision Library) is one of the most widely used libraries for computer vision tasks. OpenCV provides functions to load, display, and manipulate images.

Here's how you can load an image using OpenCV:

```
import cv2

# Load an image using OpenCV
image = cv2.imread('image.jpg')  # Provide the path to the image file

# Check if image is loaded correctly
if image is None:
    print("Error: Image not found")
else:
    print("Image loaded successfully")

# Display the image in a window
cv2.imshow('Loaded Image', image)

# Wait until a key is pressed and close the image window
cv2.waitKey(0)
cv2.destroyAllWindows()
cv2.imread(): This function reads an image from a specified file and returns the image as a numpy array.
cv2.imshow(): This function displays the image in a window.
cv2.waitKey(0): Waits for a key event to close the image window.
```

```
cv2.destroyAllWindows(): Closes all OpenCV windows.
```

1.2 Using Pillow (PIL)

Pillow is another popular Python library used for image processing. It is a fork of the Python Imaging Library (PIL) and is simpler for basic image manipulation tasks.

Here's how to load an image using Pillow:

```python
from PIL import Image

# Load an image using Pillow
image = Image.open('image.jpg')  # Provide the path to the image file

# Check the image size and format
print(f"Image size: {image.size}")
print(f"Image format: {image.format}")

# Display the image
image.show()
Image.open(): This function opens an image file and returns an image object.
image.show(): This function displays the image using the default image viewer.
```

2. Image Preprocessing and Manipulation

Once an image is loaded, we can perform a variety of preprocessing and manipulation tasks to prepare it for further analysis. These operations may include resizing, cropping, converting color spaces, and transforming images for feature extraction.

2.1 Resizing Images

Sometimes, images need to be resized to fit a specific input size for a neural network or to standardize image dimensions. You can resize an image using both OpenCV and Pillow.

Using OpenCV:

```python
# Resize image using OpenCV
```

```
resized_image = cv2.resize(image, (300, 300))  # Resize to 300x300 pixels
cv2.imshow('Resized Image', resized_image)
cv2.waitKey(0)
cv2.destroyAllWindows()
```

Using Pillow:

```
# Resize image using Pillow
resized_image = image.resize((300, 300))  # Resize to 300x300 pixels
resized_image.show()
```

2.2 Grayscale Conversion

Converting an image to grayscale simplifies many computer vision tasks and reduces the amount of data. In grayscale images, pixel values represent shades of gray, making them easier to process.

Using OpenCV:

```
# Convert image to grayscale using OpenCV
gray_image = cv2.cvtColor(image, cv2.COLOR_BGR2GRAY)
cv2.imshow('Grayscale Image', gray_image)
cv2.waitKey(0)
cv2.destroyAllWindows()
```

Using Pillow:

```
# Convert image to grayscale using Pillow
gray_image = image.convert('L')  # 'L' mode stands for grayscale
gray_image.show()
```

2.3 Image Cropping

Sometimes, you may want to focus on a specific region of an image. Cropping an image allows you to extract a portion of the image.

Using OpenCV:

```
# Crop an image using OpenCV (coordinates: top-left, bottom-right)
crop_image = image[50:200, 50:200]  # Crop region from row 50-200, column 50-200
cv2.imshow('Cropped Image', crop_image)
cv2.waitKey(0)
cv2.destroyAllWindows()
```

Using Pillow:

```
# Crop an image using Pillow
crop_image = image.crop((50, 50, 200, 200))  # (left, upper, right, lower)
crop_image.show()
```

2.4 Image Rotation

Rotating an image is a common operation, especially when preprocessing images for neural networks or augmenting data for training models.

Using OpenCV:

```
# Rotate image using OpenCV
height, width = image.shape[:2]
center = (width // 2, height // 2)
rotation_matrix = cv2.getRotationMatrix2D(center, 45, 1.0)  # Rotate by 45 degrees
rotated_image = cv2.warpAffine(image, rotation_matrix, (width, height))
cv2.imshow('Rotated Image', rotated_image)
cv2.waitKey(0)
cv2.destroyAllWindows()
```

Using Pillow:

```
# Rotate image using Pillow
rotated_image = image.rotate(45)  # Rotate by 45 degrees
rotated_image.show()
```

2.5 Image Normalization

Normalization is a process of adjusting the pixel values of an image to fit within a certain range. This is useful in machine learning to ensure consistent input data.

Using OpenCV:

```
# Normalize image using OpenCV (convert pixel values to range [0, 1])
normalized_image = image.astype('float32') / 255.0
cv2.imshow('Normalized Image', normalized_image)
cv2.waitKey(0)
cv2.destroyAllWindows()
```

Using Pillow:

```
import numpy as np

# Convert the image to a numpy array and normalize
normalized_image = np.array(image) / 255.0
```

3. Image Augmentation

In machine learning, particularly when training deep learning models, data augmentation helps artificially expand the size of a dataset by applying random transformations like rotations, flips, zooms, and shifts to the images. This increases the model's robustness.

Using Keras (for deep learning models):

```
from keras.preprocessing.image import ImageDataGenerator

# Create an ImageDataGenerator instance for augmentation
datagen = ImageDataGenerator(
    rotation_range=30,
    width_shift_range=0.2,
    height_shift_range=0.2,
    shear_range=0.2,
    zoom_range=0.2,
    horizontal_flip=True,
    fill_mode='nearest'
)
```

```
# Reshape the image and apply augmentation
image_array = np.array(image)
image_array = image_array.reshape((1, *image_array.shape))

# Generate augmented images
i = 0
for      batch      in      datagen.flow(image_array,      batch_size=1,
save_to_dir='augmented_images', save_prefix='aug', save_format='jpeg'):
   i += 1
   if i > 20:  # Generate 20 augmented images
      break
```

4. Saving Processed Images

After manipulating or processing an image, you may want to save the result. Here's how you can do it using both OpenCV and Pillow.

Using OpenCV:

```
# Save processed image using OpenCV
cv2.imwrite('processed_image.jpg', gray_image)
```

Using Pillow:

```
# Save processed image using Pillow
gray_image.save('processed_image.jpg')
```

In this section, we covered the essential techniques for loading and processing images in Python. We explored two powerful libraries—OpenCV and Pillow—that enable you to load images, resize, crop, convert to grayscale, rotate, normalize, and even augment images for training machine learning models. These preprocessing steps are essential in preparing visual data for more complex computer vision tasks, such as object detection, image classification, and facial recognition.

As you continue to work with computer vision applications, mastering these fundamental image manipulation techniques will provide you with the tools needed to handle and prepare your visual data effectively.

10.3 Using Pre-Trained Models for Image Classification

In computer vision, image classification is the task of assigning a label or category to an image based on its content. While you can build a model from scratch for image classification, leveraging pre-trained models is a more efficient and powerful approach, especially for beginners. Pre-trained models have been trained on large datasets like ImageNet, which contains millions of labeled images, and they can recognize a wide variety of objects, animals, and scenes.

In this section, we will explore how to use pre-trained models to perform image classification. We'll focus on popular models like VGG16, ResNet, and InceptionV3 that are available in deep learning frameworks such as TensorFlow/Keras and PyTorch.

1. What Are Pre-Trained Models?

Pre-trained models are neural network models that have been trained on large datasets and are available for use in your own applications. Instead of starting from scratch and training a model for hours or days, you can fine-tune these pre-trained models for your specific task. This approach is particularly useful when you don't have access to a large labeled dataset or the computational resources required to train a model from scratch.

These models have learned feature representations for common objects and patterns, which they can transfer to other tasks like:

- Image Classification
- Object Detection
- Semantic Segmentation
- Feature Extraction

The most commonly used pre-trained models for image classification are:

- VGG16
- ResNet50
- InceptionV3
- MobileNet
- EfficientNet

These models have been trained on ImageNet, a large dataset containing over 14 million images across 1,000 categories. When used for image classification, they can predict the most likely class for an input image based on the features they've learned.

2. Using Pre-Trained Models in TensorFlow/Keras

Keras, a high-level neural networks API that runs on top of TensorFlow, provides easy access to several pre-trained models. Here's how to use them for image classification.

2.1 Loading a Pre-Trained Model

You can load a pre-trained model in Keras with just a few lines of code. Let's demonstrate how to load the VGG16 model, which is a deep convolutional neural network (CNN) for image classification.

```python
import tensorflow as tf
from tensorflow.keras.applications import VGG16
from tensorflow.keras.preprocessing import image
from tensorflow.keras.applications.vgg16 import preprocess_input, decode_predictions
import numpy as np

# Load the VGG16 pre-trained model
model = VGG16(weights='imagenet')

# Load an image and resize it to 224x224 (the input size for VGG16)
img_path = 'cat.jpg'  # Replace with your image path
img = image.load_img(img_path, target_size=(224, 224))

# Convert the image to a numpy array
img_array = image.img_to_array(img)

# Expand dimensions to fit the model input shape
img_array = np.expand_dims(img_array, axis=0)

# Preprocess the image
img_array = preprocess_input(img_array)

# Make a prediction
predictions = model.predict(img_array)
```

```
# Decode the predictions
decoded_predictions = decode_predictions(predictions, top=3)[0]

# Print the top 3 predictions
for i, (imagenet_id, label, score) in enumerate(decoded_predictions):
    print(f"{i+1}. {label}: {score:.2f}")
```

Explanation of the Code:

- **VGG16(weights='imagenet'):** Loads the VGG16 model pre-trained on ImageNet.
- **image.load_img():** Loads an image and resizes it to the required input size (224x224) for VGG16.
- **image.img_to_array():** Converts the image to a NumPy array, which is the format expected by the model.
- **np.expand_dims():** Expands the dimensions of the array to match the model's expected input shape.
- **preprocess_input():** Prepares the image by scaling pixel values according to the model's requirements.
- **model.predict():** Makes a prediction on the input image.
- **decode_predictions():** Decodes the model's prediction into human-readable labels.

2.2 Using Other Pre-Trained Models (ResNet, InceptionV3)

You can easily switch to other pre-trained models like ResNet50 or InceptionV3 by changing the import statement and the model name. Here's how to use ResNet50:

```
from tensorflow.keras.applications import ResNet50
from        tensorflow.keras.applications.resnet50        import        preprocess_input,
decode_predictions

# Load the ResNet50 pre-trained model
model = ResNet50(weights='imagenet')

# Load and preprocess the image as done earlier
img = image.load_img(img_path, target_size=(224, 224))
img_array = image.img_to_array(img)
img_array = np.expand_dims(img_array, axis=0)
img_array = preprocess_input(img_array)
```

```
# Make predictions
predictions = model.predict(img_array)

# Decode predictions
decoded_predictions = decode_predictions(predictions, top=3)[0]

# Print the top 3 predictions
for i, (imagenet_id, label, score) in enumerate(decoded_predictions):
    print(f"{i+1}. {label}: {score:.2f}")
```

The process is essentially the same, with different models loaded depending on the task.

3. Fine-Tuning a Pre-Trained Model

Sometimes, you may need to fine-tune a pre-trained model for a specific task. Fine-tuning involves training the model on a smaller dataset specific to your task, allowing the model to adjust to new data while retaining the knowledge learned during its initial training.

Here's how to fine-tune a model in Keras:

3.1 Freezing the Base Layers

To prevent the pre-trained weights from being updated during training, you can freeze the base layers and only train the top layers. For example, in VGG16:

```
# Freeze the base layers of the VGG16 model
for layer in model.layers:
    layer.trainable = False

# Add custom layers on top for fine-tuning
from tensorflow.keras import layers, models
x = model.output
x = layers.Flatten()(x)
x = layers.Dense(1024, activation='relu')(x)
x = layers.Dropout(0.5)(x)
x = layers.Dense(1, activation='sigmoid')(x)  # Binary classification example
custom_model = models.Model(inputs=model.input, outputs=x)
```

```
# Compile the model
custom_model.compile(optimizer='adam',          loss='binary_crossentropy',
metrics=['accuracy'])
```

3.2 Training the Fine-Tuned Model

After adding your custom layers, you can train the model on your dataset:

```
# Assuming you have training and validation data (train_data, val_data)
custom_model.fit(train_data, epochs=5, validation_data=val_data)
```

During this process, only the custom layers (on top of the pre-trained model) will be trained while the base layers remain frozen.

4. Using Pre-Trained Models in PyTorch

PyTorch is another popular deep learning framework that also provides access to pre-trained models. Here's how to use ResNet18 in PyTorch for image classification.

4.1 Loading a Pre-Trained Model in PyTorch

```
import torch
from torchvision import models, transforms
from PIL import Image

# Load a pre-trained ResNet18 model
model = models.resnet18(pretrained=True)
model.eval()  # Set the model to evaluation mode

# Load and preprocess the image
img = Image.open('cat.jpg')  # Replace with your image path
preprocess = transforms.Compose([
    transforms.Resize(256),
    transforms.CenterCrop(224),
    transforms.ToTensor(),
    transforms.Normalize(mean=[0.485, 0.456, 0.406], std=[0.229, 0.224, 0.225]),
])
```

```
img_tensor = preprocess(img)
img_tensor = img_tensor.unsqueeze(0)  # Add batch dimension

# Make a prediction
with torch.no_grad():
    outputs = model(img_tensor)
    _, predicted_class = torch.max(outputs, 1)

# Load class labels (ImageNet classes)
LABELS = {i: label for i, label in enumerate(open('imagenet_class_index.json').readlines())}

# Print the predicted class
print(f"Predicted Class: {LABELS[predicted_class.item()]}")
```

Using pre-trained models for image classification is one of the most powerful techniques in computer vision. Instead of training a deep neural network from scratch, you can leverage these pre-trained models to save time and computational resources, while achieving high accuracy in a variety of tasks. In this section, we covered how to load and use pre-trained models such as VGG16, ResNet50, and InceptionV3 with TensorFlow/Keras and PyTorch.

By understanding how to use and fine-tune these models, you can apply them to real-world image classification tasks, and even enhance your model by adding custom layers or fine-tuning them on domain-specific datasets.

10.4 Building a Custom Image Classifier

In the world of computer vision, creating a custom image classifier is a vital skill, especially when you have a unique set of images that a pre-trained model might not recognize. While pre-trained models like VGG16, ResNet, and InceptionV3 are fantastic for general image classification tasks, they may not always be the best choice for specialized applications, such as identifying specific objects or classes in your own dataset.

In this section, we'll walk through the process of building a custom image classifier using TensorFlow/Keras. We'll cover everything from data preparation to model building and evaluation.

1. Collecting and Preparing Data

Before building a custom image classifier, you need a labeled dataset. For image classification, your data must be organized into folders, where each folder corresponds to a class, and the images in that folder are the instances of that class.

For example, if you're building a classifier to distinguish between cats and dogs, you might organize your data like this:

```
/dataset
  /train
    /cats
        cat1.jpg
        cat2.jpg
        ...
    /dogs
        dog1.jpg
        dog2.jpg
        ...
  /validation
    /cats
        cat3.jpg
        cat4.jpg
        ...
    /dogs
        dog3.jpg
        dog4.jpg
        ...
```

To get started, you need to split your dataset into at least two parts:

- **Training data**: Used to train the model.
- **Validation data**: Used to evaluate the model during training to check its generalization ability.

In some cases, you may also use a test set for final evaluation.

1.1 Image Augmentation

Image augmentation is a technique that artificially enlarges your dataset by applying random transformations like rotation, zoom, flipping, and shifting. This is useful for improving the robustness and generalization of your model, especially if you have a small dataset.

In Keras, you can use ImageDataGenerator for augmentation:

```python
from tensorflow.keras.preprocessing.image import ImageDataGenerator

train_datagen = ImageDataGenerator(
    rescale=1./255,            # Normalize pixel values
    rotation_range=40,         # Randomly rotate images
    width_shift_range=0.2,     # Randomly shift images horizontally
    height_shift_range=0.2,    # Randomly shift images vertically
    shear_range=0.2,           # Randomly shear images
    zoom_range=0.2,            # Randomly zoom into images
    horizontal_flip=True,      # Randomly flip images
    fill_mode='nearest'        # Fill empty areas after transformations
)

validation_datagen = ImageDataGenerator(rescale=1./255)   # Only rescale for validation

train_generator = train_datagen.flow_from_directory(
    'dataset/train',
    target_size=(150, 150), # Resize images to 150x150
    batch_size=32,
    class_mode='binary' # Use 'categorical' for multi-class problems
)

validation_generator = validation_datagen.flow_from_directory(
    'dataset/validation',
    target_size=(150, 150),
    batch_size=32,
    class_mode='binary'
)
```

2. Building the Custom Model

Now that you have your data ready, it's time to build the image classification model. In Keras, you can build a convolutional neural network (CNN) with multiple layers, which is typically used for image classification tasks.

2.1 Convolutional Neural Network (CNN) Architecture

The architecture of your custom image classifier will consist of several components:

- **Convolutional layers**: These layers apply filters to the input image, extracting low- and high-level features such as edges, textures, and shapes.
- **MaxPooling layers**: These layers downsample the image, reducing its size while retaining important information.
- **Flatten layer**: This converts the 2D feature maps into a 1D vector.
- **Fully connected (Dense) layers**: These layers are used for classification, where the model makes its predictions.

Let's build a basic CNN architecture using Keras:

```python
from tensorflow.keras import layers, models

# Initialize the model
model = models.Sequential()

# Add convolutional layers with ReLU activation
model.add(layers.Conv2D(32, (3, 3), activation='relu', input_shape=(150, 150, 3)))
model.add(layers.MaxPooling2D((2, 2)))

model.add(layers.Conv2D(64, (3, 3), activation='relu'))
model.add(layers.MaxPooling2D((2, 2)))

model.add(layers.Conv2D(128, (3, 3), activation='relu'))
model.add(layers.MaxPooling2D((2, 2)))

# Flatten the feature maps into a 1D vector
model.add(layers.Flatten())

# Add fully connected layers
model.add(layers.Dense(128, activation='relu'))
model.add(layers.Dropout(0.5))  # Dropout layer to reduce overfitting
```

```
model.add(layers.Dense(1, activation='sigmoid'))   # Use 'softmax' for multi-class
problems

# Compile the model
model.compile(optimizer='adam',
        loss='binary_crossentropy',  # Use 'categorical_crossentropy' for multi-class
        metrics=['accuracy'])
```

2.2 Explanation of the Architecture:

- **Conv2D**: Convolutional layer that learns filters from the input images. The number of filters (32, 64, 128) defines how many feature maps the layer will generate.
- **MaxPooling2D**: Downsampling layer to reduce the size of the feature maps.
- **Flatten**: Converts the 2D feature maps into a 1D vector to feed into the fully connected layers.
- **Dense**: Fully connected layers used for making the final classification.
- **Dropout**: A regularization technique that helps prevent overfitting by randomly setting a fraction of input units to 0 during training.
- **Sigmoid**: Activation function for binary classification. For multi-class problems, you would use softmax.

3. Training the Model

With the model built, you can now train it using the fit() function in Keras, providing it with the training data, validation data, and the number of epochs.

```
history = model.fit(
    train_generator,
    steps_per_epoch=train_generator.samples // train_generator.batch_size,
    epochs=10,
    validation_data=validation_generator,
    validation_steps=validation_generator.samples // validation_generator.batch_size
)
```

This will train the model for 10 epochs. You can adjust the number of epochs depending on your dataset and the model's performance.

4. Evaluating the Model

After training, it's essential to evaluate the performance of your custom classifier on the validation data. You can do this using the evaluate() method in Keras:

```
loss, accuracy = model.evaluate(validation_generator)
print(f"Validation Accuracy: {accuracy*100:.2f}%")
```

If the model performs well, you can proceed to use it for predictions. If the accuracy is low, you may need to adjust the architecture, increase the data augmentation, or add more training data.

5. Saving the Model

Once the model is trained, you can save it for later use:

```
model.save('custom_image_classifier.h5')
```

Later, you can load the model with:

```
from tensorflow.keras.models import load_model
model = load_model('custom_image_classifier.h5')
```

Building a custom image classifier involves several key steps, including data preparation, building and training the model, and evaluating its performance. In this section, we showed how to collect and prepare data, build a convolutional neural network (CNN) using Keras, and train the model on the dataset. By applying techniques like data augmentation, CNN architectures, and model evaluation, you can create a powerful custom image classifier suited to your specific task.

Once your model is trained and fine-tuned, you can use it to make predictions on new, unseen images and improve it iteratively with new data or more sophisticated techniques, such as transfer learning or deeper network architectures.

11. AI for Predictions

Prediction is one of the most powerful applications of AI, used to forecast trends, behaviors, and outcomes across various domains. In this chapter, you'll learn how to harness the power of machine learning to make predictions using Python. You'll start by exploring regression models that help predict continuous values, such as sales figures or stock prices. You'll dive into techniques like linear regression and decision trees to build models that can make accurate predictions based on historical data. Additionally, you'll learn how to evaluate your models' performance and fine-tune them for better accuracy. By the end of this chapter, you'll be ready to apply AI to solve real-world predictive problems, from forecasting market trends to predicting customer behavior.

11.1 Understanding Time-Series Data

Time-series data is a sequence of data points or observations that are recorded or measured at successive, evenly spaced intervals over time. This type of data is particularly valuable in fields such as finance, economics, meteorology, healthcare, and many others, where understanding trends, patterns, and behaviors over time is crucial for prediction, analysis, and decision-making.

In this section, we'll dive deep into understanding time-series data, its components, and how to work with it effectively using Python.

What is Time-Series Data?

Time-series data is any data that is collected sequentially over time. The primary characteristic that distinguishes time-series data from other types of data is the temporal order. This ordering allows for the analysis of trends, cycles, and patterns that unfold over time. The key component here is time itself.

For instance, if we look at the daily temperature in a city, each measurement is taken at a specific point in time—let's say every 24 hours. These measurements together form a time-series dataset.

Time-series data can have a variety of different structures, depending on the context:

- **Irregular**: Data collected at inconsistent time intervals.

- **Regular**: Data collected at consistent intervals, such as every minute, hour, day, week, or month.

A time-series dataset often includes several different data points at each time interval, which could represent anything from stock prices to weather observations to sensor data.

Components of Time-Series Data

Time-series data is often made up of several key components, each of which reflects a different underlying pattern:

Trend: The long-term movement in the data. It can be increasing, decreasing, or remaining relatively stable over time. For example, in economic data, a steady increase in GDP over years is an example of a trend.

Seasonality: The repeating short-term patterns or cycles in the data. Seasonality is often linked to a time of the year, a week, or a day. For example, retail sales tend to increase during the holiday season, and temperatures typically rise in summer and fall in winter.

Noise: The random fluctuations in the data that cannot be explained by the trend or seasonality. Noise represents the unpredictable, non-systematic variations in time-series data.

Cyclic Patterns: Similar to seasonality, but unlike seasonality, cyclical patterns are not of fixed period. These patterns may be related to economic cycles, business cycles, or other long-term phenomena. Unlike seasonality, which happens at a predictable interval, cyclic patterns do not follow a consistent time period.

Level: This refers to the baseline value of the time-series. It is the central value around which the trend and seasonality fluctuate.

Examples of Time-Series Data

Time-series data can be found in many different fields and industries:

Finance: Stock prices, bond yields, currency exchange rates, and interest rates are all examples of financial time-series data. Financial data is collected at regular intervals (e.g., daily, minute-wise), and analysts often look for trends and patterns to predict future market behavior.

Weather and Climate: Temperature, rainfall, wind speed, and humidity are all examples of time-series data in meteorology. Such data is typically collected at regular intervals, like every hour or every day, to track changes over time and make forecasts.

Healthcare: Time-series data in healthcare may include patient vitals such as blood pressure, heart rate, or temperature over time. This data is crucial in diagnosing diseases and monitoring the progress of treatment.

Retail: Sales data from stores or online platforms are time-series data that helps businesses forecast demand, plan inventory, and optimize marketing strategies.

IoT (Internet of Things): Sensors placed in various environments often collect time-series data. For instance, a smart thermostat records temperature data over time to adjust heating and cooling.

Visualizing Time-Series Data

Visualizing time-series data is a critical step in understanding its structure. Common plots include:

Line Plot: This is the most basic and widely used plot to visualize time-series data. The x-axis represents time, and the y-axis represents the variable of interest (e.g., temperature, stock prices).

```
import matplotlib.pyplot as plt

# Example of a simple line plot
import pandas as pd

data = pd.read_csv('time_series_data.csv', parse_dates=['Date'], index_col='Date')
data['Value'].plot(figsize=(10, 6))
plt.title('Time-Series Data')
plt.xlabel('Date')
plt.ylabel('Value')
plt.show()
```

Seasonal Decomposition Plot: This plot splits the time-series data into trend, seasonal, and residual (noise) components. It's helpful for understanding the individual effects of trend and seasonality.

```
from statsmodels.tsa.seasonal import seasonal_decompose

# Decompose the time-series data
decomposition = seasonal_decompose(data['Value'], model='additive', period=12)

# Plot the decomposed components
decomposition.plot()
plt.show()
```

Autocorrelation Plot: This plot shows the correlation of the time-series data with its own past values. It's used to detect seasonality and cyclic patterns.

```
from pandas.plotting import lag_plot

# Plotting the autocorrelation of the time-series data
lag_plot(data['Value'])
plt.show()
```

Time-Series Analysis and Forecasting

Analyzing time-series data is important for understanding underlying patterns and predicting future values. Key steps in time-series analysis include:

Stationarity: A time-series is stationary if its properties (like mean, variance, and autocorrelation) do not change over time. Stationarity is important because many forecasting models (like ARIMA) assume that the time-series is stationary. If a series is non-stationary, transformations like differencing or logarithmic scaling may be used to make it stationary.

```
from statsmodels.tsa.stattools import adfuller

# Perform Augmented Dickey-Fuller test to check for stationarity
result = adfuller(data['Value'])
print('ADF Statistic:', result[0])
print('p-value:', result[1])
```

Decomposition: Decomposing the time-series data into trend, seasonal, and noise components can help in understanding the underlying factors contributing to the data's behavior.

Forecasting: Time-series forecasting techniques, such as ARIMA (AutoRegressive Integrated Moving Average), Exponential Smoothing, and machine learning models like Long Short-Term Memory (LSTM) networks, are widely used for predicting future values.

Time-series data is everywhere, and its analysis is critical for making informed decisions in fields ranging from finance to healthcare. In this section, we covered the key components of time-series data, including trend, seasonality, noise, and cyclic patterns. We also discussed visualization techniques, such as line plots and autocorrelation plots, to understand the data's structure and behavior.

By mastering time-series analysis and forecasting techniques, you will be able to extract valuable insights and predict future trends, helping you make data-driven decisions. Whether you're dealing with stock prices, weather data, or sensor readings, time-series analysis will provide you with the tools you need to make sense of temporal data and prepare for what lies ahead.

11.2 Data Preprocessing for Prediction Models

Data preprocessing is a critical step in any machine learning or artificial intelligence project, especially when working with time-series data. Raw data typically comes with various issues like missing values, outliers, and noise that can significantly affect the performance of prediction models. Effective preprocessing is essential to clean, transform, and structure the data in a way that makes it suitable for training prediction models, such as regression, classification, and forecasting.

In this section, we'll cover the essential steps involved in data preprocessing for time-series prediction models, focusing on key techniques to improve data quality and prepare the data for machine learning.

1. Handling Missing Values

One of the first challenges when working with time-series data is dealing with missing values. Missing data points are common in real-world datasets, and handling them properly is crucial to ensure that the model learns effectively. There are several strategies for dealing with missing values:

1.1 Removing Missing Data

If missing values are sparse and don't constitute a significant portion of your dataset, one option is to remove the rows (or columns) that contain missing data.

```
# Remove rows with missing values
data_cleaned = data.dropna()
```

1.2 Imputation

For time-series data, you might want to impute missing values rather than discarding them. Imputation refers to filling missing values with estimated values, which can be done using different techniques depending on the nature of your data.

Forward Fill: This method propagates the last observed value forward to fill missing values. It works well for many time-series datasets where data points are expected to be similar over short periods.

```
data['Value'] = data['Value'].fillna(method='ffill')
```

Backward Fill: This method fills missing values using the next available value.

```
data['Value'] = data['Value'].fillna(method='bfill')
```

Linear Interpolation: This approach estimates missing values based on a linear interpolation between the previous and next available data points.

```
data['Value'] = data['Value'].interpolate(method='linear')
```

Mean/Median Imputation: You can fill missing values with the mean or median of the observed values in the dataset.

```
data['Value'] = data['Value'].fillna(data['Value'].mean())
```

Choosing the right imputation strategy depends on the characteristics of your data and the problem you are solving.

2. Handling Outliers

Outliers are data points that significantly deviate from the overall pattern of the dataset. They can distort the results of predictive models, especially linear models and time-series forecasts. It's important to identify and handle outliers properly.

2.1 Identifying Outliers

You can use various techniques to identify outliers:

Visualization: Boxplots and scatter plots are effective for visually detecting outliers.

```
import seaborn as sns

sns.boxplot(x=data['Value'])
```

Statistical Methods: Outliers can also be identified using statistical methods, such as the Z-score or IQR (Interquartile Range).

For Z-score-based identification:

```
from scipy.stats import zscore

z_scores = zscore(data['Value'])
outliers = data[abs(z_scores) > 3]  # Z-score > 3 is typically considered an outlier
```

For IQR-based identification:

```
Q1 = data['Value'].quantile(0.25)
Q3 = data['Value'].quantile(0.75)
IQR = Q3 - Q1

outliers = data[(data['Value'] < (Q1 - 1.5 * IQR)) | (data['Value'] > (Q3 + 1.5 * IQR))]
```

2.2 Handling Outliers

Once outliers are identified, you have several options for handling them:

Removal: Simply remove the outliers if they are not meaningful or are data entry errors.

```
data_cleaned = data[~data.index.isin(outliers.index)]
```

Transformation: Use logarithmic or square root transformations to reduce the impact of extreme values.

```
import numpy as np
data['Value'] = np.log(data['Value'])
```

Imputation: Replace the outliers with a calculated value such as the median or a rolling mean.

```
data['Value'] = np.where(data['Value'] > threshold, data['Value'].median(), data['Value'])
```

3. Scaling and Normalizing Data

Machine learning models often perform better when the features (input variables) are on a similar scale. For time-series data, especially when using models that are sensitive to scale (like regression models or neural networks), it's essential to scale or normalize the data.

3.1 Min-Max Scaling

Min-max scaling rescales the data to a fixed range, typically [0, 1].

```
from sklearn.preprocessing import MinMaxScaler

scaler = MinMaxScaler(feature_range=(0, 1))
data['Scaled_Value'] = scaler.fit_transform(data[['Value']])
```

3.2 Standardization (Z-score Normalization)

Standardization transforms the data so that it has a mean of 0 and a standard deviation of 1, making it suitable for models that rely on Gaussian assumptions.

```
from sklearn.preprocessing import StandardScaler

scaler = StandardScaler()
data['Standardized_Value'] = scaler.fit_transform(data[['Value']])
```

Scaling is especially important when using machine learning algorithms like K-Nearest Neighbors (KNN), Support Vector Machines (SVM), or Neural Networks, as these algorithms are distance-based and can be affected by the magnitude of the features.

4. Feature Engineering for Time-Series Data

Feature engineering is the process of creating new features from the raw data that might help improve the model's performance. In time-series forecasting, this typically involves extracting temporal features from the data, such as:

4.1 Date/Time Features

Extract useful time-related features from the date and time column (if available). These could include:

- **Year, Month, Day of the week**: Helps to capture seasonality and time-related trends.
- **Hour of the day**: Useful for data collected at hourly intervals.
- **Week of the year**: Identifies periodicity in the data.

Is holiday flag: Flags whether the data point corresponds to a holiday.

```
data['Year'] = data.index.year
data['Month'] = data.index.month
data['DayOfWeek'] = data.index.dayofweek
data['IsHoliday'] = data['Date'].isin(holidays)
```

4.2 Lag Features

Time-series forecasting often involves using previous time steps to predict future ones. A common approach is to create lag features that represent the previous values of the time-series. For instance, you might want to create a feature that represents the value of the time series at the previous time step.

```
data['Lag_1'] = data['Value'].shift(1)
data['Lag_2'] = data['Value'].shift(2)
```

4.3 Rolling Features

Rolling features, such as the rolling mean or rolling standard deviation, are calculated using a sliding window over the time-series data. These features can capture the temporal trends in the data and help smooth out short-term fluctuations.

```
data['Rolling_Mean'] = data['Value'].rolling(window=5).mean()
data['Rolling_Std'] = data['Value'].rolling(window=5).std()
```

Rolling features are especially useful when the time-series data exhibits noise or short-term fluctuations that are not relevant for forecasting.

5. Train-Test Split

When working with time-series data, it's essential to split the data into training and testing sets without introducing data leakage. Time-based splitting should be used, where the training set consists of the earlier data points, and the test set consists of the later data points.

```
train_size = int(len(data) * 0.8)
train, test = data[:train_size], data[train_size:]
```

Data preprocessing for time-series prediction models is an essential step that determines the quality and reliability of your model's predictions. By handling missing values, outliers, and scaling the data, you ensure that the model learns from clean and meaningful information. Feature engineering, such as adding date/time features, lag features, and rolling statistics, allows the model to capture the temporal patterns and trends inherent in the data.

A well-preprocessed dataset is key to improving the accuracy and performance of your prediction models. With the right preprocessing techniques in place, you can move forward to build robust time-series forecasting models that can generate accurate predictions for the future.

11.3 Implementing a Predictive Model with Scikit-Learn

Building a predictive model is a crucial step in leveraging time-series data for forecasting and decision-making. Scikit-learn, a powerful Python library for machine learning, offers a wide range of tools to implement various predictive models. In this section, we will walk through the process of implementing a predictive model for time-series forecasting using Scikit-learn. We will focus on applying a machine learning algorithm to predict future values of a time-series dataset.

Step-by-Step Process for Implementing a Predictive Model

To implement a predictive model, we need to follow a structured process:

Prepare the Data: We must first preprocess the time-series data, clean missing values, remove outliers, and generate relevant features (such as lag and rolling features). This ensures that the dataset is ready for model training.

Choose a Machine Learning Model: Scikit-learn provides several regression algorithms that can be used for time-series forecasting. For simplicity, we'll use Linear Regression as a starting point. Linear regression is a good choice when we expect linear relationships between the input features and the target variable. Other models can also be explored later based on performance.

Split the Data into Training and Testing Sets: It's essential to split the data chronologically because time-series data is sequential. This ensures that the training set contains the earlier data points, and the test set contains the later data points, to simulate real-world forecasting.

Train the Model: After splitting the data, we will train the model on the training data.

Evaluate the Model: Once the model is trained, we will evaluate its performance using appropriate metrics (such as Mean Squared Error or R^2). We will use the test set to simulate real-time prediction and assess how well the model generalizes to unseen data.

1. Preparing the Data

First, we need to import the necessary libraries and preprocess the data. Let's assume we are working with a time-series dataset (e.g., daily sales, stock prices, etc.).

```
import pandas as pd
import numpy as np
import matplotlib.pyplot as plt
from sklearn.model_selection import train_test_split
from sklearn.linear_model import LinearRegression
from sklearn.metrics import mean_squared_error, r2_score

# Load the dataset
data = pd.read_csv('time_series_data.csv', parse_dates=['Date'], index_col='Date')

# Check for missing values and handle them (for simplicity, we will use forward fill)
data['Value'] = data['Value'].fillna(method='ffill')

# Feature engineering: create lag features and rolling mean features
data['Lag_1'] = data['Value'].shift(1)
data['Lag_2'] = data['Value'].shift(2)
data['Rolling_Mean_3'] = data['Value'].rolling(window=3).mean()

# Drop rows with NaN values due to lagging
data.dropna(inplace=True)
```

2. Splitting the Data into Training and Testing Sets

When working with time-series data, it is important to split the dataset chronologically. This means the training data consists of earlier points in time, and the test data consists of later points in time. Here, we split the data into training and test sets, with the training set being 80% of the data and the test set the remaining 20%.

```
# Split the data into training and testing sets (chronologically)
train_size = int(len(data) * 0.8)
train, test = data[:train_size], data[train_size:]

# Define features (X) and target variable (y)
X_train = train[['Lag_1', 'Lag_2', 'Rolling_Mean_3']]
y_train = train['Value']
X_test = test[['Lag_1', 'Lag_2', 'Rolling_Mean_3']]
y_test = test['Value']
```

3. Choosing and Training the Model

For this example, we will use Linear Regression, a simple and effective machine learning model. The model will learn the relationship between the lagged values and the rolling mean of the data to predict the target variable (Value).

```
# Instantiate the Linear Regression model
model = LinearRegression()

# Train the model on the training data
model.fit(X_train, y_train)
```

4. Making Predictions

Once the model is trained, we can use it to make predictions on the test set. This simulates the process of forecasting future values.

```
# Make predictions on the test set
y_pred = model.predict(X_test)
```

5. Evaluating the Model

After making predictions, we need to evaluate the performance of the model. Common evaluation metrics for regression tasks include:

Mean Squared Error (MSE): Measures the average squared difference between the actual and predicted values. Lower MSE indicates a better fit.

R^2 (Coefficient of Determination): Represents how well the model explains the variability in the target variable. An R^2 value of 1 indicates perfect predictions, while 0 means the model performs no better than simply predicting the mean of the target.

```
# Calculate the Mean Squared Error (MSE) and R² score
mse = mean_squared_error(y_test, y_pred)
r2 = r2_score(y_test, y_pred)

print(f'Mean Squared Error (MSE): {mse}')
print(f'R² Score: {r2}')
```

6. Visualizing the Results

It's helpful to visualize the model's performance by plotting the actual values against the predicted values. This allows us to visually assess how well the model fits the data and whether it captures the underlying patterns.

```python
# Plot the actual vs predicted values
plt.figure(figsize=(10, 6))
plt.plot(test.index, y_test, label='Actual Values', color='blue')
plt.plot(test.index, y_pred, label='Predicted Values', color='red', linestyle='--')
plt.title('Actual vs Predicted Values')
plt.xlabel('Date')
plt.ylabel('Value')
plt.legend()
plt.show()
```

Optimizing the Model

After implementing the initial predictive model, you may want to experiment with different machine learning algorithms and techniques to improve performance. Here are some options:

Model Tuning: Try hyperparameter tuning for algorithms like Random Forests, Gradient Boosting, or SVR (Support Vector Regression) to optimize performance.

Feature Engineering: Introduce more advanced features, such as rolling windows, external variables (weather data, economic indicators), or more sophisticated time-based features (seasonality, holidays).

Time-Series Models: For better accuracy, especially for highly seasonal data, consider more advanced models specifically designed for time-series forecasting, such as ARIMA, SARIMA, or XGBoost for time-series.

Cross-Validation: Use techniques like TimeSeriesSplit in Scikit-learn for more robust evaluation in time-series data.

In this section, we demonstrated how to implement a predictive model using Scikit-learn for time-series data. We went through the process of preparing and preprocessing the data, creating features, splitting the data into training and testing sets, training a linear regression model, and evaluating the model's performance.

By following these steps, you can start predicting future values of time-series data, such as stock prices, sales data, and more. While Linear Regression is a good starting point, you can experiment with other algorithms, improve your feature engineering, and fine-tune your models for better performance.

11.4 Visualizing Predictions

Visualization plays a crucial role in understanding how well a predictive model is performing, especially in the context of time-series forecasting. By plotting the predictions alongside actual values, we can assess the model's accuracy, identify trends, and detect patterns that may not be captured. Visualizing predictions provides valuable insights into how the model behaves over time and whether it captures the underlying trends or seasonal effects.

In this section, we'll explore how to visualize predictions effectively, using various types of plots and techniques. We will focus on visualizing the actual vs. predicted values, assessing the forecasting errors, and interpreting trend patterns using Python's visualization libraries.

1. Visualizing Actual vs. Predicted Values

The first and most basic visualization involves plotting both the actual and predicted values over time. This gives us a clear view of how the model is performing and how close the predictions are to the actual values.

1.1 Plotting Actual vs. Predicted Values

```
import matplotlib.pyplot as plt

# Plot the actual vs predicted values
plt.figure(figsize=(12, 6))
plt.plot(test.index, y_test, label='Actual Values', color='blue')
plt.plot(test.index, y_pred, label='Predicted Values', color='red', linestyle='--')
plt.title('Actual vs Predicted Values')
plt.xlabel('Date')
plt.ylabel('Value')
plt.legend()
```

```
plt.grid(True)
plt.show()
```

Explanation:

- The blue line represents the actual values from the test dataset.
- The red dashed line represents the predicted values from the model.
- By comparing these two lines, we can visually assess how well the model follows the pattern of the actual data.

If the two lines are close together, the model has learned the underlying trends of the data effectively. If they are far apart, the model is likely underperforming.

2. Visualizing Forecast Errors

Forecasting errors are the differences between the actual and predicted values. Plotting the errors can provide insight into whether the model consistently overestimates or underestimates the values and if any patterns exist in the errors (such as seasonality or trends).

2.1 Calculating and Plotting the Errors

```
# Calculate the errors (residuals)
errors = y_test - y_pred

# Plot the forecast errors
plt.figure(figsize=(12, 6))
plt.plot(test.index, errors, label='Forecast Errors', color='orange')
plt.axhline(y=0, color='black', linestyle='--')
plt.title('Forecasting Errors')
plt.xlabel('Date')
plt.ylabel('Error (Actual - Predicted)')
plt.legend()
plt.grid(True)
plt.show()
```

Explanation:

- The orange line represents the forecast errors.

- The horizontal dashed black line represents zero error. Points above this line indicate overestimations (positive error), while points below indicate underestimations (negative error).

If the forecast errors are randomly distributed around zero, it suggests that the model is unbiased. However, if there's a clear pattern (e.g., larger errors at specific times), it indicates that the model may not have fully captured the underlying seasonality or trends.

3. Visualizing Rolling Forecasts

A rolling forecast refers to the process of making predictions for future time periods using a sliding window of training data. You can visualize a rolling forecast by plotting the predictions made at each step, especially for out-of-sample data (i.e., for time points beyond the training set).

3.1 Rolling Forecast Visualization

```
# Plot rolling forecast (predictions made over time)
plt.figure(figsize=(12, 6))
plt.plot(train.index, y_train, label='Training Data', color='blue')
plt.plot(test.index, y_test, label='Actual Values', color='green')
plt.plot(test.index, y_pred, label='Rolling Predictions', color='red', linestyle='--')
plt.title('Rolling Forecast: Actual vs Predicted')
plt.xlabel('Date')
plt.ylabel('Value')
plt.legend()
plt.grid(True)
plt.show()
```

Explanation:

- The blue line represents the training data (used to train the model).
- The green line shows the actual values from the test set.
- The red dashed line represents the predictions made by the model for the test data.

This visualization helps illustrate how the model progressively forecasts the future values. It can be particularly useful for time-series models that make predictions incrementally as new data becomes available.

4. Visualizing Model Performance with Confidence Intervals

For certain types of models (such as regression models), you can also plot confidence intervals around the predicted values. Confidence intervals provide a range of values within which the true value is likely to fall. This can be especially helpful for understanding the uncertainty of the model's predictions.

4.1 Plotting Predictions with Confidence Intervals

```
from sklearn.model_selection import train_test_split
from sklearn.linear_model import LinearRegression
import numpy as np

# Calculate the standard deviation of the errors
std_error = np.std(errors)

# Generate upper and lower confidence intervals (assuming normal distribution of
errors)
confidence_interval_upper = y_pred + 1.96 * std_error
confidence_interval_lower = y_pred - 1.96 * std_error

# Plot predictions with confidence intervals
plt.figure(figsize=(12, 6))
plt.plot(test.index, y_test, label='Actual Values', color='green')
plt.plot(test.index, y_pred, label='Predicted Values', color='red', linestyle='--')
plt.fill_between(test.index,    confidence_interval_lower,    confidence_interval_upper,
color='gray', alpha=0.3, label='95% Confidence Interval')
plt.title('Predictions with 95% Confidence Interval')
plt.xlabel('Date')
plt.ylabel('Value')
plt.legend()
plt.grid(True)
plt.show()
```

Explanation:

- The green line represents actual values.
- The red dashed line shows predicted values.
- The gray shaded area represents the 95% confidence interval, which means that 95% of the time, the actual values will fall within this range.

This visualization allows us to assess not only the accuracy of the predictions but also the degree of certainty about those predictions. The narrower the confidence interval, the more confident the model is about its predictions.

5. Visualizing Seasonal and Trend Components

In some cases, it might be helpful to visualize the trend and seasonal components of your time-series data. Decomposition techniques can help break down a time-series into three main components: trend, seasonality, and residual (noise). This can be useful for understanding the underlying patterns in the data and for validating whether the model captures these patterns.

5.1 Decomposing the Time-Series

```
from statsmodels.tsa.seasonal import seasonal_decompose

# Decompose the time-series data into trend, seasonal, and residual components
decomposition = seasonal_decompose(data['Value'], model='additive', period=365)

# Plot the decomposed components
plt.figure(figsize=(12, 8))
plt.subplot(411)
plt.plot(decomposition.observed, label='Observed')
plt.legend(loc='best')
plt.subplot(412)
plt.plot(decomposition.trend, label='Trend')
plt.legend(loc='best')
plt.subplot(413)
plt.plot(decomposition.seasonal, label='Seasonal')
plt.legend(loc='best')
plt.subplot(414)
plt.plot(decomposition.resid, label='Residual')
plt.legend(loc='best')
plt.tight_layout()
plt.show()
```

Explanation:

- The observed plot shows the original time-series data.

- The trend plot shows the long-term movement in the data.
- The seasonal plot represents recurring patterns or seasonality.
- The residual plot shows the noise or unexplained variation.

Decomposition helps to visually separate the different aspects of the time-series, allowing you to identify whether your predictive model is capturing the seasonal and trend components.

Visualizing predictions is a powerful tool for evaluating the performance of time-series forecasting models. By plotting actual vs. predicted values, forecasting errors, and confidence intervals, you can assess how well your model is performing and where improvements might be needed. Additionally, decomposing time-series data into trend, seasonal, and residual components provides valuable insights into the underlying patterns of the data, enabling you to create more accurate predictive models.

Visualization is an essential part of any model evaluation process, and by incorporating these techniques, you can gain a deeper understanding of how your predictive models behave and how well they generalize to unseen data.

12. Deploying Your AI Model

Building a successful AI model is just the first step; the real challenge comes in deploying it for real-world use. In this chapter, you'll learn how to take your trained AI model and deploy it so that it can be accessed and used by others. You'll explore key deployment concepts, including creating a web-based interface, setting up APIs, and integrating your model into a user-friendly application. With tools like Flask for web development and Heroku for cloud deployment, you'll get hands-on experience with deploying your model in a way that's scalable and efficient. By the end of this chapter, you'll have the skills to turn your AI projects into fully functioning applications, ready for real-world deployment.

12.1 Introduction to Model Deployment

Model deployment is the process of making a machine learning model available for use in a production environment, where it can interact with real-world data and provide insights, predictions, or automation. Once a model has been developed, trained, and evaluated, the next critical step is deployment—ensuring that the model can be accessed, used, and updated effectively by other systems or users.

In the context of Artificial Intelligence (AI) and machine learning (ML), deployment refers to the integration of a trained model into a real-world application, whether it's a web service, a mobile app, or an embedded system. Deployment not only involves delivering the model but also ensuring that it works in the production environment in a reliable, scalable, and efficient manner.

Why Model Deployment is Crucial

Deployment is essential for transforming machine learning and AI models from theoretical concepts to practical, usable tools. A model may be able to achieve high accuracy during testing and evaluation, but in a real-world environment, it must perform consistently and efficiently. Deployment also allows businesses, researchers, or developers to apply the model's predictions to solve specific problems or drive key decisions.

Here are some reasons why deployment is an essential phase in the ML workflow:

Real-World Application: A model needs to be deployed so that it can be used to make predictions, automate processes, or support decision-making in real-time applications.

Continuous Updates: In real-world environments, data continuously changes. Therefore, models need to be updated periodically to remain effective and accurate. A robust deployment pipeline can help manage updates and improvements.

Scalability and Accessibility: Deployment enables the model to be accessed by different users or systems, making it scalable across various use cases (e.g., web apps, business dashboards, IoT devices).

Efficiency: Deploying a model properly ensures it runs efficiently, making predictions or executing tasks with minimal delays.

Business Value: Successful deployment of a model directly translates to measurable business value—whether that's driving revenue, reducing costs, or improving user experience.

Stages of Model Deployment

Model deployment involves several stages that help transition a model from a development environment to a production environment. These stages typically include:

Pre-Deployment:

- **Model Selection**: Selecting the best model based on performance metrics.
- **Model Evaluation**: Testing and validating the model on unseen data to ensure it meets desired accuracy and reliability.
- **Model Packaging**: The model is packaged into a format that can be easily transferred and used in the deployment environment (e.g., a serialized file or a containerized service).

Deployment:

- **Integration**: The model is integrated with other systems, such as a web service or application. This could be an API, a cloud service, or a microservice.
- **Serving**: The model is made available to external users or systems, often via a REST API or similar interface.
- **Infrastructure Setup**: This includes setting up the necessary cloud resources (e.g., compute, storage), databases, and networking configurations to support the model in production.

Post-Deployment:

- **Monitoring**: Once the model is deployed, continuous monitoring is necessary to track its performance, ensure its reliability, and catch potential issues (such as model drift, where the model's performance degrades over time).
- **Scaling**: If the model needs to handle an increasing volume of requests, it must be scalable. Auto-scaling and load balancing may be used to ensure the model can handle varying workloads.
- **Model Updates**: As new data comes in or the business requirements evolve, the model may need to be retrained or adjusted. A proper deployment pipeline ensures that updates can be made with minimal downtime or disruption.
- **Logging and Feedback**: Continuous feedback from users or other systems can help refine the model. It's important to log the model's predictions and compare them with real-world outcomes to further improve its accuracy.

Deployment Methods

There are several ways to deploy machine learning models, depending on the needs of the application and infrastructure. Here are a few common deployment methods:

Batch Deployment:

In batch deployment, predictions are made on a batch of data at regular intervals, rather than in real-time. This method is commonly used for processes like daily reports, trend analysis, and scheduled predictions.

Real-Time Deployment:

In real-time deployment, the model makes predictions on live, incoming data as soon as it is available. This is used for applications where quick decisions are required, such as fraud detection, recommendation systems, and dynamic pricing.

Edge Deployment:

In edge deployment, the model is deployed directly on devices (e.g., IoT devices, mobile phones) rather than on a server or cloud. This is useful in scenarios where low latency and offline prediction are necessary, such as in autonomous vehicles or remote sensors.

Cloud Deployment:

Cloud-based deployment is one of the most popular methods, where the model is hosted on a cloud service (such as AWS, Google Cloud, or Microsoft Azure). This approach offers scalability, flexibility, and access to cloud-native services like compute, storage, and machine learning tools.

Deployment Challenges

While deploying a model is essential, it comes with its own set of challenges. Some of these challenges include:

Model Drift: Over time, a model's performance can degrade as the underlying data changes. Monitoring and retraining the model periodically are necessary to prevent this.

Scalability: Ensuring the model can handle large volumes of data or user requests without performance degradation.

Latency: Minimizing the delay between receiving input data and making predictions. In real-time applications, high latency can be a significant issue.

Version Control: Managing different versions of the model and ensuring smooth transitions between updates can be complex, particularly when dealing with multiple teams or environments.

Security: Ensuring that the model and its predictions are secure and that sensitive data is protected during inference and storage.

Model Interpretability: In many cases, it is important to be able to explain the model's decisions, especially in high-stakes environments like healthcare or finance. This can be more challenging for complex models like deep learning.

Tools for Model Deployment

There are several tools and frameworks available to facilitate model deployment. Some of the popular ones include:

Flask and FastAPI: These are lightweight Python web frameworks for building APIs to serve machine learning models. Flask is simple and easy to use, while FastAPI is optimized for speed.

TensorFlow Serving: A tool designed for serving TensorFlow models in production environments.

Docker: Docker is used to package a model along with its dependencies into a container, which can be deployed consistently across different environments.

Kubernetes: For scaling containerized applications, Kubernetes is widely used. It orchestrates the deployment, scaling, and management of containerized services.

MLflow: An open-source platform that manages the machine learning lifecycle, including deployment, tracking, and packaging.

AWS SageMaker and Google AI Platform: These cloud services provide managed environments for deploying, scaling, and monitoring machine learning models.

Model deployment is the final, but crucial, step in taking an AI model from the development phase to real-world application. Understanding the deployment process— pre-deployment preparation, integration, monitoring, scaling, and post-deployment maintenance—is essential for ensuring the model's success in production. Whether you're deploying a model for real-time use, batch processing, or edge devices, careful planning and execution will enable you to effectively leverage your AI model's full potential.

12.2 Using Flask to Create an AI API

Flask is a lightweight, easy-to-use Python web framework that is ideal for creating APIs to serve machine learning models. It allows you to wrap your trained machine learning models into an API (Application Programming Interface) that can be accessed by other systems or applications. By using Flask, you can take your trained AI model, deploy it as a service, and provide real-time predictions via HTTP requests.

In this section, we'll walk through the process of creating an AI-powered API using Flask. This will involve loading a trained machine learning model, building the API, and serving predictions through HTTP requests.

Why Flask for AI APIs?

Flask is an excellent choice for serving machine learning models because:

- **Lightweight and Simple**: Flask is minimalistic, which makes it fast to get started. It doesn't impose too many constraints, allowing for flexibility when building APIs.
- **Extensible**: While Flask is simple, it also has many extensions that can add features like authentication, database integration, and more.
- **Easy to Deploy**: Flask applications can be deployed easily to cloud services like AWS, Google Cloud, or on-premise servers.
- **Well-Suited for REST APIs**: Flask is ideal for creating RESTful APIs, which are commonly used to serve AI models, enabling them to be accessed by various clients like web apps, mobile apps, or other services.

Steps to Create an AI API using Flask

1. Install Flask and Required Libraries

To create an API using Flask, you need to install Flask itself, along with other dependencies such as NumPy, Pandas, or any other libraries that your AI model may require. Additionally, you'll need to have your trained model saved, typically as a .pkl or .h5 file.

Start by installing Flask and any other necessary libraries using pip:

```
pip install Flask scikit-learn numpy pandas
```

If you're using a deep learning model, you may also need libraries like TensorFlow or PyTorch.

2. Load Your Trained Model

Before creating the API, you need to load your pre-trained machine learning model. For this example, let's assume you've trained a simple model using scikit-learn and saved it as a .pkl file.

Here's how you can load the model using the joblib library:

```
import joblib

# Load the trained model
model = joblib.load('path_to_your_trained_model.pkl')
```

If you are using a deep learning model in TensorFlow or Keras, you would load it like this:

```
from tensorflow.keras.models import load_model

# Load a TensorFlow/Keras model
model = load_model('path_to_your_model.h5')
```

3. Define the Flask API

Now, let's set up a Flask app and define the routes for serving predictions. A simple structure would involve one route (/predict) that receives data as input, runs the prediction through the model, and returns the output.

Here's an example of a simple Flask API to serve the model:

```
from flask import Flask, request, jsonify
import joblib
import numpy as np

# Initialize Flask app
app = Flask(__name__)

# Load the trained machine learning model
model = joblib.load('path_to_your_trained_model.pkl')

@app.route('/')
def home():
    return "Welcome to the AI model API!"

@app.route('/predict', methods=['POST'])
def predict():
    try:
        # Get the JSON data from the request
        data = request.get_json()

        # Extract features from the data
        # Assuming the data is a list of feature values
        features = np.array(data['features']).reshape(1, -1)
```

```
    # Make a prediction using the model
    prediction = model.predict(features)

    # Return the prediction as a JSON response
    return jsonify({'prediction': prediction[0]})

  except Exception as e:
    # Handle exceptions and errors gracefully
    return jsonify({'error': str(e)}), 400

if __name__ == '__main__':
  # Run the Flask app
  app.run(debug=True)
```

Explanation:

Flask App Setup: The Flask object initializes the web application. @app.route decorators define the different routes, or endpoints, of the API.

Home Route: The / route is a simple welcome message to test if the API is running correctly.

Prediction Route: The /predict route handles POST requests and accepts JSON data. This route:

- Retrieves input data (features) from the request.
- Reshapes it into the format required by the model.
- Passes the data to the model to get the prediction.
- Returns the prediction as a JSON response.

Error Handling: If there's any issue with the data or prediction, an error message is returned with a 400 HTTP status code.

4. Test Your Flask API Locally

Once you have your Flask app defined, you can run the application locally. Flask will start a local server that listens for incoming HTTP requests.

Run the Flask app using:

```
python app.py
```

Your API should now be running on http://127.0.0.1:5000/. You can test the /predict route using a tool like Postman or cURL to send a POST request with JSON data.

Here's an example of sending a POST request using cURL:

```
curl -X POST -H "Content-Type: application/json" -d '{"features": [1.2, 3.4, 5.6, 7.8]}' http://127.0.0.1:5000/predict
```

This would return a JSON response with the model's prediction:

```
{
  "prediction": 15.6
}
```

5. Deploying the Flask API

Once you've tested your API locally and everything is working, the next step is to deploy it to a production environment so it can be accessed by others.

You can deploy your Flask app to cloud services such as Heroku, AWS, Google Cloud, or Microsoft Azure. Let's briefly discuss the deployment process for Heroku, which is one of the simplest cloud platforms for Flask apps.

Create a requirements.txt file: This file lists all the libraries your app depends on. You can generate it using:

```
pip freeze > requirements.txt
```

Create a Procfile: This file tells Heroku how to run your app. For a Flask app, the content of the Procfile would be:

```
web: python app.py
```

Initialize a Git Repository:

```
git init
git add .
git commit -m "Initial commit"
```

Create a Heroku App:

```
heroku create your-app-name
```

Deploy to Heroku:

```
git push heroku master
```

Open the deployed app:

```
heroku open
```

Your Flask app will now be accessible from a public URL, and you can make API calls to the /predict endpoint from anywhere.

Using Flask to create an AI-powered API is a straightforward and effective way to serve machine learning models. Flask provides the flexibility and simplicity needed to deploy models quickly, and it works seamlessly with Python's machine learning ecosystem. Once your API is running, you can expose your trained model to any application that can make HTTP requests, making it an ideal solution for real-time predictions and integration into larger systems.

By following the steps outlined in this section, you've learned how to:

- Create a basic Flask API to serve an AI model.
- Test the API locally and send prediction requests.
- Deploy the Flask app to a cloud platform like Heroku for production use.

Whether you are building a recommendation system, a predictive model, or a chatbot, Flask can be the foundation for serving your AI model in production environments.

12.3 Building a Web Interface for Your AI Model

Creating a web interface for your AI model allows users to interact with your machine learning model through a user-friendly graphical interface, without needing to interact with code or APIs directly. Whether you're building a recommendation system, a chatbot, or an image classifier, a web interface provides a way to present results and collect input data from users in an intuitive manner.

In this section, we'll walk through how to build a simple web interface for your AI model using Flask and HTML/CSS. The goal is to have a clean, functional, and interactive interface where users can input data, submit it to the model, and view the model's prediction in response.

Why Build a Web Interface?

A web interface is essential for making your AI model accessible to a broader audience. While APIs are great for programmatically integrating models into applications, a web interface allows non-technical users to easily interact with the model. Some reasons to create a web interface for your AI model include:

- **Ease of Use**: A well-designed web interface makes interacting with your model more accessible, even to users without technical expertise.
- **User Interaction**: A web interface allows users to input data and interact with your model in real-time, which is especially useful for models that require human input, such as chatbots or recommendation systems.
- **Visualization**: Web interfaces make it easier to visualize predictions and present the results in a clear and concise manner.
- **Interactivity**: A web app enables dynamic, interactive features like form submissions, real-time predictions, and result displays.

Steps to Build a Web Interface for Your AI Model

1. Set Up the Flask App

Before building the web interface, ensure that you have a working Flask API (as discussed in the previous section). You will need to modify the Flask app slightly to serve the web pages in addition to serving predictions.

Here's a simple Flask app that includes a route to serve the HTML interface and a route to handle predictions:

```python
from flask import Flask, render_template, request, jsonify
import joblib
import numpy as np

# Initialize Flask app
app = Flask(__name__)

# Load the trained machine learning model
model = joblib.load('path_to_your_trained_model.pkl')

# Route to serve the homepage with the form
@app.route('/')
def home():
    return render_template('index.html')

# Route to handle the prediction request
@app.route('/predict', methods=['POST'])
def predict():
    try:
        # Get the data from the HTML form
        features = [float(x) for x in request.form.values()]
        features = np.array(features).reshape(1, -1)

        # Make the prediction using the model
        prediction = model.predict(features)

        # Render the prediction on a new page
        return render_template('result.html', prediction=prediction[0])

    except Exception as e:
        # Handle exceptions gracefully
        return jsonify({'error': str(e)}), 400

if __name__ == '__main__':
    app.run(debug=True)
```

Explanation:

- **home():** This route serves the homepage, which will be the HTML form where users input their data.
- **predict():** This route handles the prediction. It receives data from the form, reshapes it, runs it through the model, and returns the prediction. The result is displayed on a new webpage.

Now, let's create the HTML templates for the web interface.

2. Creating the Web Interface

Flask uses Jinja2 templating, which allows you to create dynamic HTML pages by embedding Python code. You'll need to create two HTML files: one for the input form (index.html) and one for displaying the results (result.html).

index.html (The Input Form):

```html
<!DOCTYPE html>
<html lang="en">
<head>
    <meta charset="UTF-8">
    <meta name="viewport" content="width=device-width, initial-scale=1.0">
    <title>AI Model Interface</title>
    <link rel="stylesheet" href="styles.css">
</head>
<body>
    <div class="container">
        <h1>AI Model Prediction</h1>
        <form action="/predict" method="POST">
            <label for="feature1">Feature 1:</label>
            <input type="number" name="feature1" required>

            <label for="feature2">Feature 2:</label>
            <input type="number" name="feature2" required>

            <label for="feature3">Feature 3:</label>
            <input type="number" name="feature3" required>

            <label for="feature4">Feature 4:</label>
            <input type="number" name="feature4" required>
```

```
            <button type="submit">Predict</button>
        </form>
    </div>
</body>
</html>
```

result.html (Displaying the Prediction):

```
<!DOCTYPE html>
<html lang="en">
<head>
    <meta charset="UTF-8">
    <meta name="viewport" content="width=device-width, initial-scale=1.0">
    <title>Prediction Result</title>
    <link rel="stylesheet" href="styles.css">
</head>
<body>
    <div class="container">
        <h1>Prediction Result</h1>
        <p><strong>Prediction:</strong> {{ prediction }}</p>
        <a href="/">Make Another Prediction</a>
    </div>
</body>
</html>
```

Explanation:

- **index.html**: This page contains a form with input fields for the features that will be used for prediction. Each feature is represented by an input field where the user can enter numeric values.
- **result.html**: This page displays the prediction made by the AI model. The prediction is passed to the template using the render_template() function in Flask, and it's displayed dynamically within the HTML.

You can customize the layout and add more features or input fields depending on the complexity of your model.

3. Adding Styling to Your Web Interface

While not essential for functionality, adding some basic CSS can help improve the user experience. Here's a simple styles.css file to give your web interface a clean and modern look:

```css
/* styles.css */
body {
    font-family: Arial, sans-serif;
    background-color: #f4f4f9;
    margin: 0;
    padding: 0;
}

.container {
    width: 80%;
    margin: 0 auto;
    padding: 30px;
    text-align: center;
}

h1 {
    color: #333;
}

form {
    display: flex;
    flex-direction: column;
    align-items: center;
    margin-top: 20px;
}

label {
    font-size: 18px;
    margin: 5px;
}

input[type="number"] {
    padding: 10px;
    margin: 5px;
    width: 50%;
    font-size: 16px;
```

```
}

button {
    padding: 12px 30px;
    background-color: #4CAF50;
    color: white;
    font-size: 16px;
    border: none;
    cursor: pointer;
    margin-top: 20px;
}

button:hover {
    background-color: #45a049;
}

a {
    text-decoration: none;
    font-size: 18px;
    color: #4CAF50;
}

a:hover {
    color: #45a049;
}
```

Explanation of Styles:

- **body**: Sets the overall font and background color for the page.
- **.container**: Centers the content and adds padding around the form.
- **form**: Flexbox is used to align the form elements in a column.
- **input and button**: Basic styling to make the inputs and buttons more visually appealing.

4. Running the Flask App

Once everything is set up, you can run your Flask app as usual:

```
python app.py
```

This will launch your web interface, and you can access it by going to http://127.0.0.1:5000/ in your browser. The input form will allow users to enter data, submit it to the AI model, and see the prediction result on a new page.

Building a web interface for your AI model is a great way to make it accessible to non-technical users. By using Flask and HTML/CSS, you can create a simple but functional web app where users can input data and receive model predictions in real-time. This is an essential step for deploying machine learning models in real-world applications, as it allows interaction with your model in an intuitive and user-friendly manner.

Key takeaways from this section:

- You've learned how to set up a Flask app to serve a machine learning model via a web interface.
- You've seen how to create HTML templates for input and results.
- You've also applied basic styling to enhance the user experience.

With this web interface, you can now share your AI model with others, enabling them to easily interact with your model and get predictions.

12.4 Hosting Your AI Model Online

Once you've developed your AI model and created a web interface for it, the next step is to make it accessible to users beyond your local machine. Hosting your AI model online allows people from anywhere in the world to interact with it through a web interface, making your project more functional and scalable.

In this section, we'll walk through the steps to deploy your AI model online, including deploying it on popular cloud platforms like Heroku, AWS, and Google Cloud, and ensuring that your model runs smoothly in a production environment.

Why Host Your AI Model Online?

Hosting your AI model online provides several advantages:

- **Scalability**: With online hosting, your AI model can handle more users and requests simultaneously, depending on the resources you allocate.

- **Accessibility**: Users can access your model from anywhere in the world, making it more versatile.
- **Reliability**: Hosting services are typically more reliable than running models on local machines, ensuring better uptime and performance.
- **Collaboration**: You can share your model with others easily, allowing for collaboration and user feedback.

There are several options for hosting AI models online, and we will explore a few common platforms that are well-suited for deploying machine learning applications.

1. Hosting on Heroku

Heroku is a cloud platform that allows you to deploy, manage, and scale applications. It's beginner-friendly and has excellent integration with Python apps. Hosting an AI model on Heroku is relatively straightforward, especially for small to medium-sized applications.

Steps to Host on Heroku:

Install Heroku CLI:

Download and install the Heroku Command Line Interface (CLI).

Create a requirements.txt file:

This file lists all the dependencies your project needs to run. You can generate it using the following command:

```
pip freeze > requirements.txt
```

Ensure that the file includes the necessary libraries like Flask, scikit-learn, pandas, numpy, etc.

Create a Procfile:

The Procfile tells Heroku how to run your application. For a Flask app, it usually contains:

```
web: python app.py
```

Deploy to Heroku:

Initialize a Git repository for your project (if you haven't already):

```
git init
```

Add all your project files and commit them:

```
git add .
git commit -m "Initial commit"
```

Log in to Heroku:

```
heroku login
```

Create a new Heroku app:

```
heroku create your-app-name
```

Deploy your app:

```
git push heroku master
```

Open the Application:

Once your app is deployed, you can open it in the browser:

```
heroku open
```

2. Hosting on AWS (Amazon Web Services)

AWS offers a wide range of hosting services. Two of the most common services for hosting machine learning models are EC2 (Elastic Compute Cloud) for creating a virtual server, and Elastic Beanstalk for easy app deployment.

Steps to Host on AWS EC2:

Set Up an EC2 Instance:

- Log in to your AWS Console.
- Navigate to EC2 and click Launch Instance.
- Select an AMI (Amazon Machine Image) such as Ubuntu or Amazon Linux.
- Choose an instance type (e.g., t2.micro for small-scale use).
- Configure your instance, including security groups (make sure port 5000 is open for Flask).
- Create a key pair (or use an existing one) to securely access the instance.

Connect to Your EC2 Instance:

After launching your instance, connect to it using SSH. On your local terminal, run:

```
ssh -i your-key.pem ubuntu@your-ec2-public-ip
```

Set Up the Environment:

On the EC2 instance, install Python and necessary libraries (e.g., Flask, numpy, scikit-learn):

```
sudo apt-get update
sudo apt-get install python3-pip
pip3 install Flask numpy scikit-learn
```

Upload Your Files:

You can upload your model files (Python scripts, trained model, etc.) to the EC2 instance using SCP or an SFTP client.

Run the Flask App:

Start the Flask app on the EC2 instance:

```
python3 app.py
```

Access the App:

Open your browser and enter your EC2 instance's public IP address (e.g., http://<EC2_PUBLIC_IP>:5000) to access the model.

3. Hosting on Google Cloud Platform (GCP)

Google Cloud provides several services for deploying AI models, such as Google App Engine and Google Kubernetes Engine. Here, we'll focus on deploying a simple Flask app using Google App Engine.

Steps to Host on Google Cloud:

Set Up Google Cloud Project:

- Sign in to your Google Cloud Console.
- Create a new project and enable App Engine.
- Set up billing for your account if necessary.

Install Google Cloud SDK:

Install the Google Cloud SDK on your local machine.

Authenticate by running:

```
gcloud auth login
```

Create an app.yaml File:

The app.yaml file tells Google Cloud how to deploy your application. Here's a basic example:

```
runtime: python39
entrypoint: gunicorn -b :$PORT app:app

instance_class: F2
gunicorn is a WSGI server for Python web apps, often used for production.
```

Deploy to Google App Engine:

Navigate to the directory where your app files are located, then deploy your application:

```
gcloud app deploy
```

Access the App:

Once deployed, Google Cloud will provide a URL where you can access your AI model. It will look something like this:

```
https://<your-project-id>.appspot.com
```

4. Additional Hosting Platforms

Apart from Heroku, AWS, and Google Cloud, there are other platforms that are well-suited for hosting AI models:

- **Microsoft Azure**: Offers services like Azure Machine Learning to deploy models at scale.
- **IBM Cloud**: Provides tools for AI model deployment and serving through Watson Machine Learning.
- **DigitalOcean**: A cost-effective cloud hosting solution where you can easily deploy models on virtual private servers (droplets).

5. Key Considerations for Hosting AI Models

When hosting your AI model online, keep these considerations in mind:

- **Scalability**: Ensure that the platform you choose can scale with traffic. If you expect heavy usage, look into load balancing and horizontal scaling.
- **Security**: Protect your model and user data by using HTTPS, securing APIs with authentication, and ensuring that sensitive data is encrypted.
- **Model Performance**: Make sure that your model performs well in a production environment, with minimal latency. You might need to optimize the model using techniques like quantization or batch processing.
- **Cost**: Hosting services can incur charges based on usage. Monitor your costs and choose a platform that fits your budget.

Hosting your AI model online is a crucial step toward making it accessible to users. Platforms like Heroku, AWS, and Google Cloud provide easy ways to deploy your machine learning models and serve them through a web interface. Once deployed, users can interact with your model, submit input data, and receive predictions, all through a seamless, web-based interface.

Key takeaways from this section:

- Learn how to deploy your AI model on platforms like Heroku, AWS, and Google Cloud.
- Set up necessary files like requirements.txt and Procfile for Heroku, or app.yaml for Google Cloud.
- Consider scalability, security, and cost when choosing a hosting platform.

By following these steps, you can successfully host and scale your AI models for real-world applications.

13. AI Ethics and Responsible Coding

As AI continues to shape the future, it's crucial to consider the ethical implications of its use. In this chapter, you'll explore the importance of ethical AI development and responsible coding practices. You'll learn about potential biases in AI models, how they can lead to unfair outcomes, and strategies to mitigate these biases during data collection and model training. You'll also dive into topics such as data privacy, transparency in AI decisions, and the social impact of automation. With real-world examples and best practices, this chapter will help you understand the ethical responsibilities of an AI developer and guide you in creating AI systems that are not only powerful but also fair, transparent, and aligned with societal values. By the end of this chapter, you'll be equipped to approach AI development with integrity and a deep understanding of its impact on the world.

13.1 Understanding Bias in AI

Artificial Intelligence (AI) has the potential to revolutionize industries, improve decision-making, and enhance everyday life. However, like all powerful technologies, AI comes with its challenges and ethical concerns. One of the most prominent issues that have emerged as AI becomes more widespread is bias. Bias in AI refers to the tendency of machine learning models and algorithms to produce outputs that are systematically prejudiced or unfair. This can lead to serious implications, including discrimination, inequality, and loss of trust in AI systems.

In this section, we'll explore what bias in AI is, how it arises, and why it's crucial to address it. Understanding bias in AI is essential for developing fairer, more ethical systems that serve all people equitably. We'll break down the different types of biases, how they impact AI models, and the steps you can take to mitigate them.

What Is Bias in AI?

Bias in AI occurs when a machine learning model or an algorithm produces outcomes that favor certain groups or outcomes over others, leading to unfair treatment. This bias can arise in many forms, depending on how the AI model is developed, trained, and used. The core issue is that AI models learn from data, and if the data itself is biased, the resulting AI predictions will also be biased.

Bias can appear in various aspects of AI systems, including:

Data Bias: If the data used to train AI models is not representative of the entire population, the model may perform poorly for underrepresented groups. For example, if a facial recognition system is trained primarily on images of lighter-skinned individuals, it may fail to accurately recognize people with darker skin tones.

Algorithmic Bias: Even if the data is unbiased, the way algorithms process and interpret that data can introduce bias. Algorithms may unintentionally prioritize certain features, leading to unfair decisions or unequal outcomes.

Human Bias: Since AI systems are built and trained by humans, they can inherit the biases of their creators. If the individuals involved in developing the model bring their own unconscious biases to the process, these biases may inadvertently shape the model's behavior.

Cultural and Social Bias: Cultural and social norms can influence data collection and how AI models are designed. This can result in biases that reflect societal inequalities and prejudices, which then become encoded into the technology.

Why Does Bias in AI Matter?

Bias in AI is a major concern because it can lead to negative consequences in many areas of society. Here are some of the reasons why it's essential to understand and address bias in AI:

Social Inequality: AI systems that are biased against certain groups can reinforce social inequalities. For example, biased hiring algorithms may favor male candidates over female candidates, or predictive policing algorithms may disproportionately target minority communities. This can perpetuate existing societal biases and lead to unfair treatment.

Legal and Ethical Concerns: Biased AI can lead to legal violations, such as discrimination in hiring, housing, or lending practices. These biases may also violate ethical principles of fairness and justice, which are fundamental to maintaining public trust in AI technologies.

Loss of Trust: If users believe that AI systems are biased or unfair, they are less likely to trust and adopt these technologies. This can hinder the widespread use of AI, especially in critical applications like healthcare, law enforcement, and finance.

Economic Impact: When AI systems make biased decisions, it can affect people's financial well-being. For example, biased loan approval algorithms may deny individuals access to credit based on characteristics like race, gender, or socioeconomic status, leading to long-term economic disadvantages.

Common Examples of Bias in AI

To better understand the various ways AI bias can manifest, let's look at a few notable examples from real-world applications:

Facial Recognition: One of the most widely discussed examples of bias in AI comes from facial recognition systems. Studies have shown that facial recognition technology tends to have higher error rates for people of color, particularly Black women. This is due to biased training data that predominantly consists of lighter-skinned individuals, which results in inaccurate recognition of darker-skinned faces.

Hiring Algorithms: Companies use AI-driven hiring tools to screen resumes, assess candidates, and even conduct interviews. However, if these systems are trained on biased data (e.g., resumes that come from predominantly male applicants), the AI can perpetuate gender biases and lead to discrimination against women or minority candidates.

Predictive Policing: Predictive policing algorithms use historical crime data to forecast where crimes are most likely to occur. If historical crime data reflects biased policing practices (e.g., disproportionately targeting Black or Hispanic neighborhoods), the AI system may predict more crimes in these areas, reinforcing existing racial biases in law enforcement.

Healthcare Decision-Making: In healthcare, AI is used to predict patient outcomes, recommend treatments, and assist with diagnoses. If training data is biased (e.g., underrepresentation of certain demographics or medical conditions), AI models may offer suboptimal or even harmful recommendations for marginalized groups, leading to health disparities.

How Bias Emerges in AI

Bias in AI doesn't appear by accident—it typically arises from one or more of the following sources:

Skewed or Incomplete Data: If the data used to train a model is not representative of the entire population, it can create biased results. For example, if a facial recognition system is trained only on images of white people, it will likely perform poorly on people of color.

Imbalanced Training Data: Machine learning models are often trained on large datasets, and if certain groups or characteristics are overrepresented or underrepresented in these datasets, the model will develop a skewed understanding of the world.

Unconscious Human Bias: Human biases—whether they are racial, gender-based, or otherwise—can unintentionally make their way into AI systems. For example, developers may unconsciously prioritize certain data features over others, affecting the fairness of the model.

Historical Bias: AI models may learn from historical data that contains patterns of discrimination or inequality. For instance, data from a biased criminal justice system could result in AI models that perpetuate unfair outcomes in the judicial process.

How to Address and Mitigate Bias in AI

Now that we understand what bias is and why it's a problem, let's discuss some approaches to identifying and mitigating bias in AI systems:

Diverse and Representative Data: Ensure that the data used to train AI models is diverse and represents all relevant groups. This includes balancing datasets with respect to race, gender, age, socioeconomic status, and other demographic factors. The more representative the data, the less likely the model is to develop biased outcomes.

Bias Audits and Fairness Testing: Regularly audit and test AI models for bias using fairness metrics. These tests should evaluate how well the model performs across different demographic groups and flag any significant disparities in performance.

Transparency and Explainability: Encourage transparency and explainability in AI decision-making. Users should be able to understand how decisions are made, especially when they directly impact individuals' lives (e.g., loan approvals or hiring decisions). Explainable AI allows for greater accountability and helps detect bias early.

Bias Mitigation Techniques: There are several technical approaches to reducing bias in machine learning, such as:

- **Data Preprocessing**: Altering the dataset to correct imbalances or biases before training the model.
- **Algorithmic Adjustments**: Modifying the learning algorithm to ensure fairness and reduce bias during training.
- **Post-processing**: Adjusting the model's predictions to account for any unfair outcomes.

Human Oversight: Even with sophisticated AI systems, human oversight is essential. AI models should be regularly monitored by diverse teams of developers, ethicists, and other stakeholders to identify and address potential biases that may arise during deployment.

Bias in AI is a critical issue that can have far-reaching consequences, especially as AI continues to be integrated into various sectors. Understanding the sources and types of bias is the first step toward developing more ethical and equitable AI systems. Addressing bias requires a multi-faceted approach, including the use of diverse data, rigorous testing for fairness, transparent algorithms, and continuous human oversight.

As AI continues to evolve, it's important for developers and practitioners to prioritize fairness and ethics to ensure that AI technologies work for everyone, without perpetuating harmful stereotypes or inequalities. By addressing bias proactively, we can build AI systems that are more inclusive, just, and beneficial for society as a whole.

13.2 Privacy and Data Protection

As artificial intelligence (AI) continues to play an increasingly prominent role in our everyday lives, privacy and data protection have become two of the most critical issues in the development and deployment of AI systems. AI systems rely on vast amounts of data to function, but much of this data is personal, sensitive, or otherwise private. From healthcare records to financial information, the data used to train and power AI models can have profound implications for individuals' privacy.

In this section, we'll explore the importance of privacy and data protection in AI, the potential risks and challenges, and the steps that developers, organizations, and policymakers can take to safeguard individuals' personal information. By understanding the balance between innovation and privacy, we can ensure that AI technologies are developed responsibly, ethically, and in compliance with privacy laws and regulations.

Why Privacy and Data Protection Matter in AI

AI systems are fundamentally dependent on data. Whether it's personal data (e.g., names, addresses, health information) or behavioral data (e.g., browsing habits, purchase histories), AI models require large datasets to function accurately and effectively. However, the use of this data raises significant concerns about individuals' privacy and security.

The potential consequences of AI mishandling sensitive data include:

Loss of Trust: People are becoming increasingly aware of the risks associated with sharing personal data. If AI systems are perceived as invasive or irresponsible in how they handle data, users may lose trust in these technologies, which could slow their adoption and harm the companies involved.

Data Breaches: AI systems process sensitive data that, if exposed, can lead to identity theft, financial fraud, and other security risks. A data breach can have devastating consequences for individuals and businesses alike, leading to reputational damage, legal consequences, and financial losses.

Unintended Use of Data: If AI systems collect and use data beyond the originally intended purpose, it can lead to unintended privacy violations. For example, a fitness tracking app could collect personal health data that, if mishandled or sold to third parties, could be used for purposes not agreed upon by the user.

Discrimination: Privacy and data protection are crucial in preventing AI systems from exploiting personal data in ways that lead to discrimination. For instance, AI models used in credit scoring could rely on sensitive attributes like race or gender, which could result in discriminatory decisions.

Key Privacy Risks in AI

AI systems can introduce a variety of privacy risks due to their reliance on vast datasets and the complex nature of their decision-making processes. Here are some of the main privacy concerns that need to be addressed:

Data Collection and Consent: One of the primary concerns regarding privacy in AI is how data is collected. In many cases, AI systems require individuals to provide consent for their data to be used. However, people may not fully understand what their data is being used for, and whether it's being collected, stored, or shared with third parties. Additionally, users may feel pressured to provide consent to use certain services without fully understanding the implications.

Solution: Clear, transparent consent mechanisms should be implemented that ensure users understand what data is being collected, how it will be used, and how long it will be stored.

Data Storage and Security: Storing vast amounts of personal data poses significant risks, especially if that data is not adequately secured. Hackers or unauthorized actors could access sensitive information, leading to privacy violations.

Solution: Organizations must employ robust security measures, including encryption, secure storage practices, and regular vulnerability testing to safeguard personal data from unauthorized access.

Anonymization and De-identification: While AI models often rely on anonymized or aggregated data to reduce privacy risks, the process of anonymization itself is not always foolproof. In some cases, advanced data analytics or machine learning techniques could re-identify individuals from anonymized datasets.

Solution: Ensuring true anonymization and de-identification, where it is impossible to re-identify individuals, is crucial. AI systems should prioritize using data that is completely anonymized or aggregated whenever possible to prevent any potential breach of privacy.

Data Sharing and Third-Party Access: AI models often rely on data that is shared across various organizations or services. This can lead to issues if third parties use personal data for purposes beyond what the individual originally consented to.

Solution: Contracts, terms of service, and transparent data-sharing policies should be in place to ensure that data shared between parties is done so securely and in accordance with privacy laws and regulations.

Data Profiling: AI systems can create detailed profiles of individuals based on their online behavior, preferences, and interactions. While profiling can offer personalized experiences, it also raises concerns about how much of individuals' personal lives are being tracked and analyzed without their knowledge.

Solution: AI systems should allow users to control their data, providing the option to opt out of certain forms of profiling or data collection. Ethical guidelines should be established to prevent excessive data profiling or the creation of overly invasive profiles.
Regulations and Laws Governing Data Protection in AI

As the use of AI grows, so too does the need for clear regulations to ensure that privacy is maintained. Several laws and regulations have been established worldwide to protect personal data and establish ethical guidelines for AI systems.

General Data Protection Regulation (GDPR): The European Union's General Data Protection Regulation (GDPR) is one of the most stringent data privacy laws in the world. It places significant obligations on organizations that process personal data, including the need to obtain explicit consent from users before collecting their data and allowing individuals to access, correct, and delete their data. GDPR also emphasizes the right to explanation, meaning that individuals must be informed about the decisions AI systems make that impact them.

Impact on AI: AI developers and companies must ensure that their models comply with GDPR requirements, including ensuring transparency, data security, and the protection of users' rights.

California Consumer Privacy Act (CCPA): The California Consumer Privacy Act (CCPA) is a landmark privacy law in the United States that gives California residents the right to control the personal data that businesses collect about them. It grants users the right to request access to their data, opt-out of data sales, and request data deletion.

Impact on AI: AI developers in California or with customers in California must adhere to the provisions of the CCPA, ensuring they provide users with clear choices regarding how their data is used and the right to be forgotten.

Health Insurance Portability and Accountability Act (HIPAA): In the healthcare sector, HIPAA provides regulations for the privacy and security of medical records. Healthcare AI systems that handle personal health data must comply with HIPAA requirements, ensuring that patient information is protected and used only for authorized purposes.

How to Protect Privacy in AI

To address the privacy concerns surrounding AI, it's important to implement a range of strategies that minimize risks and maximize transparency and control for users:

Data Minimization: When designing AI systems, it's important to collect only the data that is necessary for the intended purpose. Avoid over-collection of data, and ensure that the data being collected is relevant and proportionate to the task.

Privacy by Design: AI systems should be built with privacy in mind from the very beginning of development. This involves integrating privacy measures into every stage of the AI lifecycle, from data collection and processing to deployment and monitoring.

User Control and Transparency: Provide users with clear options for controlling their data. This can include allowing users to opt-out of data collection, offering data access, and providing tools for users to delete or modify their data. Additionally, users should be informed about how their data will be used and how long it will be retained.

Secure Data Handling: Implement strong data encryption and storage protocols to ensure that sensitive data is protected from unauthorized access. Regular security audits and vulnerability assessments should be performed to identify and fix potential weaknesses in the system.

Bias and Fairness Considerations: Privacy concerns are closely related to issues of bias and fairness. AI systems that rely on biased or discriminatory data can perpetuate privacy violations, particularly for marginalized groups. Developers should ensure that AI systems are fair, transparent, and designed with ethical principles in mind.

Privacy and data protection are fundamental aspects of AI development that must be addressed proactively. As AI systems continue to evolve and handle increasingly sensitive data, developers and organizations must prioritize the responsible use of personal information. By adhering to privacy regulations, implementing robust security practices, and giving users control over their data, we can build AI systems that respect privacy and foster trust among users. Ultimately, striking a balance between innovation and privacy will enable AI to reach its full potential while safeguarding individuals' rights.

13.3 AI Safety and Security

As artificial intelligence (AI) continues to develop and integrate into more aspects of our daily lives, ensuring the safety and security of AI systems is becoming increasingly important. AI's potential to revolutionize industries such as healthcare, finance, transportation, and entertainment is enormous, but with great power comes great responsibility. AI systems can have unintended consequences, and these systems are vulnerable to malicious attacks. Therefore, maintaining the safety, robustness, and security of AI systems is critical in preventing harm, ensuring reliability, and promoting trust among users and stakeholders.

In this section, we'll delve into the various dimensions of AI safety and security, including potential risks, the importance of secure development practices, and strategies to ensure that AI systems operate safely and securely. Addressing these challenges is essential for the continued success and responsible deployment of AI technologies.

Why AI Safety and Security Matter

The significance of AI safety and security cannot be overstated. From autonomous vehicles to medical diagnostic systems, AI is increasingly being trusted with high-stakes decision-making processes. A failure in safety or security could result in real-world harm, including loss of life, financial losses, and damage to societal trust in AI technologies. There are several reasons why AI safety and security are paramount:

Unintended Consequences: AI systems are designed to perform tasks and make decisions based on the data they are given. However, due to the complexity of these systems, unintended consequences can arise. For example, an AI model trained on biased data could make discriminatory decisions, or a self-driving car could fail to react appropriately in a dangerous situation due to errors in its perception system. These errors may not be immediately apparent and could result in harmful outcomes.

Vulnerability to Attacks: AI systems, like any other software, are vulnerable to cyberattacks. Attackers may exploit weaknesses in the AI model or manipulate the input data (e.g., adversarial attacks) to cause the AI to behave in undesirable ways. For instance, in a security setting, adversarial attacks could trick AI models into failing to recognize malicious activity, leading to a breach.

Loss of Control: As AI systems become more sophisticated and autonomous, there is an increasing risk that humans may lose control over the system. For example, an AI system could act in ways that were not intended by its developers, leading to unpredictable or unsafe behaviors. This is especially concerning in critical areas like military applications or nuclear safety.

Ethical and Social Risks: AI safety and security are also closely tied to ethical concerns. AI systems must operate in a way that aligns with ethical principles and social norms. For instance, if an AI system makes a decision that adversely impacts a specific group of people, such as profiling, discrimination, or exclusion, it raises significant ethical concerns.

Key Challenges in AI Safety and Security

AI safety and security are multi-faceted challenges that span a wide range of domains. Some of the primary challenges include:

Robustness and Reliability: AI systems need to be robust, meaning they can function correctly and predictably in a variety of real-world situations. Unfortunately, even the most well-designed models can break down when exposed to unexpected conditions or adversarial inputs. For example, an AI-based facial recognition system might perform well under typical lighting conditions but could fail or misidentify subjects in low-light or chaotic environments. Ensuring AI systems can handle these variations is a significant safety concern.

Solution: To improve robustness, AI systems should be trained on diverse datasets, including edge cases and outlier conditions, to help them generalize well in different environments. Regular stress testing and simulation under various conditions should also be part of the development process.

Adversarial Attacks: One of the most pressing security concerns with AI is its vulnerability to adversarial attacks. These attacks involve subtly altering input data in a way that causes the AI to make incorrect predictions or decisions. For instance, a small change to an image could cause a neural network to misclassify the object, even though the change is imperceptible to humans. In the context of cybersecurity, adversarial attacks could be used to bypass security systems or cause damage to AI-powered infrastructure.

Solution: Techniques like adversarial training (exposing AI models to adversarial examples during training) can help improve the model's ability to detect and defend against such attacks. Additionally, security measures such as robust encryption and real-time monitoring of AI systems can be used to mitigate risks.

Explainability and Transparency: Many AI models, especially deep learning models, are often referred to as "black boxes" because they make decisions in ways that are not easily understandable to humans. This lack of transparency poses a risk to AI safety. If developers and end-users do not fully understand how an AI system makes decisions, they may struggle to trust its results, spot potential errors, or fix problems when they arise. Additionally, when something goes wrong, understanding why it happened is crucial for preventing similar issues in the future.

Solution: Explainable AI (XAI) is an emerging field that focuses on creating models that provide human-readable explanations for their decisions. This could involve using simpler models, providing visualizations of how a model makes decisions, or developing techniques to interpret complex models.

Autonomous Systems and Loss of Control: As AI systems become more autonomous, there is a risk that humans may lose control of their decision-making processes. For example, an AI system designed to optimize supply chain logistics might autonomously reassign delivery routes without human oversight, potentially causing significant disruptions. The issue becomes even more critical in high-stakes fields like autonomous vehicles, military drones, or medical devices.

Solution: One approach to mitigating this risk is through the concept of "human-in-the-loop" systems, where humans retain the ability to intervene and correct the AI's behavior. Additionally, AI models should be designed to operate within clearly defined boundaries and constraints that align with human values and safety standards.

Bias and Fairness: AI systems can unintentionally perpetuate or even exacerbate societal biases. If an AI model is trained on biased data (e.g., data that reflects historical inequalities), the model may make biased decisions, such as discriminating against certain groups. This not only raises safety concerns but also ethical concerns, especially in sensitive areas like hiring, criminal justice, and lending.

Solution: Developers should prioritize fairness by using diverse and representative datasets for training AI systems. Moreover, fairness audits and bias detection techniques should be implemented to identify and mitigate bias before the system is deployed.

Best Practices for Ensuring AI Safety and Security

Ensuring the safety and security of AI systems requires a comprehensive approach that incorporates technical, ethical, and regulatory considerations. Here are some best practices for AI safety and security:

Comprehensive Testing and Validation: AI systems should undergo extensive testing to ensure they are safe and secure. This includes testing for robustness in a variety of real-world scenarios, testing against adversarial attacks, and verifying that the system behaves as expected under different conditions.

Secure Development Lifecycle: Security practices should be integrated into the entire AI development lifecycle. From data collection and preprocessing to model deployment and monitoring, every stage should be designed with security in mind. This may involve code audits, penetration testing, and vulnerability assessments to identify potential weaknesses.

Ethical Guidelines and Standards: AI developers should adhere to ethical guidelines that promote fairness, transparency, and accountability. Clear ethical frameworks, such as the IEEE Global Initiative on Ethics of Autonomous and Intelligent Systems, should guide AI development to ensure that these systems serve the public good.

Collaboration Across Industries: AI safety and security are not issues that any single company or organization can tackle alone. Collaboration among AI developers, researchers, policymakers, and regulatory bodies is essential to creating global standards for AI safety and security. This collaborative approach can help ensure that AI technologies are developed responsibly and with the necessary safeguards in place.

Continuous Monitoring and Updates: AI systems should be continuously monitored after deployment to ensure they remain safe and secure. This includes tracking performance, detecting anomalies, and updating the models as needed to address emerging threats or vulnerabilities. Regular updates and patching of vulnerabilities are essential to maintain the system's safety.

AI safety and security are vital concerns that must be addressed as AI systems become more integrated into society. These systems hold great promise, but without proper safeguards, they can pose significant risks to privacy, safety, and fairness. Developers, organizations, and policymakers must work together to ensure that AI is developed with security and ethical considerations in mind. By implementing robust security measures, ensuring transparency, addressing bias, and adhering to ethical guidelines, we can build AI systems that are safe, trustworthy, and beneficial to society. As AI technology advances, maintaining a focus on safety and security will be crucial for the sustainable and responsible use of AI.

13.4 Best Practices for Ethical AI Development

As artificial intelligence continues to permeate every facet of our lives, from healthcare to finance and beyond, it's crucial that AI development is carried out in an ethically responsible manner. AI systems have the potential to bring about transformative benefits to society, but they also pose significant risks if not carefully developed and deployed. Ethical AI development is about ensuring that AI technologies are used for good, avoid harm, and are aligned with human values and societal norms.

This section outlines key best practices for ensuring that AI development remains ethical, fair, and beneficial to all.

Why Ethical AI Matters

The importance of ethical AI development cannot be overstated. AI systems have the potential to influence decisions that impact people's lives in profound ways. Whether it's hiring decisions made by an AI model, medical diagnoses powered by AI algorithms, or automated vehicles on the road, AI is becoming a tool that can significantly shape the future. Ethical AI development ensures that these systems are transparent, accountable, and fair while avoiding harmful consequences such as discrimination, bias, or job displacement.

Furthermore, public trust in AI technologies depends on transparency and ethical practices. Without these principles, society may become wary of AI's potential, hindering its widespread adoption and benefits.

Best Practices for Ethical AI Development

Ensure Transparency and Explainability

AI models, especially complex ones like deep learning, often operate as "black boxes," meaning that their decision-making process is not easily understandable by humans. This lack of transparency can lead to mistrust and even harmful decisions that are difficult to identify or correct. Explainable AI (XAI) is a crucial aspect of ethical AI development, ensuring that users, developers, and stakeholders can understand why and how an AI system makes a particular decision.

Best Practices:

- Use interpretable models when possible or develop techniques to explain complex models.
- Provide clear explanations for AI decision-making, especially in critical areas like healthcare, finance, and justice.
- Regularly audit and review models to ensure their decisions align with the expected outcomes.

Prioritize Fairness and Mitigate Bias

One of the most significant ethical challenges in AI development is the risk of bias. AI models can unintentionally perpetuate or even exacerbate social biases, leading to unfair outcomes. For example, a recruitment AI might favor candidates from certain demographics based on biased historical data. Bias can also manifest in facial recognition systems, leading to misidentification or discrimination against certain racial or ethnic groups.

Best Practices:

- Use diverse and representative datasets during training to avoid biased outcomes.
- Regularly audit AI systems for bias and fairness, using fairness metrics and techniques to assess their performance.
- Implement fairness algorithms that actively address disparities in model outcomes.
- Ensure that decisions made by AI are evaluated based on their fairness, not just accuracy or performance.

Respect Privacy and Data Protection

AI systems rely on vast amounts of data, and this data often includes sensitive information about individuals. Privacy violations can occur when data is misused, shared without consent, or accessed by unauthorized individuals. Ethical AI development requires ensuring that data privacy is maintained and that AI systems comply with data protection laws and regulations.

Best Practices:

- Collect and use data with the informed consent of individuals, and ensure transparency in how data is collected, stored, and used.
- Anonymize personal data where possible to protect individuals' identities.
- Regularly update security protocols to prevent unauthorized access to sensitive data.
- Adhere to data protection regulations such as GDPR (General Data Protection Regulation) and CCPA (California Consumer Privacy Act) to ensure compliance.

Accountability and Responsibility

One of the key ethical principles of AI development is accountability. When AI systems make decisions, it's important to know who is responsible for those decisions, especially if something goes wrong. This is especially critical in fields like healthcare, autonomous driving, and criminal justice, where AI decisions can have serious consequences. Ethical AI systems should be designed with accountability in mind.

Best Practices:

- Implement clear accountability structures, outlining who is responsible for AI decisions and outcomes.
- Create mechanisms for human oversight, allowing experts to intervene if AI decisions are incorrect or harmful.
- Establish clear lines of responsibility for the development, deployment, and maintenance of AI systems.

Design for Safety and Robustness

Ethical AI development requires that AI systems are safe and reliable. An AI system that can fail or behave unpredictably in critical situations can pose significant risks to people's lives and property. In sectors such as healthcare, autonomous vehicles, and energy, safety is paramount.

Best Practices:

- Design AI systems that are robust and can handle unexpected inputs or edge cases without causing harm.
- Perform extensive testing under various conditions to identify potential failures and weaknesses in AI systems.
- Implement redundant safety mechanisms (e.g., "kill switches") that can stop an AI system's operation in case of malfunction.

Promote Inclusivity and Social Good

Ethical AI development should prioritize inclusivity, ensuring that the benefits of AI are accessible to everyone and that AI technologies serve the public good. This includes designing AI systems that are not only fair and unbiased but also consider social, environmental, and economic factors.

Best Practices:

- Involve diverse teams of people, including those from underrepresented communities, in AI development to ensure the perspectives and needs of various groups are taken into account.

- Design AI systems that aim to improve societal well-being, such as AI solutions for climate change, healthcare, and education.
- Strive for accessibility, ensuring that AI technologies are accessible to individuals with disabilities or those from marginalized communities.

Establish Ethical Guidelines and Regulations

As AI technology becomes more widespread, establishing clear ethical guidelines and regulations is essential to ensure that its development remains aligned with societal values. Governments, organizations, and independent bodies can play a critical role in setting ethical standards for AI development, deployment, and usage.

Best Practices:

- Stay informed about the latest ethical guidelines and standards for AI development, such as those from the IEEE, the European Commission, or other regulatory bodies.
- Follow established industry best practices for ethical AI development, including the principles of fairness, transparency, accountability, and privacy.
- Engage with policymakers to help shape laws and regulations that govern AI development and deployment, ensuring that AI technologies serve the public good and are used responsibly.

Foster Public Awareness and Education

A critical component of ethical AI development is public awareness and education. People need to understand AI's capabilities, its limitations, and the potential risks it may pose. By fostering an informed and educated public, we can ensure that AI is developed and used in ways that align with societal values.

Best Practices:

- Promote public awareness campaigns about the ethical implications of AI technologies.
- Provide educational resources to help individuals better understand AI, its potential benefits, and its risks.
- Encourage open discussions about AI's societal impact, including its role in shaping the future of work, privacy, and decision-making.

Ethical AI development is an essential aspect of ensuring that AI technologies benefit society in a responsible and sustainable manner. By adhering to best practices such as ensuring transparency, promoting fairness, respecting privacy, and fostering inclusivity, developers can create AI systems that are not only technically effective but also aligned with societal values and human rights. AI is a powerful tool, but without a strong ethical foundation, its potential for harm is equally significant. By integrating ethical considerations into every stage of AI development, we can build a future where AI serves the public good, promotes equity, and ensures safety and trust.

14. Advanced AI Topics Preview

As you build a solid foundation in AI, the next step is exploring more advanced concepts and techniques that push the boundaries of what AI can achieve. In this chapter, we'll introduce you to some of the cutting-edge topics in the field, including deep learning, reinforcement learning, and neural networks. You'll get an overview of how deep learning models, such as convolutional neural networks (CNNs) and recurrent neural networks (RNNs), are used for complex tasks like image generation and language translation. We'll also explore the basics of reinforcement learning, where machines learn through trial and error, making decisions that maximize long-term rewards. By the end of this chapter, you'll have a preview of the exciting areas of AI that you can explore further as you continue your learning journey. Whether you aim to specialize in deep learning or dive into reinforcement learning, this chapter will inspire and prepare you for the next steps in mastering AI.

14.1 Deep Learning: The Next Step in AI

Deep learning is often hailed as the next frontier in artificial intelligence (AI), representing a significant leap forward from traditional machine learning techniques. As the name implies, deep learning involves the use of deep neural networks—models inspired by the human brain that are capable of learning from vast amounts of data to perform highly complex tasks. While machine learning is the broader field that encompasses a variety of algorithms designed to help computers learn from data, deep learning takes this a step further by using networks with many layers, hence the term "deep."

In this chapter, we will explore what deep learning is, how it works, and why it is revolutionizing AI. We will dive into its applications, the types of neural networks that power deep learning, and its key components. Deep learning has made remarkable strides in recent years, driving breakthroughs in fields such as computer vision, natural language processing, and autonomous systems. This chapter will serve as an introduction to the core concepts and potential of deep learning, giving you the foundation needed to explore more advanced topics in subsequent chapters.

What is Deep Learning?

At its core, deep learning refers to a subset of machine learning techniques that use neural networks with many layers (hence "deep") to model complex patterns in large datasets. These models are designed to automatically learn features from raw data, eliminating the need for manual feature extraction. In traditional machine learning, a human expert would typically design the features that the model uses to make predictions, but in deep learning, the network learns these features automatically by adjusting its internal parameters during training.

Deep learning models are particularly useful in scenarios where the relationships between input data and the output are so intricate or nonlinear that traditional machine learning algorithms cannot capture them. For example, in tasks like speech recognition, image classification, and language translation, deep learning has outperformed conventional methods by a wide margin.

How Deep Learning Works

Deep learning models consist of multiple layers of neurons (also called nodes or units) connected in a network. Each layer processes the input data in some way, extracting progressively more abstract and complex features as it moves through the network. The basic architecture of a deep learning model can be broken down into three key parts:

Input Layer: This layer receives the raw data—whether it's an image, a text sentence, or any other type of information. The data is then passed through the next layers of the network for processing.

Hidden Layers: These layers perform the bulk of the computation in a deep learning model. Each hidden layer consists of many neurons, and each neuron takes input from the previous layer, performs some mathematical operations (e.g., a weighted sum), and passes the result through an activation function (such as ReLU, Sigmoid, or Tanh). The purpose of these layers is to extract high-level features from the data. For example, in an image recognition task, the first layers might identify edges or textures, while deeper layers recognize complex objects like faces or animals.

Output Layer: After data passes through the hidden layers, it reaches the output layer, where the final decision or prediction is made. In a classification task, the output layer typically produces a probability distribution across different classes. For example, in a cat vs. dog image classification task, the model would output the probability that an image belongs to each category.

The deep learning model is trained using large amounts of labeled data. During training, the model adjusts its internal parameters (i.e., the weights of the connections between neurons) to minimize the error in its predictions. This process is typically achieved through a technique called backpropagation, which calculates the gradient of the error with respect to each weight and updates the weights using an optimization algorithm like stochastic gradient descent (SGD) or Adam.

Types of Deep Learning Models

There are several types of deep learning architectures, each suited for specific types of tasks. Below are some of the most common models used in deep learning:

Convolutional Neural Networks (CNNs):

- CNNs are specialized for processing grid-like data, such as images. They are designed to recognize patterns and spatial hierarchies in data by using convolutional layers, which apply filters to extract features from input data.
- CNNs have been the foundation for advances in image recognition, object detection, and video analysis. Popular applications include facial recognition, medical image analysis, and autonomous driving.

Recurrent Neural Networks (RNNs):

- RNNs are designed to handle sequential data, such as time series or natural language. They have loops that allow information to persist, making them well-suited for tasks like speech recognition, language modeling, and time-series prediction.
- A specialized version of RNNs, called Long Short-Term Memory (LSTM) networks, helps address the issue of vanishing gradients, allowing RNNs to capture long-term dependencies in sequences.

Generative Adversarial Networks (GANs):

- GANs consist of two networks: a generator and a discriminator. The generator creates synthetic data (e.g., fake images), while the discriminator attempts to distinguish between real and fake data. Through a process called adversarial training, the two networks improve over time, with the generator producing increasingly realistic data.
- GANs have been used in applications like image generation, data augmentation, and even creating deepfakes.

Autoencoders:

- Autoencoders are a type of neural network used for unsupervised learning, often for dimensionality reduction, anomaly detection, or image denoising. They work by encoding input data into a lower-dimensional representation (the "encoding") and then decoding it back to the original data (the "decoding").
- Autoencoders are also used in tasks like data compression and feature extraction.

Applications of Deep Learning

Deep learning has unlocked new possibilities across many industries, thanks to its ability to model highly complex data. Some of the most impactful applications include:

Computer Vision: Deep learning has revolutionized image and video analysis, enabling machines to perform tasks like facial recognition, object detection, and image segmentation. CNNs are commonly used in this field for tasks ranging from medical imaging to autonomous vehicles.

Natural Language Processing (NLP): Deep learning has powered major advances in NLP, including machine translation, sentiment analysis, and chatbots. Models like transformers (e.g., GPT-3, BERT) have significantly improved tasks such as text generation, question answering, and summarization.

Speech Recognition: Deep learning models are behind the success of voice assistants like Siri, Alexa, and Google Assistant. RNNs and CNNs are used to transcribe speech, recognize accents, and perform speaker identification.

Autonomous Vehicles: Deep learning plays a key role in enabling self-driving cars to interpret their environment. CNNs are used to recognize pedestrians, traffic signs, and other vehicles, while RNNs help track movement over time and make driving decisions.

Healthcare: In medicine, deep learning is used to analyze medical images (such as X-rays, MRIs, and CT scans), predict patient outcomes, and even assist in drug discovery. CNNs have been particularly successful in identifying patterns in medical data.

Why Deep Learning is the Next Step in AI

Deep learning represents the next leap in AI for several reasons:

Ability to Handle Large, Complex Data: Deep learning is uniquely capable of handling large and high-dimensional data, such as images, audio, and text, making it ideal for tasks that traditional machine learning cannot tackle effectively.

Improved Accuracy: Thanks to its multi-layered architecture, deep learning models often outperform traditional machine learning methods in terms of accuracy, particularly in complex tasks like image classification and language processing.

Automation of Feature Extraction: Unlike traditional machine learning algorithms, which rely on humans to manually engineer features, deep learning networks learn features automatically, improving efficiency and accuracy over time.

Scalability: Deep learning models can improve with more data and computational power. As AI researchers and developers have access to more data and more powerful hardware (e.g., GPUs), deep learning models continue to grow in their capabilities.

Deep learning is reshaping the AI landscape, offering powerful tools for tackling some of the most challenging problems in technology and society. By utilizing deep neural networks with many layers, deep learning is able to automatically learn complex features from data, leading to breakthroughs in fields like computer vision, natural language processing, and healthcare. As we continue to advance in AI, understanding deep learning and its applications will be essential for anyone looking to harness the power of this transformative technology.

14.2 Reinforcement Learning: Teaching AI to Make Decisions

Reinforcement Learning (RL) is a powerful branch of machine learning that empowers artificial intelligence (AI) to make decisions autonomously, learn from its actions, and improve its performance over time through interactions with its environment. Unlike supervised learning, where AI models are trained on labeled data, or unsupervised learning, where the model identifies patterns in data without explicit labels, reinforcement learning involves teaching AI agents to perform actions in an environment to maximize a cumulative reward. This process of trial and error, where the agent learns from the consequences of its actions, is what sets reinforcement learning apart.

In this chapter, we will explore the fundamental concepts of reinforcement learning, its core components, how it works, and its wide array of applications. We will also dive into the exploration-exploitation trade-off, the challenges RL agents face, and some of the techniques and algorithms used to train agents, such as Q-learning and policy gradient methods.

What is Reinforcement Learning?

At the heart of reinforcement learning lies the concept of an agent interacting with an environment to achieve a goal. The environment is the world in which the agent operates, and the agent's goal is to maximize a cumulative reward by taking actions that lead to favorable outcomes. The agent learns by receiving feedback from the environment in the form of rewards or punishments for the actions it takes.

The learning process in reinforcement learning can be broken down into the following components:

Agent: The entity that makes decisions and interacts with the environment. It can be a robot, software, or even a game-playing AI.

Environment: The external system or context in which the agent operates. It provides feedback based on the agent's actions.

Action: The set of possible moves or choices the agent can make within the environment.

State: The current condition or situation of the environment that the agent can observe. This represents the context in which the agent will make decisions.

Reward: A numerical value that the agent receives after taking an action. Positive rewards are given for desirable outcomes, while negative rewards (or penalties) are given for unfavorable ones. The agent's goal is to maximize this cumulative reward over time.

Policy: A strategy or rule that the agent follows to decide which action to take in a given state. It can be deterministic or probabilistic.

Value Function: A function that estimates how good a particular state is in terms of the expected future reward. It helps the agent decide which states to prioritize.

Q-Function (Quality Function): A function that estimates the value of a specific action taken in a particular state. It helps the agent evaluate not only the states but also the actions within those states.

How Reinforcement Learning Works

Reinforcement learning operates in an iterative cycle of interactions between the agent and the environment:

Initialization: The agent starts in an initial state in the environment, typically with little or no knowledge about how to navigate the environment or what actions lead to favorable outcomes.

Exploration: The agent selects an action based on its current policy. The policy may involve random exploration to gather information about the environment or following a strategy if some prior knowledge exists.

Interaction with the Environment: After taking an action, the agent transitions to a new state in the environment. The environment provides feedback in the form of a reward or penalty based on the agent's action and the resulting state.

Learning: The agent uses the feedback (reward) to update its policy, seeking to maximize the total cumulative reward over time. It may also update its value function or Q-function to improve its future decisions.

Iteration: The agent repeats this process, taking actions, receiving feedback, updating its policy, and gradually refining its decision-making process.

Through this process, the agent learns to map states to actions in a way that maximizes the total reward, which is known as policy optimization.

Key Concepts in Reinforcement Learning

Exploration vs. Exploitation Trade-Off: One of the central challenges in reinforcement learning is balancing exploration and exploitation.

- Exploration refers to the agent trying new actions to discover potentially better strategies, even if these actions may not immediately lead to a high reward.
- Exploitation refers to the agent exploiting what it already knows to maximize rewards by choosing actions that have yielded positive outcomes in the past.

The challenge is that if the agent explores too much, it may miss out on high rewards, but if it exploits too early, it might get stuck in a suboptimal strategy. The agent must strike a balance between the two, typically using strategies like epsilon-greedy (where the agent sometimes chooses random actions with probability epsilon and follows the best-known action the rest of the time).

Markov Decision Process (MDP): Reinforcement learning problems are often modeled as Markov Decision Processes (MDPs). An MDP is a mathematical framework that defines the environment in terms of states, actions, rewards, and transitions. The key property of MDPs is that the future state of the system only depends on the current state and action, and not on the history of past states and actions (known as the Markov property). This simplification makes it easier to model and solve RL problems.

Reinforcement Learning Algorithms

There are several reinforcement learning algorithms, each with its unique approach to solving decision-making problems. Some of the most common ones include:

Q-Learning:

Q-learning is a model-free reinforcement learning algorithm that focuses on learning an optimal action-value function (Q-function). The Q-function provides a value for each state-action pair, indicating how good an action is in a particular state. The agent updates its Q-values based on the observed rewards and the maximum Q-value of the subsequent state.

The formula for updating Q-values is:

$$Q(s,a) = Q(s,a) + \alpha \left(r + \gamma \max_{a'} Q(s',a') - Q(s,a) \right)$$

where:

- $Q(s,a)$ is the current Q-value for state s and action a.

- r is the immediate reward.

- γ is the discount factor that determines how much future rewards are valued.

- α is the learning rate.

- s' is the new state after taking action a.

- a' represents possible future actions.

Policy Gradient Methods:

Policy gradient methods directly optimize the policy by adjusting the probability distribution over actions rather than using a value function. This approach is useful for environments where the action space is large or continuous (e.g., robot control).

These methods use gradient ascent to maximize the expected reward by adjusting the policy parameters in the direction of the greatest improvement.

Deep Reinforcement Learning (DRL):

- In deep reinforcement learning, deep neural networks are used to approximate the Q-function or policy, allowing RL agents to scale to more complex environments with high-dimensional inputs (e.g., images, video).
- Techniques like Deep Q-Networks (DQNs) combine Q-learning with deep learning to handle high-dimensional data and improve performance in challenging tasks like playing video games or robotic control.

Applications of Reinforcement Learning

Reinforcement learning has gained immense popularity in recent years, especially in complex decision-making tasks. Here are some of the notable applications of RL:

Game Playing:

RL has demonstrated remarkable success in training agents to play complex games. AlphaGo, developed by DeepMind, used RL to defeat human champions in the game of Go, a task previously thought to be too complex for computers. RL is also behind the success of AI agents in playing video games such as Dota 2 and StarCraft II.

Robotics:

RL is widely used in training robots to perform tasks such as walking, grasping objects, and navigation. Robots learn through trial and error, refining their actions to achieve optimal performance in dynamic environments.

Autonomous Vehicles:

RL is integral to the development of self-driving cars, where the agent (car) learns to navigate roads, avoid obstacles, and make safe decisions based on the environment. The agent is trained to make real-time decisions in complex, unpredictable scenarios.

Healthcare:

RL can be used in personalized medicine, where the agent learns to optimize treatment strategies for individual patients. It can also assist in designing drug discovery processes and optimizing hospital resource management.

Finance:

RL is used for portfolio optimization, algorithmic trading, and financial decision-making. It can help maximize returns by learning optimal trading strategies based on market conditions.

Challenges in Reinforcement Learning

Despite its potential, reinforcement learning comes with several challenges:

- **Sample Efficiency**: RL often requires a large number of interactions with the environment to learn effective policies, which can be time-consuming and computationally expensive.
- **Exploration Issues**: Striking the right balance between exploration and exploitation remains a challenging aspect of RL.
- **Stability and Convergence**: Deep reinforcement learning can suffer from instability, making it hard to converge to an optimal solution.

Reinforcement learning is a dynamic and rapidly growing field within AI that allows machines to learn from their own experiences and make decisions autonomously. By simulating a trial-and-error process, RL agents can improve their performance over time, solving complex problems across a range of domains, from gaming to robotics, healthcare, and beyond.

14.3 AI in Robotics and Automation

Artificial Intelligence (AI) has become a cornerstone of modern robotics and automation, revolutionizing industries across the globe. AI enables robots to learn, adapt, and make decisions autonomously, transforming how machines interact with the world and perform complex tasks. Robotics combined with AI is allowing machines to perform jobs that were once thought to be exclusively within human capabilities, from manufacturing to service industries, healthcare, and even home environments.

In this chapter, we will explore the role of AI in robotics and automation, focusing on the key principles and technologies that drive the field, as well as the practical applications of AI-powered robots. From intelligent decision-making to advanced sensor systems, we will look at how AI is enabling robots to become more capable, flexible, and autonomous, and how these technologies are shaping the future of automation.

What is AI in Robotics?

AI in robotics involves integrating advanced machine learning, computer vision, natural language processing, and decision-making algorithms to create intelligent robots that can perform tasks in dynamic and unpredictable environments. The goal of AI in robotics is to allow robots to perceive their environment, reason about the situation, make decisions, and take actions to achieve a specific goal without human intervention. AI provides the intelligence that enables robots to perform complex tasks autonomously, learn from experience, adapt to new situations, and improve their performance over time.

In traditional robotics, machines typically follow a set of predefined instructions or programmed behaviors. However, AI enhances a robot's ability to handle real-time, unforeseen challenges, by enabling it to:

- **Perceive the environment**: Using sensors, cameras, and machine learning algorithms to understand the surroundings.
- **Process data**: Interpreting data from various sensors to make informed decisions.
- **Plan actions**: Deciding on the best course of action based on the analysis of the environment.
- **Learn and adapt**: Improving performance by learning from past experiences and changing conditions.

The integration of AI techniques such as machine learning, deep learning, reinforcement learning, and computer vision allows robots to become autonomous problem solvers.

Key Components of AI in Robotics

To understand the impact of AI in robotics, it's crucial to look at the key components that make intelligent robots work:

Perception:

- **Computer Vision**: Robots use computer vision to interpret visual information from cameras and other sensors, enabling them to recognize objects, navigate spaces, and understand their surroundings. Deep learning-based algorithms, such as convolutional neural networks (CNNs), are commonly used for tasks like object detection, recognition, and classification.

- **Sensors**: Robots are equipped with various sensors (e.g., LIDAR, infrared, ultrasonic, and tactile sensors) that help them perceive the environment, measure distances, detect obstacles, and gauge object properties.

Decision-Making and Planning:

- AI-based robots need to plan and decide on actions. This is often done using Reinforcement Learning (RL), where robots learn from trial and error to optimize actions based on rewards. Decision Trees, Markov Decision Processes (MDPs), and Monte Carlo Tree Search (MCTS) are some of the techniques used to determine the best course of action.
- Path Planning is a crucial aspect of robot decision-making. Robots must plan routes or trajectories to navigate around obstacles and complete tasks in an efficient manner. AI-based path-planning algorithms can optimize robot movements in real-time.

Control and Actuation:

- Robots use control systems to execute the actions planned by the decision-making process. AI-driven control systems make use of adaptive algorithms that adjust the robot's movement based on feedback from the environment, such as speed, direction, and force.
- Inverse Kinematics and Motion Control are key methods used in robotics to translate high-level planning decisions into physical movements, ensuring accuracy in robot actions.

Learning and Adaptation:

- Machine Learning (ML) algorithms, particularly deep learning models, are used to help robots improve their performance over time by learning from experience. For example, robots can learn to recognize objects better or perform tasks more efficiently by processing large datasets of real-world examples.
- Transfer Learning allows robots to apply knowledge gained in one task or environment to another, speeding up the learning process and reducing the need for extensive training in new scenarios.
- Reinforcement Learning (RL) plays a major role in enabling robots to optimize their behavior autonomously by rewarding the robot for successful actions and penalizing it for undesirable outcomes.

Applications of AI in Robotics and Automation

AI-driven robotics and automation are transforming various sectors, making processes more efficient, cost-effective, and accurate. Below are some key applications:

Manufacturing and Industrial Automation:

AI-powered robots are increasingly used in assembly lines, quality control, and material handling. They can perform repetitive tasks with precision, accuracy, and speed, allowing manufacturers to boost productivity.

- **Collaborative Robots (Cobots):** These are robots designed to work alongside humans. AI enables cobots to interact safely with human workers, assisting them in tasks such as lifting heavy objects, assembling components, and packaging goods.
- **Predictive Maintenance**: AI is used to predict when industrial robots and machines are likely to fail, based on sensor data and machine learning models. This allows for preventative maintenance, reducing downtime and maintenance costs.

Autonomous Vehicles:

AI is a key enabler of autonomous driving technology. Robots in the form of self-driving cars use AI algorithms, including deep learning, computer vision, and reinforcement learning, to navigate roads, detect obstacles, follow traffic rules, and make driving decisions in real-time.

AI-powered robots in logistics, such as autonomous drones and delivery robots, are reshaping supply chains by performing tasks like parcel delivery, inventory management, and warehouse organization.

Healthcare Robotics:

- **Surgical Robots**: AI-powered robots, such as the da Vinci Surgical System, assist surgeons with minimally invasive procedures. These robots offer enhanced precision, reduce human error, and can even learn from previous surgeries to improve future performance.
- **Robotic Prosthetics**: AI is being used to design advanced prosthetic limbs that adapt to the user's movements and feedback, providing a more natural experience.

- **Rehabilitation Robots**: AI-driven robotic devices help patients with physical rehabilitation. These robots assist patients in exercises and therapies while learning from the patient's performance to optimize treatment.

Agricultural Robotics:

- AI-powered agricultural robots are transforming the farming industry by automating tasks like planting, watering, harvesting, and pest control. Robots equipped with AI and computer vision can detect crop diseases and nutrient deficiencies, helping farmers improve crop yield and reduce waste.
- **Autonomous Tractors**: AI enables autonomous tractors and harvesters that can navigate fields without human intervention, improving efficiency and reducing labor costs.

Service Robotics:

- **Robotic Assistants**: Robots with AI are used in hotels, restaurants, and hospitals to assist with customer service tasks such as greeting guests, delivering items, and cleaning rooms.
- **Personal Robots**: AI-powered personal robots are designed for domestic tasks, such as vacuuming, lawn mowing, and cooking. These robots learn about their environment and improve their efficiency over time.

Search and Rescue Operations:

AI-powered robots are deployed in disaster-stricken areas to search for survivors, assess damage, and deliver supplies. These robots can navigate hazardous environments, such as collapsed buildings, where it may be dangerous for human rescuers to enter.

Challenges and Future of AI in Robotics

While AI in robotics has achieved significant advancements, several challenges remain:

- **Safety and Reliability**: Ensuring that robots can perform tasks safely and reliably in dynamic environments, especially when interacting with humans, is a critical concern.
- **Ethical Concerns**: The increasing use of robots in workplaces and service industries raises ethical questions about job displacement, privacy, and the potential for robots to make biased decisions.

- **Complex Environments**: Robots are still struggling to operate efficiently in highly unstructured or dynamic environments where unpredictable changes occur frequently.

Looking to the future, AI in robotics will continue to evolve and expand its capabilities. More sophisticated AI models will enable robots to tackle even more complex tasks with higher degrees of autonomy and flexibility. The integration of Edge Computing and 5G networks will allow robots to process data in real-time, improving performance and responsiveness. Additionally, AI will continue to enhance human-robot collaboration, enabling robots to act as assistive partners in numerous fields.

AI is the driving force behind the transformation of robotics and automation, making machines smarter, more adaptable, and more capable of handling complex tasks. From manufacturing to healthcare, transportation, and agriculture, the integration of AI with robotics has the potential to revolutionize industries and improve our quality of life. As AI technology continues to advance, we can expect even greater breakthroughs in robotics, bringing us closer to a future where intelligent robots coexist and collaborate with humans to solve global challenges.

14.4 Exploring Quantum AI

Quantum computing is one of the most promising and rapidly evolving fields in computer science, and when combined with Artificial Intelligence (AI), it opens the door to groundbreaking possibilities. The concept of Quantum AI brings together the principles of quantum mechanics and AI algorithms, promising to revolutionize data processing, optimization problems, and machine learning tasks that classical computers struggle to solve efficiently. In this chapter, we will dive into the fascinating world of Quantum AI, exploring how quantum computers work, how they can enhance AI capabilities, and the potential applications of this fusion.

What is Quantum Computing?

To understand Quantum AI, we first need to understand the basics of quantum computing. Quantum computing uses quantum-mechanical phenomena, such as superposition, entanglement, and quantum interference, to perform calculations in ways that classical computers cannot. Unlike classical bits, which can represent either a 0 or a 1, quantum bits (qubits) can exist in a superposition of both 0 and 1 at the same time. This ability allows quantum computers to process information much faster than traditional computers when solving certain complex problems.

Key principles of quantum computing include:

Superposition: A qubit can exist in multiple states at once. For example, instead of being in a state of just 0 or 1, a qubit can be in a state of 0 and 1 simultaneously. This allows quantum computers to explore multiple solutions to a problem at the same time.

Entanglement: When qubits become entangled, the state of one qubit is dependent on the state of another, even if they are far apart. This property allows quantum computers to perform complex computations with much more efficiency and speed.

Quantum Interference: Quantum interference helps to combine different probabilities in a way that leads to correct solutions, amplifying the right answers and canceling out the wrong ones.

Quantum computers operate on these principles to solve certain types of problems exponentially faster than classical computers. While quantum computers are still in the early stages of development, the combination of quantum computing with AI algorithms holds immense potential.

How Quantum AI Works

Quantum AI takes the power of quantum computing and applies it to AI algorithms, particularly in areas such as optimization, data processing, and machine learning. The idea is that quantum computers can handle much larger datasets, perform computations on more variables simultaneously, and solve complex problems that would take classical computers thousands of years to compute.

Key areas where quantum computing can enhance AI include:

Quantum Machine Learning (QML): Quantum machine learning is a growing area that explores how quantum computing can be used to enhance machine learning models. Traditional machine learning algorithms rely heavily on classical computation and may struggle with large datasets or computationally expensive models. Quantum computers, with their ability to process vast amounts of data simultaneously, could make these tasks much faster and more efficient.

Some areas where quantum machine learning holds promise include:

- **Supervised and Unsupervised Learning**: Quantum computing could speed up the training process for machine learning models by solving optimization problems faster, allowing for more efficient model fitting and predictions.
- **Quantum Support Vector Machines (QSVM):** This is a quantum version of classical support vector machines (SVMs), a popular machine learning algorithm for classification tasks. By using quantum computing to enhance SVMs, it is possible to process larger datasets and improve the accuracy of classification.
- **Quantum Neural Networks**: Quantum neural networks use quantum algorithms to enhance traditional neural network architectures, potentially leading to faster training times and more accurate models for complex tasks.

Optimization Problems: Optimization is one of the biggest challenges in many AI and machine learning problems. Problems like minimizing a loss function, finding the best path, or choosing the most efficient option among many are examples of optimization challenges that AI must solve. Quantum computers excel at solving certain types of optimization problems that are computationally hard for classical computers.

Quantum Annealing: Quantum annealing is a process that can be used to solve optimization problems. It is based on the quantum principle of tunneling, where the system can explore multiple solutions simultaneously to find the optimal one. This method has been successfully applied to problems like finding the most optimal routes in logistics or the best parameters in machine learning models.

Quantum-inspired Algorithms: Even though large-scale quantum computing hardware is still in development, certain quantum-inspired algorithms have already been applied to AI and optimization problems. These algorithms are designed to take advantage of quantum computing's properties, offering performance improvements over classical methods.

Speeding Up Data Processing: Quantum computing can dramatically speed up the process of training machine learning models and processing massive datasets. For example, quantum computers can perform matrix multiplications (a core operation in machine learning algorithms) much faster than classical computers. This can lead to improvements in tasks such as image recognition, natural language processing, and reinforcement learning, which rely on processing vast amounts of data quickly.

Quantum-enhanced AI Algorithms: Many AI algorithms are based on complex statistical models and data distributions. Quantum computing can enhance these algorithms by providing better ways to sample from large probability distributions, optimize over large parameter spaces, and find the best solution to problems with numerous variables.

Applications of Quantum AI

The combination of quantum computing and AI has the potential to revolutionize numerous industries and fields. Some key applications of Quantum AI include:

Healthcare: Quantum AI could be used to speed up drug discovery and genomics. By processing vast datasets of genetic information and performing simulations of molecular interactions, quantum computers can help identify potential drug candidates much faster than classical computers. In addition, quantum-enhanced AI algorithms can optimize treatment plans and predict patient outcomes with higher accuracy.

Finance: In finance, quantum AI has the potential to optimize portfolios, predict stock prices, and assess risk more effectively. Quantum computing can also help with fraud detection and financial modeling by processing large amounts of transactional data quickly and identifying hidden patterns that classical methods may miss.

Optimization in Logistics: Quantum AI can transform industries that rely on complex logistics, such as transportation, delivery services, and supply chains. By leveraging quantum-enhanced optimization algorithms, companies can find more efficient routes for deliveries, optimize inventories, and reduce operational costs.

Artificial General Intelligence (AGI): AI research has long aimed at creating AGI, a system that can learn and perform any intellectual task that a human can do. While AGI is still a distant goal, quantum computing has the potential to accelerate its development. Quantum AI could enable AGI systems to process vast amounts of information and adapt to new tasks more effectively, ultimately leading to more powerful and flexible AI systems.

Cybersecurity: Quantum computing can enhance AI-based cybersecurity systems by identifying vulnerabilities and potential security breaches more efficiently. Quantum-enhanced AI algorithms can analyze massive amounts of data from network traffic and detect anomalies in real-time, helping to protect sensitive information and prevent cyberattacks.

Challenges and Limitations of Quantum AI

While Quantum AI holds great promise, it is still in its infancy, and there are several challenges and limitations:

Quantum Hardware Limitations: Building large-scale, error-free quantum computers is still a significant challenge. Current quantum computers, known as Noisy Intermediate-Scale Quantum (NISQ) devices, are prone to errors and are limited in the number of qubits they can support. As a result, the full potential of Quantum AI cannot yet be realized.

Algorithm Development: Quantum AI algorithms are still being developed and refined. It is not yet clear which quantum algorithms will be most effective for AI and machine learning applications. Researchers are working to identify algorithms that will provide a clear advantage over classical approaches.

Interdisciplinary Knowledge: Quantum AI requires a deep understanding of both quantum computing and AI, making it a challenging field for researchers to master. The lack of experts in both areas is slowing down progress, but as the field grows, more interdisciplinary knowledge will be shared.

Quantum AI is an exciting and emerging field that combines the power of quantum computing with the potential of artificial intelligence. By leveraging the unique properties of quantum mechanics, Quantum AI has the potential to revolutionize machine learning, optimization, data processing, and much more. While there are still many challenges to overcome, the possibilities are vast, and Quantum AI could unlock new frontiers in fields such as healthcare, finance, logistics, cybersecurity, and beyond. As quantum hardware continues to improve and algorithms are developed, we may soon witness a new era of AI powered by quantum computers, bringing us closer to solving some of the most complex problems in science and technology.

15. Your AI Journey Ahead

Congratulations on completing your first steps into the world of AI! In this final chapter, we'll help you chart the path forward, whether you want to deepen your knowledge or apply what you've learned to real-world projects. You'll discover resources, tools, and advanced learning opportunities that will help you continue building your AI expertise. We'll discuss how to stay updated with the rapidly evolving field of AI, join AI communities, and contribute to open-source projects. Additionally, we'll offer advice on how to pursue a career in AI, including the skills and qualifications employers are looking for, and how to position yourself for success in the AI job market. Your journey in AI is just beginning, and with the knowledge and skills you've gained, you are now ready to tackle more advanced challenges and create innovative AI applications. The possibilities are endless, and the future is yours to shape.

15.1 Learning Paths: Where to Go Next

As you reach the end of this book, you're now equipped with the foundational knowledge of Python and Artificial Intelligence (AI). Whether you're a beginner or have some experience, the journey of learning AI is ongoing and dynamic. AI is a rapidly evolving field, and the skills you've learned so far will serve as a stepping stone to more advanced concepts and practical applications. In this section, we'll explore some possible learning paths to help you advance further in your AI journey, whether you're looking to specialize in a particular subfield, gain more hands-on experience, or contribute to the cutting-edge research happening in the world of AI.

1. Mastering Advanced AI Techniques

Now that you've learned the basics, it's time to dive deeper into more advanced AI topics. The next step would be to gain expertise in more complex and specialized areas of AI. This will provide you with deeper knowledge of how AI works in real-world applications. Here are some advanced topics you can focus on:

Deep Learning:

Deep learning is a subset of machine learning, focused on algorithms inspired by the structure and function of the human brain (artificial neural networks). If you're interested in cutting-edge AI technologies like image recognition, speech recognition, and autonomous vehicles, deep learning is the way forward. You can study frameworks like

TensorFlow, Keras, and PyTorch in more depth to understand how to build complex neural networks.

Recommended Resources:

- Deep Learning by Ian Goodfellow, Yoshua Bengio, and Aaron Courville (Book)
- Coursera's "Deep Learning Specialization" by Andrew Ng

Reinforcement Learning:

Reinforcement learning (RL) is an area of machine learning concerned with how agents should take actions in an environment to maximize a cumulative reward. It's the foundation of many AI systems that learn from trial and error, including AI playing games like chess, Go, or autonomous driving.

Recommended Resources:

- Reinforcement Learning: An Introduction by Richard S. Sutton and Andrew G. Barto (Book)
- Coursera's "Deep Learning and Reinforcement Learning" by the University of Alberta

Natural Language Processing (NLP):

NLP is another essential field for AI that focuses on the interaction between computers and human languages. With tools like GPT-3, BERT, and other transformer models, NLP is becoming increasingly powerful. If you're passionate about working with text data, chatbots, sentiment analysis, or machine translation, this is a great area to explore.

Recommended Resources:

- "Speech and Language Processing" by Daniel Jurafsky and James H. Martin (Book)
- "Natural Language Processing with Deep Learning" by Stanford University (Online Course)

Computer Vision:

Computer Vision focuses on enabling machines to interpret and understand visual information. It powers technologies such as facial recognition, object detection, and self-driving cars. Mastering computer vision techniques, particularly deep learning models, will give you the ability to create powerful image-processing systems.

Recommended Resources:

- "Deep Learning for Computer Vision" by Rajalingappaa Shanmugamani (Book)
- Coursera's "Convolutional Neural Networks" by Andrew Ng (Course)

2. Working on AI Projects and Competitions

One of the best ways to solidify your learning is by working on real-world projects. AI is not only about theory but also about practical application. Here are some ways to enhance your skills:

Participate in Competitions:

Competitions like Kaggle and DrivenData allow you to solve real-world problems and compete with other data scientists and AI practitioners. By participating in these competitions, you can learn new techniques, sharpen your problem-solving abilities, and build your portfolio. These platforms also provide access to datasets and challenges from different domains, ranging from healthcare to finance to natural language processing.

Recommended Resources:

- Kaggle (www.kaggle.com) for machine learning challenges
- DrivenData (www.drivendata.org) for data science competitions for social good

Start Open-Source AI Projects:

Contributing to open-source projects is a fantastic way to collaborate with others and gain experience in coding and solving practical AI problems. GitHub hosts many open-source AI repositories that you can contribute to, such as TensorFlow, PyTorch, or scikit-learn.

Recommended Resources:

- Explore AI repositories on GitHub (www.github.com)
- Find open-source AI projects through organizations like AI for Good or TensorFlow.

Create Personal Projects:

Building personal projects is one of the most effective ways to learn. You could start small by creating a simple AI model or application, then expand it as your skills grow. For example, you can develop a chatbot, create an image classifier, or build an AI for predictive analytics using real-world datasets.

Project Ideas:

- Build a recommendation system (e.g., for movies, products, etc.)
- Create an AI to predict house prices based on historical data.
- Build a sentiment analysis tool that reads social media posts or product reviews.

3. Specializing in a Subfield

As you continue your learning, you might find certain areas of AI more appealing and decide to specialize in them. AI is broad, and by focusing on a niche, you can develop a deeper understanding of that area. Here are some specialization options:

AI in Robotics:

Robotics combines AI and mechanical engineering to build machines that can perform tasks autonomously. Understanding how AI is applied to control robotic movements, perception (e.g., object detection), and decision-making (e.g., reinforcement learning) can open doors in industries such as healthcare, manufacturing, and autonomous vehicles.

Recommended Resources:

- "Introduction to Robotics" by John J. Craig (Book)
- MIT's "Robotics" course (Online Course)

AI for Healthcare:

AI in healthcare has immense potential, from diagnosing diseases to predicting patient outcomes and personalizing treatment. Specializing in medical AI will allow you to work on solving real-world problems in the healthcare industry, such as building predictive models for medical conditions or creating computer-aided diagnostics tools.

Recommended Resources:

- "Artificial Intelligence in Healthcare" by Parashar Shah and S. P. S. Gill (Book)

- AI in Healthcare Specialization by Stanford University (Online Course)

AI in Finance:

AI in finance is another rapidly growing field. You can specialize in areas such as algorithmic trading, fraud detection, or risk analysis. With the increasing amount of financial data available, AI can be used to make more informed and accurate decisions in real-time.

Recommended Resources:

- "Artificial Intelligence in Finance" by Yves Hilpisch (Book)
- Coursera's "AI in Finance" by the University of Michigan (Online Course)

AI for Cybersecurity:

With the rise of digital threats, AI plays an important role in identifying and responding to cybersecurity attacks. Specializing in AI for cybersecurity will allow you to apply your skills to protect systems from malicious activities, such as identifying abnormal patterns of activity or predicting cyber-attacks.

Recommended Resources:

- "Machine Learning for Cybersecurity" by Shlomi Dolev (Book)
- Online tutorials and courses on cybersecurity and AI-based anomaly detection

4. Contributing to AI Research and Development

If you're interested in pushing the boundaries of AI, pursuing a career in research or contributing to the development of new AI technologies could be an exciting path. This path involves working in academic or industrial research labs, contributing to the development of AI theories, algorithms, or models.

Pursue Advanced Degrees:

Many AI professionals opt for a Master's or Ph.D. in Computer Science, Data Science, or AI, where they can dive deeper into the theoretical aspects of AI and contribute to academic research. A graduate degree often provides the necessary foundation for research and development positions in top tech companies or universities.

Recommended Resources:

- Explore AI programs at leading institutions such as Stanford, MIT, or Carnegie Mellon.
- Research papers and journals like the Journal of Artificial Intelligence Research (JAIR) and ArXiv for the latest AI research.

Engage in AI Research Communities:

To stay on top of the latest developments, it's helpful to participate in AI research communities. Conferences such as NeurIPS, ICML, and CVPR are excellent opportunities to network with researchers, share ideas, and learn from experts in the field.

Your journey into AI doesn't end with this book; it's just the beginning. By diving deeper into more advanced topics, working on projects, exploring subfields, and engaging with the AI community, you will continue to expand your knowledge and refine your skills. Remember, AI is a rapidly evolving field, and the key to mastering it is persistence, curiosity, and hands-on experience. Wherever you choose to go next, stay curious and keep learning. Your AI journey is bound to be exciting and full of opportunities!

15.2 Joining the AI Community and Open Source Contributions

As you embark on your AI journey, one of the most rewarding and impactful ways to continue learning and growing is by joining the broader AI community. The field of Artificial Intelligence is vast, constantly evolving, and filled with passionate professionals, researchers, and enthusiasts who contribute to its advancement. By participating in the AI community and engaging in open-source contributions, you not only expand your own knowledge but also play a role in shaping the future of AI.

In this section, we will explore the importance of being part of the AI community, the benefits of collaborating with others, and how you can contribute to open-source projects. Whether you're an AI beginner or an experienced developer, community involvement is a crucial aspect of professional growth and innovation in the AI space.

1. The Importance of Joining the AI Community

The AI community is vast and global, encompassing individuals from diverse backgrounds, including computer science, engineering, data science, business, healthcare, and more. Here are some reasons why joining the community is beneficial:

Learning from Experts: By participating in AI forums, attending conferences, or collaborating with researchers, you gain access to the latest trends, innovations, and breakthroughs in AI. This can accelerate your learning and help you stay up-to-date with rapidly advancing technologies.

Networking and Collaboration: Being part of the AI community opens the door to networking with professionals and experts in the field. Collaborating on projects or discussing challenges with others can provide new perspectives and ideas, ultimately improving your skills and projects.

Inspiration and Motivation: Engaging with like-minded individuals who are passionate about AI can inspire you to push your own boundaries. Whether it's tackling challenging projects, solving real-world problems, or working on exciting applications, the community is a great source of motivation.

Career Opportunities: AI conferences, workshops, and meetups are excellent networking opportunities that may lead to internships, job offers, or collaborations on research projects. Many employers value community involvement and open-source contributions when evaluating potential candidates.

2. Engaging with the AI Community

There are many ways to engage with the AI community, whether online or in-person. Here are some popular avenues for building connections and expanding your knowledge:

Online Communities and Forums:

- **Reddit**: Subreddits like r/MachineLearning, r/DataScience, and r/ArtificialIntelligence are great places to engage with the community, ask questions, and stay updated on the latest developments.
- **Stack Overflow**: A go-to platform for solving coding problems, discussing AI-related queries, and providing answers to others. Contributing to discussions and helping fellow AI enthusiasts can build your reputation as an expert.
- **AI Research and Discussion Forums**: Sites like AI Alignment Forum and Cross Validated (on Stack Exchange) host in-depth discussions and research-focused conversations related to AI theories, algorithms, and practical applications.

Conferences and Meetups:

- Conferences like NeurIPS, ICML, CVPR, and AAAI bring together AI researchers and practitioners from around the world to present new research, share insights, and network. These conferences offer workshops, lectures, and panels on state-of-the-art AI topics.
- Meetup.com is another excellent platform where you can find local AI meetups, workshops, and hackathons in your area. These events often focus on collaboration and networking, making them perfect for meeting others in the AI field.

Social Media:

- Twitter and LinkedIn are two popular social media platforms used by AI professionals to share research, ideas, tutorials, and articles. Following influential AI researchers, developers, and organizations can help you stay updated on industry trends and innovations.
- Medium and Substack are platforms where you can find insightful blog posts from AI experts and enthusiasts, exploring everything from theoretical concepts to practical AI applications.

Hackathons and Competitions:

- Participating in AI-driven hackathons is an excellent way to engage with the AI community, improve your skills, and solve real-world challenges. Websites like Devpost and Hackathon.com list upcoming hackathons, some of which focus on AI-specific problems.
- Competitions like Kaggle or DrivenData allow you to apply AI techniques to solve data-driven problems. These platforms are filled with vibrant AI communities, where you can collaborate with others, share ideas, and learn from your peers.

3. Contributing to Open Source AI Projects

Open-source contributions are a powerful way to engage with the AI community and make a meaningful impact on the development of AI tools and frameworks. When you contribute to open-source projects, you help improve existing tools, share new ideas, and collaborate with developers from all over the world. In the AI space, many popular libraries, frameworks, and models are open-source, and there is always a need for contributors.

Here's how you can start contributing to AI open-source projects:

Identify Your Area of Interest:

Open-source AI projects span a wide range of topics, from deep learning frameworks like TensorFlow, PyTorch, and Keras to data manipulation tools like Pandas and NumPy. By identifying your area of interest (such as natural language processing, computer vision, or reinforcement learning), you can narrow down your focus and find relevant projects to contribute to.

Find Projects on GitHub:

- GitHub is the primary platform for hosting open-source AI projects. Use the search bar to find repositories related to AI, machine learning, or specific technologies you're interested in. Many of these repositories have open issues that you can help solve, from bug fixes to feature requests.
- Explore projects with a "good first issue" label to find beginner-friendly contributions.

Contribute to Documentation:

Not all contributions have to be code-based. Helping with documentation, tutorials, or creating example use cases for open-source projects is incredibly valuable. Clear documentation allows others to learn from and contribute to the project more effectively.

Bug Fixes and Feature Requests:

If you find an issue or bug in an AI project, you can contribute by diagnosing the problem, submitting a fix, and creating a pull request (PR). This is a great way to practice your coding skills and learn more about the underlying codebase.

Open-source projects often welcome contributions for new features or improvements. If you have an idea for something that would make the project better or more efficient, you can submit a feature request or a PR with your suggested changes.

Collaborate with Other Contributors:

Open-source contributions are collaborative. Interacting with other contributors, reviewing code, and sharing feedback helps foster a sense of community and improves the quality of the project. Collaborative efforts often lead to innovative solutions and new ways of approaching AI problems.

Learn from Established AI Libraries:

Contributing to or reviewing the source code of widely-used AI libraries, such as scikit-learn, OpenCV, or spaCy, will give you hands-on experience with high-quality code and industry-standard tools. These projects are well-documented, have a large community of contributors, and provide excellent learning opportunities for beginners and experts alike.

4. Mentorship and Giving Back

As you progress in your AI journey, one of the best ways to continue your growth is by giving back to the community. Mentorship is an invaluable way to help others learn and build your own leadership skills. Here's how you can get involved:

Mentor Newcomers:

As you become more experienced, consider mentoring those who are just starting out. You can offer guidance on learning resources, coding practices, or how to approach AI problems. Online platforms like Codementor or AI-related Slack channels provide opportunities to mentor others.

Host Meetups or Workshops:

If you feel comfortable sharing your knowledge, consider organizing local meetups or virtual workshops where people can learn together. You could teach basic AI concepts, run hackathons, or offer hands-on coding tutorials.

Share Your Knowledge Through Blogs:

Writing blog posts on Medium, Dev.to, or your own personal website is an excellent way to share your AI journey, discuss concepts you've learned, and help others. Blogging allows you to explain complex topics in simple terms and helps you build a portfolio that demonstrates your expertise.

Joining the AI community and contributing to open-source projects is an enriching experience that will accelerate your learning, provide networking opportunities, and allow you to make a real impact in the field. Whether you're interacting with fellow learners, contributing code to open-source libraries, or mentoring others, the AI community is full of opportunities for personal and professional growth. So, get involved, collaborate, and continue your journey toward mastering AI!

15.3 Building Your AI Portfolio

As you progress in your AI journey, one of the most important steps you can take is to build a solid portfolio. An AI portfolio is not just a collection of your work, but also a way to showcase your skills, demonstrate your experience, and highlight your ability to solve real-world problems using Artificial Intelligence. Whether you're looking to land a job in AI, collaborate on open-source projects, or even freelance, a well-curated portfolio can be your ticket to standing out in a competitive job market.

In this section, we'll discuss how to effectively build your AI portfolio, the types of projects to include, and how to present your work in a way that showcases your expertise. By the end of this chapter, you will have a clear understanding of how to create a portfolio that will impress potential employers or collaborators.

1. Why Build an AI Portfolio?

In today's fast-paced and competitive AI job market, your portfolio serves as proof of your practical skills and understanding of AI concepts. Here's why building a portfolio is essential:

Demonstrates Practical Skills: Employers want to see that you can apply what you've learned in real-world scenarios. A strong portfolio shows that you're capable of working on projects beyond theoretical knowledge.

Highlights Problem-Solving Abilities: AI is all about solving complex problems using data. Through your portfolio, you can demonstrate your ability to approach and solve problems with machine learning, data science, and AI techniques.

Personal Branding: A well-organized portfolio helps build your personal brand. It shows that you are proactive in developing your skills, staying up-to-date with the latest technologies, and actively contributing to the AI field.

Opens Career Opportunities: Your portfolio can be used as a powerful tool when applying for jobs, internships, or freelance work. It gives potential employers a concrete understanding of your abilities, making it easier for them to assess if you're a good fit for their team.

2. Essential Components of an AI Portfolio

Now that we understand why an AI portfolio is important, let's look at the key components you should include in your portfolio. These components will demonstrate your technical skills, creativity, and ability to tackle various challenges in the field of AI.

a) Personal Introduction

The first section of your portfolio should be an introduction that provides some background about who you are, your interests, and why you're passionate about AI. This introduction should be brief but impactful, giving the reader an insight into your professional journey and motivations.

Skills and Expertise: Highlight the AI, machine learning, data science, and programming skills you possess (e.g., Python, TensorFlow, PyTorch, Scikit-learn, NLP, Computer Vision, etc.).

Your AI Goals: Share the types of AI problems or industries you're most interested in (e.g., healthcare, finance, robotics, or autonomous systems).

b) Project Portfolio

The bulk of your AI portfolio should consist of projects you've worked on. These projects should demonstrate your ability to solve different types of problems using AI techniques. Here's how to structure each project:

Project Title: Choose a clear and descriptive name for each project.

Problem Statement: Briefly describe the problem you were trying to solve and the context behind it. For example, did you work on a prediction model? Build a chatbot? Solve a classification problem?

AI Techniques Used: Mention the key AI and machine learning techniques you applied to solve the problem. This could include deep learning models, regression algorithms, neural networks, or reinforcement learning.

Tools and Technologies: List the libraries, frameworks, and programming languages you used for each project. Mention tools like Python, NumPy, Pandas, Scikit-learn, TensorFlow, or PyTorch.

Approach and Solution: Describe the methodology you used to solve the problem, such as how you preprocessed data, trained your model, and evaluated its performance.

Results and Evaluation: Include the results of your model or solution. This could be accuracy, precision, recall, F1-score, or any other metric relevant to your problem. If applicable, mention how the model performed on unseen data.

Challenges and Learning: Talk about any challenges you encountered during the project and how you overcame them. Discuss what you learned and how it improved your skills.

Link to Code and Documentation: Provide links to the project code on platforms like GitHub or GitLab. Also, include any relevant documentation or readme files that explain the project's purpose and usage.

Example Projects to Include:

Image Classification: A project where you built a convolutional neural network (CNN) to classify images from a dataset (e.g., CIFAR-10, MNIST).

Natural Language Processing (NLP): A project where you applied NLP techniques, such as text classification or sentiment analysis, on a real-world dataset (e.g., Twitter data, movie reviews).

Time Series Forecasting: A project where you used machine learning algorithms to predict future data points, such as stock prices or sales data.

Chatbot Development: A project where you built a chatbot using machine learning, such as a simple rule-based chatbot or one using deep learning techniques like sequence-to-sequence models.

Reinforcement Learning: A project where you implemented an agent that learns by interacting with an environment, such as playing a game or solving a maze.

3. Showcasing Your Skills

Alongside your projects, you should also include sections that highlight your skills and accomplishments in the AI field. These sections should give potential employers or collaborators a comprehensive understanding of what you bring to the table.

a) Skills Section

This section should be a bullet-point list of the technical skills you've mastered, including programming languages, AI algorithms, and frameworks.

- **Programming Languages**: Python, R, JavaScript, etc.
- **Machine Learning Libraries**: TensorFlow, PyTorch, Scikit-learn, Keras, etc.
- **Data Manipulation**: Pandas, NumPy, SQL, etc.
- **Data Visualization**: Matplotlib, Seaborn, Plotly, etc.
- **Cloud Platforms**: AWS, Google Cloud, Azure (if applicable).

b) Certifications and Courses

Include any AI-related certifications, online courses, or academic qualifications that you have completed. These can add credibility to your expertise and show that you have a solid foundation in the AI field.

- **Coursera**: Machine Learning by Andrew Ng, Deep Learning Specialization, etc.
- **Udacity**: AI Programming with Python Nanodegree, Data Scientist Nanodegree, etc.
- **Kaggle Competitions**: Mention any notable rankings or achievements in Kaggle competitions.

c) AI Blog or Articles

If you have a blog where you write about AI, or if you've contributed articles to Medium, Dev.to, or other platforms, link to them in your portfolio. Sharing your insights on AI trends, coding tutorials, and project walkthroughs shows that you are an active member of the AI community and a thought leader.

4. Making Your Portfolio Accessible and User-Friendly

The presentation of your portfolio is just as important as the content. A clean, easy-to-navigate, and visually appealing portfolio can make a big difference in how potential employers perceive you. Here are some tips:

Portfolio Website: Build your portfolio on a personal website using platforms like GitHub Pages, WordPress, Wix, or Squarespace. Make sure it is easy to navigate and looks professional.

Organize Projects: Group similar projects together (e.g., NLP projects, computer vision projects, etc.) to make it easier for visitors to find relevant work.

Clear Layout: Ensure your portfolio has a clear layout with sections for your introduction, skills, projects, and contact information. Use visuals like screenshots, graphs, and charts to make the portfolio more engaging.

Responsive Design: Make sure your portfolio is mobile-friendly so it can be accessed easily on any device.

5. Final Tips for Building an Impressive AI Portfolio

Keep it Updated: Regularly update your portfolio with new projects, skills, and achievements. This shows that you are continuously learning and growing in the field.

Showcase Collaboration: If you have worked on collaborative projects, be sure to mention them. Collaboration is highly valued in the AI field, so demonstrating that you can work effectively in teams is essential.

Be Creative: While demonstrating technical skills is important, it's also valuable to showcase your creativity. Try to come up with innovative project ideas or approaches to existing problems.

Get Feedback: Before making your portfolio public, get feedback from peers, mentors, or professionals in the AI community. They can offer valuable insights and help you improve it.

Building a strong AI portfolio is one of the most effective ways to demonstrate your abilities, impress potential employers, and stand out in the competitive world of Artificial Intelligence. By carefully curating your projects, showcasing your skills, and presenting your work in a user-friendly format, you can create a portfolio that highlights your expertise and passion for AI. Keep building, keep learning, and let your portfolio reflect your journey as an AI practitioner.

15.4 Preparing for AI Careers and Certifications

As the AI field continues to evolve rapidly, pursuing a career in Artificial Intelligence (AI) is an exciting and rewarding journey. Whether you're just starting or are already deep into the world of machine learning and AI, there are several ways to prepare for a successful career. One of the most effective ways to advance in the AI field is by acquiring relevant certifications and actively preparing for job roles that require AI expertise.

In this section, we will cover key strategies to help you prepare for a career in AI, including the types of AI roles available, necessary skills and knowledge, and how AI certifications can help boost your credibility and job prospects. By the end of this chapter, you'll be equipped with practical guidance on how to navigate your AI career path and make informed decisions about certifications.

1. Exploring Career Opportunities in AI

The AI industry is broad, and there are numerous career opportunities depending on your interests, skills, and level of experience. AI professionals can specialize in various roles such as machine learning engineering, data science, AI research, robotics, and more. Here are some of the most common career paths in AI:

a) Machine Learning Engineer

Machine learning engineers develop and implement machine learning models and algorithms. They work on building models that can predict outcomes, recognize patterns, and automate tasks. The role requires strong programming skills (Python, R, etc.) and expertise in ML algorithms, deep learning, and software engineering.

Key Skills: Machine learning algorithms, model evaluation, Python programming, deep learning frameworks (TensorFlow, PyTorch), data preprocessing.

b) Data Scientist

Data scientists focus on analyzing complex data to uncover trends, patterns, and insights that can help organizations make informed decisions. They often work with large datasets, using statistical and machine learning techniques to perform data analysis.

Key Skills: Data cleaning, statistical analysis, machine learning, programming (Python, R), data visualization (Matplotlib, Seaborn), SQL, big data tools (Spark, Hadoop).

c) AI Researcher

AI researchers contribute to advancing the field of AI by developing new algorithms, theories, and methodologies. They often work in academic settings, research labs, or corporate research teams, exploring areas like reinforcement learning, neural networks, and computer vision.

Key Skills: Strong mathematical foundation, research skills, familiarity with AI theories, advanced algorithms, neural networks, AI model optimization.

d) AI Software Engineer

AI software engineers design, develop, and integrate AI solutions into software products. They focus on creating scalable AI systems and ensuring that AI models can be seamlessly integrated into business processes or applications.

Key Skills: Software development, AI model integration, cloud computing, AI architecture design, coding best practices.

e) Robotics Engineer

Robotics engineers build robots that interact with the environment and perform tasks autonomously or semi-autonomously. AI plays a critical role in enabling robots to perceive, learn, and make decisions based on real-time data.

Key Skills: Control systems, robotics algorithms, computer vision, machine learning, sensors, and actuators.

f) AI Consultant

AI consultants help organizations adopt AI technologies to solve business problems. They assess an organization's AI needs, design AI solutions, and guide companies through the implementation process. This role often requires both technical expertise and an understanding of business objectives.

Key Skills: AI solution design, client-facing communication, problem-solving, understanding business operations, knowledge of industry-specific AI applications.

2. Key Skills Required for AI Careers

Regardless of the specific career path you choose, there are several core skills that AI professionals should master:

a) Programming Skills

- **Python**: Python is the go-to programming language for AI and machine learning due to its rich ecosystem of libraries and frameworks (TensorFlow, PyTorch, Scikit-learn).
- **R**: R is useful for statistical analysis and data visualization and is often used in data science roles.
- **Other languages**: Some roles may also require proficiency in other programming languages, such as C++, Java, and Julia.

b) Mathematics and Statistics

AI and machine learning are built on strong mathematical foundations, including:

- **Linear Algebra**: Essential for understanding machine learning algorithms like matrix operations used in neural networks.
- **Calculus**: Used in optimization algorithms (e.g., gradient descent) and in understanding backpropagation in neural networks.
- **Probability and Statistics**: Key for understanding models, evaluating uncertainty, and making predictions in AI systems.

c) Machine Learning & Deep Learning

- **Supervised and Unsupervised Learning**: Understanding the differences between these two learning paradigms and how to apply algorithms like decision trees, support vector machines (SVM), and k-means clustering.
- **Deep Learning**: Expertise in neural networks, CNNs (convolutional neural networks), RNNs (recurrent neural networks), and reinforcement learning.
- **Natural Language Processing (NLP):** A specialized field focusing on the interaction between computers and human language, involving text classification, sentiment analysis, and chatbot development.
- **Computer Vision**: Techniques that allow machines to interpret and understand visual information, such as image recognition and object detection.

d) Data Engineering

- **Data Preprocessing**: The ability to clean, normalize, and transform raw data into a format that can be fed into machine learning models.
- **Big Data Tools**: Familiarity with platforms like Apache Hadoop, Spark, and NoSQL databases (e.g., MongoDB) can be helpful in dealing with large datasets.

- **SQL**: Proficiency in SQL for data retrieval from relational databases is essential for data-related roles.

e) Soft Skills

In addition to technical expertise, soft skills such as communication, problem-solving, and teamwork are highly valued in AI careers. AI professionals often work in cross-disciplinary teams and need to communicate complex technical concepts to non-technical stakeholders.

3. AI Certifications: Why They Matter

Certifications can provide a competitive edge when applying for AI roles. They demonstrate your commitment to learning, validate your skills, and give employers confidence in your ability to perform on the job. Here are some of the top AI certifications you might consider:

a) Google Professional Machine Learning Engineer

Google offers a certification that focuses on machine learning concepts, including the design and implementation of ML models. This certification also tests your ability to use Google Cloud's machine learning tools and platforms.

b) Microsoft Certified: Azure AI Engineer Associate

This certification is designed for professionals working with AI on the Microsoft Azure platform. It covers topics such as machine learning, deep learning, and conversational AI.

c) TensorFlow Developer Certificate

Offered by Google, this certification is specifically for those who want to demonstrate their proficiency in using TensorFlow for machine learning and deep learning projects.

d) IBM Data Science Professional Certificate

This certification focuses on the foundational skills required for data science and AI, including Python programming, data analysis, and machine learning.

e) Coursera and Udacity AI Nanodegrees

Courses from platforms like Coursera and Udacity offer AI-specific certifications and nanodegrees, such as Udacity's AI Programming with Python and Coursera's AI for Everyone by Andrew Ng. These can be especially valuable if you are looking to transition into AI from a different background.

4. How to Prepare for AI Job Interviews

Landing an AI job involves not only acquiring the right skills but also preparing for technical interviews. Here are some tips to help you succeed in AI interviews:

Practice Coding Challenges: Many AI job interviews include coding challenges that test your problem-solving ability. Platforms like LeetCode, HackerRank, and Codewars are great places to practice.

Understand Data Structures and Algorithms: A strong understanding of algorithms and data structures is essential for solving complex problems in AI and machine learning. Be prepared to discuss algorithm efficiency and optimization techniques.

Prepare for System Design Interviews: AI-related roles often require knowledge of how to design scalable systems. You may be asked to design a recommendation system or discuss how to implement an AI model in production.

Stay Updated: AI is a fast-evolving field, and interviewers may ask about the latest trends, tools, and research papers. Keep up with AI news, research, and advancements by following journals, blogs, and conferences.

Build Real-World Projects: During interviews, be ready to showcase projects from your portfolio. Be prepared to explain the problem-solving approach, the algorithms used, and the results achieved.

5. Building a Career Path in AI

To ensure long-term success in AI, it's important to continue learning and growing in your field. Here are some ways to advance your AI career:

Specialize: Focus on a specific AI domain, such as NLP, computer vision, or reinforcement learning. Specializing can help you become an expert in that area and stand out from the competition.

Collaborate and Network: Join AI communities, attend conferences, and contribute to open-source projects. Building relationships with other professionals in the AI field can open doors to new opportunities.

Continue Your Education: AI is a field that requires constant learning. Consider pursuing advanced degrees (e.g., a master's or PhD in AI) or taking specialized online courses to stay updated with the latest research and technologies.

Building a career in AI is an exciting and fulfilling pursuit, but it requires a combination of technical skills, certifications, and real-world experience. By actively learning, preparing for key AI job roles, and obtaining relevant certifications, you can set yourself up for success in this rapidly growing field. Stay committed to your learning journey, and always look for ways to challenge yourself and contribute to the AI community.

Artificial Intelligence is shaping the future, and Python is the key to unlocking its potential. **Python for AI: A Beginner's Guide to Coding Intelligence** is your first step into the world of AI development, designed for beginners with no prior programming experience.

This book takes you on a structured journey, starting with the fundamentals of Python programming before gradually introducing essential AI concepts, machine learning techniques, and hands-on projects. You'll learn how to manipulate data, train AI models, and even build real-world applications like chatbots and image recognition systems.

Through clear explanations, practical exercises, and step-by-step guidance, you'll gain the confidence to write code, experiment with AI algorithms, and understand how intelligence is coded into machines. By the end of this book, you'll have a strong foundation in both Python and AI, preparing you for more advanced topics in artificial intelligence.

Your journey into AI doesn't stop here—this book is just the beginning. As the first installment in the AI from Scratch series, it sets the stage for deeper exploration into deep learning, neural networks, and beyond.

The future of AI is waiting. Are you ready to be a part of it?

Dear Reader,

Thank you for embarking on this journey into the world of Python and Artificial Intelligence with me. Writing Python for AI: A Beginner's Guide to Coding Intelligence has been a labor of love, and I am truly grateful that you chose this book as your starting point in AI.

Learning something new—especially a field as exciting and complex as AI—takes patience, curiosity, and persistence. Whether you're a beginner taking your first steps in coding or someone looking to expand your knowledge, I appreciate the time and effort you've invested in this book. Your willingness to explore, experiment, and challenge yourself is what makes this learning journey meaningful.

A heartfelt thank you to my readers, supporters, and the amazing community of AI enthusiasts worldwide. Your passion for knowledge and innovation is what drives progress in technology, and I'm honored to be a small part of your learning experience.

I also want to express my gratitude to the open-source community, whose incredible contributions have made AI accessible to learners across the globe. The knowledge shared by researchers, developers, and educators continues to inspire and empower the next generation of AI creators—including you!

If this book has helped you in any way, I would love to hear about your learning experience. Your feedback, thoughts, and ideas inspire me to continue writing and sharing knowledge. Feel free to connect with me, share your AI projects, or simply say hello!

Once again, thank you for your trust, your time, and your curiosity. The future of AI is bright, and I can't wait to see what you create. Keep learning, keep coding, and keep pushing the boundaries of what's possible!

With gratitude,

Gilbert Gutiérrez